ARCHB

MAGISTRATES' COURTS CRIMINAL PRACTICE

2010

SUPPLEMENT TO THE 2010 EDITION
UP TO DATE TO MARCH 2010

EDITOR

BARBARA BARNES District Judge (Magistrates' Courts)

CONTRIBUTING EDITORS

GAYNOR HOUGHTON-JONES LL.B. Hons
of Gray's Inn, Barrister

WILLIAM CARTER, B.A. (OXON)
of Gray's Inn, Barrister

JEREMY COLEMAN
District Judge (Magistrates' Courts)

GILLIAN JONES, LL.B. (EC) Hons
of 18 Red Lion Court, Barrister

KEVIN McCORMAC, O.B.E., M.A. (OXON)
Barrister

STEPHEN LEAKE LL.M.
of the Middle Temple, Barrister

STEPHEN SHAY B.A. (OXON.)
of the Middle Temple, Barrister

ASSISTANT EDITOR

LOUISE COWEN , B.A. (CANTAB), M.PHIL (CANTAB)

SWEET & MAXWELL
2010

Published in 2010 by
Sweet & Maxwell Ltd of
100 Avenue Rd, London, NW3 3PF
(http://www.sweetandmaxwell.co.uk)
Typeset by Sweet and Maxwell Ltd, London
and printed in the UK by
CPI William Clowes Beccles NR34 7TL

No natural forests were destroyed to make this product; only farmed timber was used and replanted.

A CIP catalogue record for this book is available from the British Library

ISBN-MAIN WORK 978–0414040885
ISBN-SUPPLEMENT 978–1847039255

SERVICE INFORMATION

The Archbold Magistrates' service *Archbold Magistrates' Courts Criminal Practice* **consists of one main text volume (including the tables and index). This volume is reissued annually, and is updated by an annual supplement.**

The supplement containing updating material for the main volume, is published once a year as part of the service. After consulting the main work on any given subject, reference should always be made to the same paragraph number in the current supplement to check that there have been no new developments since the main text volume was published. The supplement will also track material which has been removed or relocated as part of the reissue process.

All references in the text to cases, statutes and statutory instruments are contained in the tables printed at the beginning of this supplement.

TABLE OF CONTENTS

TABLE OF CASES

TABLE OF STATUTES

[Paragraph numbers in bold type denote where the text of the statute is printed]

TABLE OF STATUTORY INSTRUMENTS

[Paragraph numbers in bold type denote where the text of the statutory instrument is printed]

Part I

Pre-trial Issues

CHAPTER 1

CRIMINAL INVESTIGATIONS

I. INVESTIGATORY POWERS

D. ENTRY, SEARCH AND SEIZURE

(2) Warrant to enter and search premises

Police and Criminal Evidence Act 1984, s.8

1–33

Power of justice of the peace to authorise entry and search of premises
The *Faisaltex* case cited in the main work is now reported at [2009] 1 Cr.App.R. 37.
The *Redknapp* case cited in the main work is now reported at [2009] 1 W.L.R. 2091. **1–34**

(5) Execution of the warrant

Police and Criminal Evidence Act 1984, s.16

The *Redknapp* case cited in the main work is now reported at [2009] 1 W.L.R. 2091. **1–50**

(10) Retention

Police and Criminal Evidence Act 1984, s.22

1–62

Retention
The *Scopelight* case referred to in the main work, and reported at [2009] 2 Cr.App.R. 22, has been reversed on appeal: *Scopelight Ltd and Others v Chief Constable of Northumbria Police and Another, The Times*, November 11, 2009, CA (Civ. Div.), where it was held that the police can retain property after the Crown Prosecution Service decide not to prosecute, if a private prosecution is being contemplated or is taking place. Section 22 ("anything which has been seized by a constable may be retained so long as is necessary in all the circumstances") requires the police to consider each case on its own individual facts, at each stage in the process of investigation and prosecution. Where a body other than the CPS wishes to pursue a private prosecution, the relevant circumstances include, but are not limited to: the potential prosecutor's identity and motive; the gravity of the allegations together with the reasons why the CPS declined to prosecute, and thus the extent to which the public have a legitimate interest in prosecution; the police view of the significance of what has been retained; and any material fact concerning the proposed defendant.

(15) Return or retention of seized property

Criminal Justice and Police Act 2001, ss.53-58

1–78

Retention of seized items

The reference to para. 7(4) of Sched. 3B to the 1990 Act came into force on October 1, 2009: *Human Fertilisation and Embryology Act 2008 (Commencement No. 1) (England) Order* 2009 (S.I. 2009 No. 2202).

(17) Construction of Pt 2 of the Criminal Justice and Police Act 2001

Criminal Justice and Police Act 2001, s.66

1–83

General interpretation of Pt 2

The amendments effected by the*Human Fertilisation and Embryology Act* 2008, s.65, and Sched. 7, para. 20, came into force on October 1, 2009: *Human Fertilisation and Embryology Act 2008 (Commencement No. 1) (England) Order 2009* (S.I. 2009 No. 2202).

(18) Powers of seizure under 2001 Act (Schedule 1)

Powers to which s.50 applies (list 1)

1–84   The reference to para. 7(1) and (2) of Sched. 3B to the 1990 Act came into force on October 1, 2009: *Human Fertilisation and Embryology Act 2008 (Commencement No. 1) (England) Order 2009* (S.I. 2009 No. 2202).

E. ARREST AND DETENTION

(5) Other statutory powers of arrest without warrant

Police and Criminal Evidence Act 1984, s.26, Sched. 2

1–112   The entries in relation to the *Army Act*, the *Air Force Act* and the *Naval Discipline Act* are now repealed.

CHAPTER 2

CONSTITUTION AND JURISDICTION

IV. IMPARTIALITY OF MAGISTRATES

E. APPARENT BIAS

In *Michel v. R*, *The Times*, November 9, 2009 the court restated the test to be applied in cases of apparent bias. This was an appeal to the Privy Council from Jersey. It was said that the right to a fair trial could be infringed by an unacceptable level of hostile and sarcastic remarks or questions from the Judge. In this case the excessive number and the character of interventions from the Judge were held to render the conviction unsafe even though the case against the defendant was formidable. It was said that what needed to be considered was not only that the defendant should feel he had had a fair trial but that the 'reasonable observer' would also regard it as such. **2–29**

But sceptical comments made by a judge in the context of a lengthy trial suggesting that a defendant's account was 'manipulative and dishonest' were held to be justified and not to amount to real or apparent bias; *Piggott* [2009] EWCA Crim 2292.

Where a magistrate had been a teacher at a defendant's school but had neither taught him nor had any other personal dealings with him but did recognise his name it was held that a 'fair-minded and informed observer' would not conclude in these circumstances that there was a real possibility of apparent bias so the conviction was upheld—*R. (on the application of B) v. Wolverhampton Youth Court* [2009] EWHC 2706 (Admin). **2–30**

CHAPTER 3

EXTRADITION

III. ARREST

(1) Part 1 warrant

Although there can be no formula for appropriate particularisation, the requested **3–10** person would need sufficient details of the circumstances of the underlying offences to enable him to understand what he has been convicted of and to consider whether any bars to extradition apply. It will almost always be necessary for a warrant to contain the number of offences of which the person has been convicted, and some information about when and where the offences were committed, and the person's participation in them, although not necessarily in the same level of detail as required in an accusation warrant. More particulars are appropriate in more complex crimes: *Sandi v. Romania* [2009] EWHC 3079 (Admin).

The Supreme Court found, dismissing the appeal, in *Louca v. Germany*, [2009] 1 W.L.R. 2550, that ss.2(4)(b) and "(6)(c) do not intend to require the executing court to be informed by the arrest warrant of the existence of another warrant which might, in some conceivable case, be of some relevance to an abuse of process argument.

(2) Part 2 warrant

In *Deuss v. Attorney General of Bermuda* [2009] UKPC 38, the statutory definition **3–19** of an "extradition crime" in relation to British territories was discussed. It was said that a magistrate is entitled to issue a provisional warrant provided he receives evidence that satisfies him that the defendant is accused of conduct within the jurisdiction of another country which would, if committed in a British territory, justify the issue of a warrant for his arrest; there is no requirement that a magistrate must satisfy himself that the conduct constitutes an extradition crime.

V. PROCEDURE

A. First Appearance Before the Court

Extradition

An extradition hearing does not begin simply because the case is called on in court **3–23** —*Gronostajski v. Poland* [2007] EWHC 3314; something has to be said or done to show that extradition has started; merely adjourning proceedings is not enough. It is sufficient for the judge to make a statement in open court that proceedings have started, even if that is followed immediately by a decision to adjourn. Although the act of ordering an adjournment is a step in the extradition process, it does not, in itself, amount to taking a step in the process: *Kozluk v. Poland* [2009] EWHC 3523 (Admin).

B. The Extradition Hearing

(1) Extradition proceedings

Extradition Act 2003, s.78

A court does not have the power to refuse extradition on the grounds that the of- **3–34** fence is trivial. The *Criminal Procedure Rules* apply to extradition proceedings but they govern procedure only; they are not to be used to modify or change Parliament's intention so as to create an additional exception to the Act: *Hubner v. Czeck Republic*, [2009] EWHC 2929 (Admin).

The triviality of an extradition offence or the imposition of a seemingly disproportionately lengthy sentence cannot amount to "striking and unusual facts" so as to render extradition a disproportionate interference with an individual's Art.8 rights: *Sandru v. Romania*, [2009] EWHC 2879 (Admin).

(2) Extradition offence

Extradition Act 2003, s.64

3–45   It is not for the court to decide whether a person should be prosecuted in England and Wales or extradited with a view to prosecution abroad; that is a decision for the Director of Public Prosecutions; and, in making his decision, it is not for him to take account of any possible violation of the person's ECHR rights were he to be extradited; the fact that a person is suffering from Asperger Syndrome, and that suicide and self harm can be associated with that disorder, falls short of establishing a risk of infringement of Art.3: *R. (on the application of McKinnon) v. Secretary of State for Home Affairs; R. (McKinnon) v. DPP* [2009] EWHC 2021 (Admin).

Extradition Act 2003, s.137

3–49   Where a warrant has alleged that a person had alienated movable property on which an Inland Revenue official had "levied an attachment", the conduct did not satisfy the dual criminality test: *Luczak v. Poland*, [2009] EWHC 2753 (Admin).

(3) Restrictions or bars to extradition ss.11–25, 79, 95, 96

Passage of time: ss.14, 82

3–54   Extradition was found to be oppressive where a person (a) had pleaded guilty straightaway but had been kept in custody for over two years before trial, (b) did not flee to return home and had resided at a contactable address throughout, (c) was not aware of his trial in absence until after it had concluded, (d) was informed of the outcome but was not told to return to France, (e) the Dutch Probation Service had told him to wait until he was summoned to return, (f) was unaware of the European arrest warrant (g) twenty years was a long time and France had waited until three years after the EAW system had come into force before making any extradition attempt and had offered no explanation for the delay: *Wenting v. France* December 15, 2009 unreported.

Speciality: ss.17, 95

3–59   Section 20(5) requires the court to decide whether a convicted person sentenced in his absence is entitled to a retrial. "Entitlement" means a right under the law of the requesting state and it is not necessary to consider what a requesting state might do in practice. It is for the requesting state to establish compliance with s.20. Where a requesting state is a member of the Council of Europe it can be assumed that, as signatories to ECHR, they are capable of protecting against an unjust trial pursuant to Art. 6; letters from the Hungarian judge were sufficient *prima facie* evidence to satisfy compliance with s.20: *Benko v. Hungary* [2009] EWHC 3530 (Admin).

(4) Other Considerations

Human Rights, s.87

3–65   "Special administrative measures" which might be imposed (i.e. special confinement of prisoners where there is a risk of death or serious bodily injury) or life without parole do not of themselves cross the Art.3 threshold for inhuman or degrading treatment so as to militate against extradition to the USA; whether the conditions of detention infringe Art.3 depends on the facts of the individual case: *R. (on the application of Bary) v. Secretary of State for the Home Department* [2009] EWHC 2068 (Admin).

VIII. CHALLENGING THE DECISIONS

Extradition Act 2003, ss.26, 27

There is an express provision in the *Civil Procedure Rules* para.5.3(9) advising that **3–82** a "fax" should not be used as a means to file a notice of appeal "except in an unavoidable emergency"

Once the time limit for appeal under Pt 1 has expired the order is final; there is no jurisdiction to judicially review the order unless an intervening circumstance of the type outlined in *R. (on the application of Navadunskis) v. Serious Organised Crime Agency* [2009] EWHC 1292 (Admin) has arisen after the time limit has expired, even if the failure has occurred through the incompetence of legal representatives: *R. (on the application of Mann) v. Westminster Magistrates' Court* [2010] EWHC 48(Admin).

Where an issue is available to be raised at an extradition hearing, that issue may be **3–84** raised on appeal to the Divisional court, even though it has not been raised before: *Hoholm v. Government of Norway* [2009] EWHC 1513 (Admin).

Extradition Act 2003, s.29

Section 29(4) is expressed in terms which appear to give the court no discretion and **3–87** the court, in order to decide whether the result would have been different if evidence had been adduced, should consider evidence which was not available at the hearing with some care; admitting evidence which would require a full rehearing in the High Court must be regarded as exceptional: *Szombathely City Court and others v. Fenyvesi and another* [2009] 4 All E.R. 324, DC.

For the purposes of s.36(2) and (3) the "required period" does not begin to run until the period permitted for applying for leave to appeal to the Supreme Court ends; it makes no difference that certification of a point of law of general public importance was requested and refused: *Owens v. City of Westminster Magistrates' Court* [2009] A.C.D. 56.

CHAPTER 4

COMMENCEMENT OF PROCEEDINGS

II. THE PROSECUTOR

C. Prosecution of Offences by Parties Other than the CPS

Where a public authority is expressly empowered by statute to prosecute particular **4–24** offences, as a body corporate with legal personality, it would also enjoy the general common law right to bring a private prosecution in respect of other offences unless expressly excluded from doing so by statute: see *R. v. Rollins; R. v. McInerney, The Times*, October 20, 2009, CA.

D. Decision to Prosecute

(2) The Code

(a) *Introduction*

The Director of Public Prosecution has issued a consultation document seeking views **4–29** on proposed changes to the Code for Crown Prosecutors. The consultation ended on January 11, 2010.

F. Cases where Consent to Prosecute is Required

Failure to Obtain Consent

Whereas the clear purpose of s.25(2) of the *Prosecution of Offences Act* 1985 is to **4–37** enable the arrest, charging and remand in custody or bail of a person against whom proceedings may have been commenced without the consent of the Attorney General or Director of Public Prosecutions having first been obtained, any prohibition in an enactment on the "institution or carrying on of proceedings" without the relevant consent applied at the point at which the person who had been arrested and charged with such an offence was brought to court following the charge and the charge was entered in the court register: *R. v. Lambert* [2009] 2 Cr.App.R. 32, CA.

IV. INSTITUTION OF PROCEEDINGS

C. Time-Limit for Laying the Information or Charge

(4) Amendment of information outside of time limit

The question of whether two offences can be said to relate to "the same misdoing" is **4–62** one that is fact specific and should not be determined by other decided cases on the same two offences: *Williams v. DPP*, unreported, July 24, 2009, DC ([2009] EWHC 2354 (Admin.) (referring to *R. (on the application of Thornhill) v. Uxbridge Magistrates' Court*, 172 J.P.297, QBD (Silber J.) and concluding on particular facts that offences of failing to supply a specimen of breath and failing to supply a specimen of urine did amount to "the same misdoing").

As to whether it was "in the interests of justice" to permit amendment after the time-limit had expired, a fundamental failure on the part of the prosecutor during the proceedings properly to comply with the case management duties arising under the

Criminal Procedure Rules 2005 (as by failing to identify at an earlier stage, including when the case had been listed for a case management hearing, that the amendment would be necessary) may be such that the interests of justice would be best served by disallowing the amendment even where the effect was that a defendant who appeared to have little defence would in fact not be convicted: see *ibid*.

(5) Time limits in other enactments

4–63   Where a statute disapplied s.127(1) of the *Magistrates' Courts Act* 1980 and provided that proceedings for an offence might be brought within a fixed period "from the date on which evidence sufficient in the opinion of the prosecutor to warrant the proceedings came to his knowledge", and that "a certificate signed by or on behalf of the prosecutor and stating the date on which evidence sufficient in his opinion to warrant the proceedings came to his knowledge shall be conclusive evidence of that fact", the certificate would normally be determinative of the issue of when the relevant period began to run, such that a court could not go behind it save where it was inaccurate on its face or fraud could be shown; but a certificate would be invalid if it stated merely that the proceedings had been brought within the specified period after "the date on which evidence sufficient in the opinion of the prosecutor came to his knowledge" and did not recite the actual date on which sufficient evidence came to the knowledge of the prosecutor: *Burwell v. DPP*, 173 J.P. 351, DC. See also *Azham v. Epping Forest DC*, unreported, October 14, 2009, DC.

Although prosecutors are not entitled to shuffle papers between officers or sit on information so as to extend a time-limit, there is no principle of law that knowledge in a prosecutor begins immediately when any employee of that prosecutor has the relevant information; there is a degree of judgment involved in bringing a prosecution, and knowledge involves an opportunity for those with appropriate skills to consider whether there is sufficient information to justify a prosecution: *RSPCA v. Johnson*, unreported, October 16, 2009, DC ([2009] EWHC 2702 (Admin.)).

E. Written Charging and Requistioning

(3) Piloting of new procedure in magistrates' courts sitting at specified locations

4–83   The *Criminal Justice Act 2003 (Commencement Order No. 23) Order* 2009 (S.I. 2009 No. 2879) brought ss.29(1) to (3), (5) and (6) (new method of instituting proceedings (written charge and requisition)) and 30 (further provision about new method) into force on November 1, 2009, for the additional purposes of:

    (a) criminal proceedings instituted by a public prosecutor within the meaning of s.29(5)(a) in Brent, Feltham, Havering or South Western magistrates' court;

    (b) criminal proceedings instituted by a public prosecutor within the meaning of s.29(5)(e), who is authorised for the purposes of the *Vehicle Excise and Registration Act* 1994, s.49, anywhere in England and Wales;

    (c) criminal proceedings instituted by a public prosecutor within the meaning of s.29(5)(e), where they are instituted by the Secretary of State for Work and Pensions or the Secretary of State for Health anywhere in England and Wales.

F. Laying of Information to Obtain Issue of Summons or Warrant of Arrest

(2) Discretion to issue summons and warrants

Exercise of the discretion

4–89   There is no invariable requirement that a private prosecutor applying for a summons or warrant under s.1 of the Magistrates' Courts Act 1980 must first have taken the matter to the police, although in a particular case it may be a relevant circumstance; thus a magistrate's decision to refuse to issue process for that reason alone without considering the whole of the relevant circumstances and without informing himself of all relevant facts would be a flawed exercise of the discretion: *R. (Barry) v. Birmingham Magistrates' Court* , unreported, October 2, 2009, DC ([2009] EWHC 2571 (Admin)).

V. ALTERNATIVES TO PROSECUTION (DIVERSION)

B. Children and Young Persons

(3) Youth conditional cautions

With effect from November 16, 2009, the youth conditional cautioning provisions in **4–118b** ss.66A to 66H of the *Crime and Disorder Act* 1998 (including the power to include a financial penalty condition) have been brought into force partially for the purposes of a pilot scheme in the police areas of Cambridgeshire, Hampshire, Humberside: *Criminal Justice and Immigration Act 2008 (Commencement No. 7) Order* 2009 (S.I. 2009 No. 860) and *Criminal Justice and Immigration Act 2008 (Commencement No. 12) Order* 2009 (S.I. 2009 No. 2780).

The offences (and description of offences) in relation to which a financial penalty condition may be attached to a youth conditional caution, and the maximum amount of the penalty that may be specified in such a condition in respect of each of those offences, are prescribed by the *Crime and Disorder Act 1998 (Youth Conditional Cautions: Financial Penalties) Order* 2009 (S.I. 2009 No. 2781).

D. Cautioning of Adults

(3) Conditional cautions

(b) *When a conditional caution may be given*

As from November 16, 2009, the substitution of subs.(3) and the insertion of new **4–124** subs.(3A) to (3C) (but not (3A)(b)) in s.22 of the *Criminal Justice Act* 2003 has been brought into force in the additional pilot areas of Hampshire and Humberside: *Police and Justice Act 2006 (Commencement No. 12) Order* 2009 (S.I. 2009 No. 2774).

Section 27 of the *Criminal Justice Act* 2003 was brought into force for all purposes **4–126** on November 16, 2009: *Criminal Justice Act 2003 (Commencement No. 22) Order* 2009 (S.I. 2009 No. 2775) (i.e bringing the Director of the Serious Fraud Office, a Secretary of State and persons specified by the Secretary of State within the definition of "relevant prosecutor").

(c) *Financial penalties*

As from November 16, 2009, the insertion of s.23A in the *Criminal Justice Act* 2003 **4–128** was brought into force in the additional pilot police areas of Hampshire and Humberside: *Police and Justice Act 2006 (Commencement No. 12) Order* 2009 (S.I. 2009 No. 2774).

The offences (and description of offences) in relation to which a financial penalty condition may be attached to a conditional caution, and the maximum amount of the penalty that may be specified in such a condition in respect of each of those offences, are prescribed by the *Criminal Justice Act 2003 (Conditional Cautions: Financial Penalties) Order* 2009 (S.I. 2009 No. 2773).

E. Penalty Notices

(1) On the spot penalties for disorderly behaviour

(c) *Penalty notices*

4–135   The requirement in the *Criminal Justice and Police Act* 2001, s.3, that penalty notices for disorderly behaviour must be in a form prescribed by regulations made by the Secretary of State was repealed (with effect from January 13, 2010) by the *Legislative Reform (Revocation of Prescribed Form of Penalty Notice for Disorderly Behaviour) Order* 2010 (S.I. 2010 No. 64). In consequence, the *Penalties for Disorderly Behaviour (Form of Penalty Notice) Regulations* 2002 (S.I. 2002 No. 1838) (and amending regulations S.I. 2004 No. 3169 and S.I. 2005 No. 630) have been revoked.

(d) *Effect of penalty notice and restriction on proceedings where penalty notice given*

4–137a   Where a person is issued with a fixed penalty notice in respect of one offence under s.2 of the *Criminal Justice and Police Act* 2001, payment of the penalty does not relieve him of any possible further proceedings if subsequently it becomes apparent that a more serious offence, and in particular a non-penalty offence, was in fact committed during the course of the incident that gave rise to the issuing of the penalty notice; no reasonable expectation of non-prosecution could be said to arise and instituting proceedings in such circumstances involved no improper escalation of charge: *R. v. Gore and Maher* [2009] 2 Cr.App.R. 27, CA.

(e) *Guidance*

4–137b   Section 6 of the *Criminal Justice and Police Act* 2001 confers a power on the Secretary of State to issue guidance in relation to the giving of penalty notices for disorder. Guidance was issued under that section in March 2005, and supplemented by additional guidance in relation to offences committed by young people aged between 16 and 17 (July 2005), offences committed by young people aged between 10 and 15 (October 2005), and use of the powers by community support officers. For the full text of the guidance documents, see *http://www.police.homeoffice.gov.uk/publications/ operational-policing/penalty-notices-guidance*.

With effect from July 16, 2009, *Ministry of Justice Circular 2009/04* sets out revised guidance on the use of the penalty notice scheme as a means to deal with offences of retail theft and criminal damage.

With effect from July 23, 2009, *Ministry of Justice Circular 2009/05* sets out self-standing guidance on the use of penalty notices as a means to deal with adult offenders in possession of cannabis and its derivatives for personal use.

Chapter 5

BAIL

I. INTRODUCTION

In August 2009 the Crown Prosecution Service issued guidance to prosecutors **5–2** deprecating the practice of acceding to technical bail for defendants already in custody on other matters. This approach had developed on the basis of administrative convenience and the saving of transport costs from custody. The new guidance makes it clear that the provisions of the *Bail Act* apply to each and every hearing and if exceptions to the right to unconditional bail exist then bail should be opposed despite the fact that the defendant is already in custody. The avoidance of remands on technical bail prevents a situation arising where a defendant may be released unexpectedly from a custodial remand being left only on unconditional bail for charges where a remand in custody or with conditions of bail may have been imposed save for the fact he was already held in custody.

The fact that the prosecution cannot give rise to an expectation on behalf of the defendant that he will get bail at court was confirmed in *R. (on the application of Burns) v. Woolwich Crown Court January* 14, 2010, unreported. The defendant was charged with offences of fraud, blackmail and possession of criminal property. No objections were made to bail at the magistrates' court and he was granted conditional bail by the court. At a Crown Court hearing full details of the offences and the defendant were asked about and the Crown Court indicated the issue of bail would be reconsidered at which stage the prosecution did object to bail which was then refused. The Crown Court said, having heard all the information about the charges and in addition that the defendant was liable to be arrested for further offences arising out of the discovery of large amounts of cash deposited in his bank account, that a change of circumstances had arisen requiring reconsideration of bail. This decision was appealed on the basis that the Crown Court was not entitled to look again at bail as there had been no relevant change in circumstances and that the decision was irrational and also went against a legitimate expectation that bail would be granted as throughout the proceedings the prosecution had never objected to bail until the intervention of the Crown Court. It was held that there was a change of circumstances since the defendant was to be charged with new offences; that the decision was rational and within the Bail Act criteria and that the prosecution cannot give any expectation of bail as that decision was for the court not the prosecution.

The *Coroners and Justice Act* 2009 removes from the magistrates' courts the power **5–2a** to make a decision on bail for defendants charged with murder. Such cases it would appear must now be sent to the Crown Court in custody to be heard by a Crown Court judge within 48 hours. This provision came into effect on February 1, 2009. Practical arrangements for the listing of such cases at the Crown Court will have to be considered.

Coroners and Justice Act 2009 s.115

Bail decisions in murder cases to be made by Crown Court judge

115.—(1) A person charged with murder may not be granted bail except by order of a judge of the Crown Court.

(2) Subsections (3) and (4) apply where a person appears or is brought before a magistrates' court charged with murder.

(3) A judge of the Crown Court must make a decision about bail in respect of the person as soon as reasonably practicable and, in any event, within the period of 48 hours beginning with the day after the day on which the person appears or is brought before the magistrates' court.

(4) The magistrates' court must, if necessary for the purposes of subsection (3), commit the person to custody to be brought before a judge of the Crown Court. excluded.

(5) For the purposes of subsections (3) and (4), it is immaterial whether the magistrates' court—

    (a) sends the person to the Crown Court for trial, or

    (b) adjourns proceedings under section 52(5) of the *Crime and Disorder Act* 1998 (c. 37) and remands the person.

(6) In this section a reference to a person charged with murder includes a person charged with murder and one or more other offences.

(7) (7) For the purposes of subsection (3), when calculating the period of 48 hours Saturdays, Sundays, Christmas Day, Good Friday and bank holidays are to be

[This section came into force on February 1, 2010 by virtue of the *Coroners and Justice Act 2009 (Commencement No.3 and Transitional Provision) Order* 2010 S.I. No. 145 of 2010]

5–3   The case of *R. (Fergus) v. Southampton Crown Court* has now been reported on appeal at *R. (On the application of F) v. Southampton Crown Court* [2009] EWHC 2206 (Admin).

III. PRINCIPLES FOR GRANTING/DENYING BAIL

(1) Statutory grounds for refusal

5–35   Part 1 of Sched. 1 to the*Bail Act* 1976 is amended by the *Coroners and Justice Act* 2009 s.114 with effect from February 1, 2010 with the insertion of a new paragraph as follows—

    6ZA. . If the defendant is charged with murder, the defendant may not be granted bail unless the court is of the opinion that there is no significant risk of the defendant committing, while on bail, an offence that would, or would be likely to, cause physical or mental injury to any person other than the defendant.

Paragraph 9 of the Schedule is also amended by the same section with effect from February 1, 2010 and reads as follows—

Decisions under paragraph 2

    9. In taking the decisions required by paragraph 2(1), or in deciding whether it is satisfied as mentioned in paragraph 2A(1), 6(1) or 6A or of the opinion mentioned in paragraph 6ZA of this part of this Schedule, the court shall have regard to such of the following considerations as appear to it to be relevant, that is to say—

    (a) the nature and seriousness of the offence or default (and the probable method of dealing with the defendant for it),

    (b) the character, antecedents, associations and community ties of the defendant

    (c) the defendant's record as respects the fulfilment of his obligations under previous grants of bail in criminal proceedings,

    (d) except in the case of a defendant whose case is adjourned for inquiries or a report the strength of the evidence of his having committed the offence or having defaulted, as well as any others which appear to be relevant,

    (e) if the court is satisfied that there are substantial grounds for believing that the defendant, if released on bail (whether subject to conditions or not), would commit an offence while on bail, the risk that the defendant may do so by engaging in conduct that would, or would be likely to, cause physical or mental injury to any person other than the defendant,.

These amendments recognise the fact that bail decisions in murder cases can now only be made by the Crown Court and in making bail decisions with regard to indictable imprisonable offences regard must be had to whether there are substantial grounds to believe there is a risk of the commission of offences which would involve physical or mental injury to others.

[These paragraphs are printed as amended by s.114 of the *Coroners and Justice Act* 2009 by virtue of the *Coroners and Justice Act 2009 (Commencement No. 3 and Transitional Provision) Order* S.I. No. 145 of 2010 which came into force on February 1, 2010]

IV. CONDITIONS OF BAIL

(1) Bail Act 1976, Sched. 1, para. 8

Post-release

The *Criminal Procedure Rules* have been amended by the *Criminal Procedure* **5–43** *(Amendment) Rules* 2009 S.I. 2009 No 2087 which came into force on the October 5, 2009 and which amend Pt 19 of the Rules which apply to bail. The new rules are designed to ensure there is proper communication between the court and those who either provide accommodation and support as part of bail conditions or those who monitor electronic curfews.

A new Rule 19.27 applies to bail granted subject to accommodation or support requirements provided by or on behalf of a local authority. Under the rules the court has a duty to inform the service provider of the details of the defendant and the offence and also to give details of the accommodation or support requirement and other bail conditions and the return date to court. The defendant must be notified by the court of the name and contact details of the service provider and the address where he must reside under the requirement. Any subsequent changes to the requirement or other bail conditions or the date must also be notified by the court to the service provider. See Appendix G.

A new Rule 19.26 is also inserted which applies to bail granted subject to a condition of electronic curfew. The court is under a duty to notify those responsible for monitoring the curfew of the details of the defendant, the offence and the specific requirements of the curfew. The court must also provide the defendant with the name of those responsible for monitoring the curfew and their contact details. The court must also notify those responsible for monitoring the curfew of any subsequent changes or variations to the curfew. These rules also appear in the *Criminal Procedure Rules* 2010 which apply from April 5, 2010. See Appendix G

In *Barrett* [2009] EWCA Crim 2213 it was confirmed that there is no obligation to give credit for time spent on bail with a curfew where it had not been electronically monitored. Although the argument to give some credit was appealing the court held that the statutory provisions did not allow for it.

V. APPEAL AND RECONSIDERATION

B. APPEAL TO MAGISTRATES' COURT IN RESPECT OF POLICE BAIL

Magistrates' Courts Act 1980, s.43B

The procedure to be adopted when application is made to a court to vary police bail **5–59** was considered in *R. (On the application of Ajaib) v. Birmingham Magistrates' Court* [2009] EWHC 2127 (Admin). An appeal was made against the refusal to vary bail conditions imposed by the police. The court heard from the officer in the case that the appellant was said to be liquidating his assets with a view to leaving the country and on this information a condition was imposed to address the fear of failure to answer bail. This decision was appealed as being unfair and in breach of Arts 5, 6, and 8 of the ECHR. It was contended that disclosure should have been ordered to clarify the origin and source of this information. On appeal it was held that no human rights had been breached and as these were pre-charge proceedings the *Criminal Procedure Rules*, especially those relating to disclosure, did not apply. It was open to the court to rely on the information given by the officer and the appellants rights were not infringed as he had the opportunity to give evidence himself and to challenge the information.

VI. ABSCONDING AND BREACH OF BAIL CONDITIONS

A. Offence of Absconding while on Bail

5–76   In *Cockburn-Smith* [2008] EWCA Crim 3159 a sentence of three months imprisonment for absconding from bail when a warrant had been outstanding for two years was upheld even though the substantive charges had not been proceeded with.

B. Liability to Arrest

Bail Act 1976, s.7

Liability to arrest for absconding or breaking conditions of bail

5–83   **7.**—(1) If a person who has been released on bail in criminal proceedings and is under a duty to surrender into the custody of a court fails to surrender to custody at the time appointed for him to do so the court may issue a warrant for his arrest.

(1A) Subsection (1B) applies if—

     (a) a person has been released on bail in connection with extradition proceedings,

     (b) the person is under a duty to surrender into the custody of a constable, and

     (c) the person fails to surrender to custody at the time appointed for him to do so.

(1B) A magistrates' court may issue a warrant for the person's arrest.

(2) If a person who has been released on bail in criminal proceedings absents himself from the court at any time after he has surrendered into the custody of the court and before the court is ready to begin or to resume the hearing of the proceedings, the court may issue a warrant for his arrest; but no warrant shall be issued under this subsection where that person is absent in accordance with leave given to him by or on behalf of the court.

(3) A person who has been released on bail in criminal proceedings and is under a duty to surrender into the custody of a court may be arrested without warrant by a constable—

     (a) if the constable has reasonable grounds for believing that that person is not likely to surrender to custody;

     (b) if the constable has reasonable grounds for believing that that person is likely to break any of the conditions of his bail or has reasonable grounds for suspecting that that person has broken any of those conditions; or

     (c) in a case where that person was released on bail with one or more surety or sureties, if a surety notifies a constable in writing that that person is unlikely to surrender to custody and that for that reason the surety wishes to be relieved of his obligations as a surety.

(4) a person arrested in pursuance of subsection (3) above—

     (a) shall, except where he was arrested within 24 hours of the time appointed for him to surrender to custody, be brought as soon as practicable and in any event within 24 hours after his arrest before a justice of the peace ; and

     (b) in the said excepted case shall be brought before the court at which he was to have surrendered to custody.

(4A) A person who has been released on bail in connection with extradition proceedings and is under a duty to surrender into the custody of a constable may be arrested without warrant by a constable on any of the grounds set out in paragraphs (a) to (c) of subsection (3).

(4B) A person arrested in pursuance of subsection (4A) above shall be brought as soon as practicable and in any event within 24 hours after his arrest before a justice of the peace for the petty sessions area in which he was arrested.

(5) A justice of the peace before whom a person is brought under subsection (4) or (4B) above may, subject to subsection (6) below, if of the opinion that that person—

     (a) is not likely to surrender to custody, or

     (b) has broken or is likely to break any condition of his bail, remand him in custody or commit him to custody, as the case may require, or alternatively, grant him bail subject to the same or to different conditions, but if not of that opinion shall grant him bail subject to the same conditions (if any) as were originally imposed.

(6) Where the person so brought before the justice is a child or young person and the justice does not grant him bail, subsection (5) above shall have effect subject to the provisions of section 23 of the Children and Young Persons Act 1969 (remands to the care of local authorities).

(7) In reckoning for the purposes of this section any period of 24 hours, no account shall be taken of Christmas Day, Good Friday or any Sunday.

(8) In the case of a person charged with murder or with murder and one or more other offences—

    (a) subsections (4) and (5) have effect as if for "justice of the peace" there were substituted "judge of the Crown Court",

    (b) subsection (6) has effect as if for "justice" (in both places) there were substituted "judge", and

    (c) (c) subsection (7) has effect, for the purposes of subsection (4), as if at the end there were added ", Saturday or bank holiday."

[This section is printed as amended by the *Coroners and Justice Act* 2009 Sched. 21(7) para.74(b) with effect from February 1, 2010]

This section has been amended to recognise the fact that decisions on bail can only be made by the Crown Court as regards any defendant charged with murder as a result of amendments made by the *Coroners and Justice Act* 2009 s.115. Any defendant charged with murder and in breach of bail will have to be produced before the Crown Court as the magistrates' court no longer has power to deal with such cases.

Chapter 6

DISCLOSURE

II. OBLIGATIONS TO DISCLOSE EVIDENCE PRE-TRIAL

A. Obligations Common to Both Parties

(2) Obligation to disclose expert evidence

The provisions in Pt 24 of the *Criminal Procedure Rules* 2005 setting out obliga- **6–04** tions on both parties to disclose expert evidence on which it is proposed to rely have been moved to new Pt 33 (expert evidence) (Appendix G-191 *et seq.* in this supplement): see the *Criminal Procedure (Amendment) Rules* 2009 (S.I. 2009 No. 2087).

III. DISCLOSURE OF PROSECUTION MATERIAL WHICH IS NOT RELIED UPON AS EVIDENCE (UNUSED MATERIAL)

F. Defence Disclosure

(2) Current requirements as to the defence statements

Implications of voluntary disclosure by accused

As to the relationship between the right to a fair trial under Art. 6 of the European **6–36** Convention on Human Rights and the provisions in s.11 of the *Criminal Procedure and Investigations Act* 1996 dealing with the drawing of adverse inferences from failure adequately to supply a defence statement, see *R. v. Essa* [2009] 5 Archbold News 2, CA. Whereas the court further indicated that no lawyer should properly advise his client not to give a defence statement, those comments were said in the context of the requirements of s.5 of the Act (relating to trial on indictment) and plainly have no application to the voluntary service of a defence statement in summary trials under s.6.

I. Nature of the Duties of Initial and Continuing Disclosure Application by the Accused

Third party disclosure

As to the duties arising in relation to material held by individuals or companies over- **6–47b** seas, see *R. v. F.* [2010] Crim.L.R. 148, CA (*post*, § 6-50a).

Bad character of Prosecution witness

As to the extent of the duty to disclose previous convictions of a prosecution witness, **6–48** (i) only those convictions which are material need to be disclosed, materiality depending on whether the information could have any possible bearing on the witness's credibility or character; disclosure of such information engaged the rights of the witness under Art. 8 of the European Convention on Human Rights, though disclosure would be justified under Art. 8(2) if it was necessary secure the accused's right to a fair trial; (ii) the decision as to what should be disclosed is for the prosecution, albeit a generous view should be taken; (iii) in case of dispute, the issue should be referred to the judge who should be supplied with the previous conviction(s) of the witness together with a brief indication, agreed with the defence, of the matter about which the witness is expected to give evidence: see *H.M. Advocate v. Murtagh*, unreported, August 3, 2009, PC ([2009] UKPC 36).

Material held overseas

6–50a   Whereas the *Criminal Procedure and Investigations Act* 1996 makes no special provision in relation to material held by individuals or companies overseas or by foreign governmental authorities or material that may be examined overseas in the course of the investigation, if it appears that there is relevant material, then the prosecution must take reasonable steps to obtain it, either informally or making use of the powers contained in the *Crime (International Co-operation) Act* 2003 and international conventions; but where the judicial or other author authorities of a non-European Union state will not make the material available there is no absolute obligation on the prosecution to disclose relevant material held overseas outside the European Union by entities not subject to the jurisdiction of these courts; the position is quite different to the position where the information is held in the UK or by a person amenable to the jurisdiction of these courts: *R. v. F.*, [2010] Crim.L.R. 148, CA.

Consequences of inadequate disclosure

6–51   Where it becomes apparent after a trial that the prosecution had failed adequately to comply with the duty to disclose unused material, the mere fact that the material satisfied the test for disclosure does not decide the question of whether the additional material, if available at trial, might reasonably have affected the decision of the tribunal to convict (not least because any potential assistance that the material gives the defence may be greatly outweighed by the help it gives the prosecution case); the question has to be decided by consideration of the overall impact of the additional material on the case: see *R. v. Kenedy,* unreported, October 9, 2008, CA ([2008] EWCA Crim. 2817); and *R. v. Pomfrett,* unreported, October 8, 2009, CA ([2009] EWCA Crim. 1939).

O. THIRD PARTY DISCLOSURE

6–69   As to the duties arising in relation to material held by individuals or companies overseas, see *R. v. F.*, [2010] Crim.L.R. 148, CA (*post,* § 6-50a).

P. PROTECTED MATERIAL

(1) Public interest immunity

Criminal Procedure rules

6–77   The provisions in Pt 25 of the *Criminal Procedure Rules* 2005 setting out provisions supplementing ss.3(6), 7A(8), 8(5), 14(2) and 16 of the *Criminal Procedure and Investigations Act* 1996 have been moved to new Pt 22 (disclosure) (Appendix G-140 *et seq.* in this supplement): see the *Criminal Procedure (Amendment) Rules* 2009 (S.I. 2009 No. 2087).

(2) Confidentiality

6–80   The provisions in Pt 26 of the *Criminal Procedure Rules* 2005 making ancillary provision in connection with matters arising under ss.17 and 18 of the *Criminal Procedure and Investigations Act* 1996 have been moved to new Pt 22 (disclosure) (Appendix G-140*et seq.* in this supplement): see the *Criminal Procedure (Amendment) Rules* 2009 (S.I. 2009 No. 2087).

CHAPTER 7

PRE-TRIAL PROCEDURE

*III. PLEA BEFORE VENUE AND MODE OF TRIAL (ALLOCATION)
PROCEDURE IN RESPECT OF EITHER WAY OFFENCES WHERE
ACCUSED AN ADULT*

C. MODE OF TRIAL PROCEDURE (ALLOCATION)

(2) Decision as to mode of trial (allocation)

Magistrates' Courts Act 1980, s.19 (not in force)

Decision as to allocation

19.—(1) The court shall decide whether the offence appears to it more suitable for summary **7–46**
trial or for trial on indictment.

(2) Before making a decision under this section, the court—

    (a) shall give the prosecution an opportunity to inform the court of the accused's
previous convictions (if any); and

    (b) shall give the prosecution and the accused an opportunity to make representa-
tions as to whether summary trial or trial on indictment would be more suitable.

(3) In making a decision under this section, the court shall consider—

    (a) whether the sentence which a magistrates' court would have power to impose for
the offence would be adequate; and

    (b) any representations made by the prosecution or the accused under subsection
(2)(b) above, and shall have regard to any allocation guidelines (or revised allocation guidelines) issued as definitive guidelines under section 170 of the *Criminal
Justice Act* 2003 [122 of the *Coroners and Justice Act* 2009].

(4) Where—

    (a) the accused is charged with two or more offences; and

    (b) it appears to the court that the charges for the offences could be joined in the
same indictment or that the offences arise out of the same or connected circumstances, subsection (3)(a) above shall have effect as if references to the sentence
which a magistrates' court would have power to impose for the offence were a
reference to the maximum aggregate sentence which a magistrates' court would
have power to impose for all of the offences taken together.

(5) In this section any reference to a previous conviction is a reference to—

    (a) a previous conviction by a court in the United Kingdom; or

    [(aa) a previous conviction by a court in another member State of a relevant offence
under the law of that State; or]

    (b) *a previous finding of guilt in*—

        (i) *any proceedings under the Army Act 1955, the Air Force Act 1955 or the
Naval Discipline Act 1957 (whether before a court-martial or any other
court or person authorised under any of those Acts to award a punishment
in respect of any offence); or*

        (ii) *any proceedings before a Standing Civilian Court.*

    [(b) a previous conviction of a service offence within the meaning of the *Armed Forces
Act* 2006 ("conviction" here including anything that under section 376(1) and (2) of
that Act is to be treated as a conviction)].

[(5A) For the purposes of subsection (5)(aa) an offence is "relevant" if the offence would
constitute an offence under the law of any part of the United Kingdom if it were done in
that part at the time when the allocation decision is made.]

(6) If, in respect of the offence, the court receives a notice under section 51B or 51C of

the *Crime and Disorder Act* 1998 (which relate to serious or complex fraud cases and to certain cases involving children respectively), the preceding provisions of this section and sections 20, 20A and 21 below shall not apply, and the court shall proceed in relation to the offence in accordance with section 51(1) of that Act.]

[The new s.19 (set out in square brackets in the main work) which is to be substituted in the Magistrates' Courts Act 1980 by the *Criminal Justice Act* 2003 as from a day to be appointed is printed as further amended (as from a day or days to be appointed) by the *Coroners and Justice Act* 2009, Scheds 17, 21, 23].

Sentencing and allocation guidelines

7–48   As from a day or days to be appointed, Ch. 1 of Pt 4 of the *Coroners and Justice Act* 2009 abolishes the Sentencing Guidelines Council and replaces it with a new Sentencing Council. Section 122 of that Act provides that the Sentencing Council may prepare "allocation guidelines" relating to decisions by a magistrates' court under s.19 of the Magistrates' Courts Act 1980 as to whether an offence is more suitable for summary trial or trial on indictment.

As to the duty of the court to have regard to definitive (as opposed to draft) sentencing guidelines when determining mode of trial (allocation), the duty in the *Criminal Justice Act* 2003, s.172(1)(b) is to be replaced by a new duty in s.125 of the 2009 Act (s.125(1)(b) refers to the exercising of "any other function relating to the sentencing of offenders", which must plainly include a decision as to mode of trial or allocation). The nature of the new duty in s.125 is somewhat more restrictive, in that the court must "follow" any relevant sentencing guideline "unless the court is satisfied that it would be contrary to the interests of justice to do so". *Cf.* the duty under s.172 of the 2003 Act (the court must "have regard to" any sentencing guideline) and the authorities interpreting that section.

(3) Procedure where summary trial appears more suitable

Preferment of further charges following election to adjust mode of trial

7–55a   *DPP v. Hammerton* has been reported at [2009] 2 Cr.App.R. 18.

VI. PREPARATION FOR SUMMARY TRIAL

(1) General

Case management hearings and pre-trial reviews

7–126b   In accordance with the case management duties arising under the *Criminal Procedure Rules* 2005, it is the obligation of any party, prior to a case management hearing or pre-trial review, carefully to look at the papers so as to apprise the court of the issues; such hearings are not exercises in formality, but are the proper occasion for each of the parties carefully to examine its case and for the justices, or their clerks, to subject the case to scrutiny so that the trial can take place efficiently by concentrating on the identified issues and the evidence needed in respect of them; if an oversight occurs, the relevant party must apply immediately to the court rather than leaving the issue unresolved until the trial, particularly in a busy court where it may be that the resources of the court do not permit an adjourned trial to take place for some time: *Williams v. DPP*, unreported, July 24, 2009, DC ([2009] EWHC 2354 (Admin)).

VII. SPECIFIC CASE MANAGEMENT POWERS

C. Preliminary, Sentencing and Other Hearing by Video Link

(1) Introduction

The *Coroners and Justice Act* 2009 prospectively amends the provisions in the **7–132a** *Crime and Disorder Act* 1998, Pt 3A. The amendments permit a single justice to give live link directions for preliminary hearings when an accused is in custody, and remove the requirements for the accused's consent to the use of a live link. Further, a new s.57F is inserted in the 1998 Act so as to permit a live link direction to be given in respect of enforcement hearings relating to confiscation orders. There are also consequential amendments to the *Police and Criminal Evidence Act* 1984, ss.46ZA (persons granted live link bail) and 46A(1ZA) (power of arrest for failure to answer police bail); and insertion in the 1984 Act of new ss.54B and 54C, which make provision for searches of accused persons answering to live link bail.

The amendments were brought into force on December 14, 2009, subject to transitional provisions and with limited effect insofar as they relate to s.57C of the 1998 Act: *Coroners and Justice Act 2009 (Commencement No. 1 and Transitional Provisions) Order* 2009 (S.I. 2009 No. 3253).

(2) Interpretation

Crime and Disorder Act 1998, s.57A

Introductory

57A.—(1) This Part— **7–133**
    (a) applies to preliminary hearings and sentencing hearings in the course of proceedings for an offence and enforcement hearings relating to confiscation orders; and
    (b) enables the court in the circumstances provided for in sections 57B, 57C, 57E and 57F to direct the use of a live link for securing the accused's attendance at a hearing to which this Part applies.

(2) The accused is to be treated as present in court when, by virtue of a live link direction under this Part, he attends a hearing through a live link.

(3) In this Part—
"confiscation order" means an order made under—
    (a) section 71 of the *Criminal Justice Act* 1988;
    (b) section 2 of the *Drug Trafficking Act* 1994; or
    (c) section 6 of the *Proceeds of Crime Act* 2002;
"custody"—
    (a) includes local authority accommodation to which a person is remanded or committed by virtue of section 23 of the *Children and Young Persons Act* 1969; but
    (b) does not include police detention;
"enforcement hearing" means a hearing under section 82 of the *Magistrates' Courts Act* 1980 to consider the issuing of a warrant of committal or to inquire into a person's means;
"live link" means an arrangement by which a person (when not in the place where the hearing is being held) is able to see and hear, and to be seen and heard by, the court during a hearing (and for this purpose any impairment of eyesight or hearing is to be disregarded);
"police detention" has the meaning given by section 118(2) of the *Police and Criminal Evidence Act* 1984;
"preliminary hearing" means a hearing in the proceedings held before the start of the trial (within the meaning of subsection (11A) or (11B) of section 22 of the 1985 Act) including, in the case of proceedings in the Crown Court, a preparatory hearing held under—
    (a) section 7 of the *Criminal Justice Act* 1987 (cases of serious or complex fraud); or
    (b) section 29 of the *Criminal Procedure and Investigations Act* 1996 (other serious, complex or lengthy cases);
"sentencing hearing" means any hearing following conviction which is held for the purpose of—

(a) proceedings relating to the giving or rescinding of a direction under section 57E;

(b) proceedings (in a magistrates' court) relating to committal to the Crown Court for sentencing; or

(c) sentencing the offender or determining how the court should deal with him in respect of the offence.

[This section is printed as amended by the *Coroners and Justice Act* 2009, s.109(2). The amendments were brought into force as from December 14, 2009: *Coroners and Justice Act 2009 (Commencement No. 1 and Transitional Provisions) Order* 2009 (S.I. 2009 No. 3253)].

(3) Live link at preliminary hearings where accused is in custody other than at the police station

Crime and Disorder Act 1998, s.57B

Use of live link at preliminary hearings where accused is in custody

7–134   **57B.**—(1) This section applies in relation to a preliminary hearing in a magistrates' court or the Crown Court.

(2) Where it appears to the court before which the preliminary hearing is to take place that the accused is likely to be held in custody during the hearing, the court may give a live link direction under this section in relation to the attendance of the accused at the hearing.

(3) A live link direction under this section is a direction requiring the accused, if he is being held in custody during the hearing, to attend it through a live link from the place at which he is being held.

(4) If a hearing takes place in relation to the giving or rescinding of such a direction, the court may require or permit a person attending the hearing to do so through a live link.

(5) The court shall not give or rescind such a direction (whether at a hearing or otherwise) unless the parties to the proceedings have been given the opportunity to make representations.

(6) If in a case where it has power to do so a magistrates' court decides not to give a live link direction under this section, it must—

(a) state in open court its reasons for not doing so; and

(b) cause those reasons to be entered in the register of its proceedings.

(7) The following functions of a magistrates' court under this section may be discharged by a single justice—

(a) giving a live link direction under this section;

(b) rescinding a live link direction before a preliminary hearing begins; and

(c) requiring or permitting a person to attend by live link a hearing about a matter within paragraph (a) or (b).

[This section is printed as amended by the *Coroners and Justice Act* 2009, s.106(2). The amendment was brought into force on December 14, 2009; but has no effect in relation to a live link direction given before that date: *Coroners and Justice Act 2009 (Commencement No. 1 and Transitional Provisions) Order* 2009 (S.I. 2009 No. 3253)].

(4) Live link at preliminary hearings where accused is in custody at the police station

Crime and Disorder Act 1998, s.57C

Use of live link at preliminary hearings where accused is at police station

7–135   **57C.**—(1) This section applies in relation to a preliminary hearing in a magistrates' court.

(2) Where subsection (3) or (4) applies to the accused, the court may give a live link direction in relation to his attendance at the preliminary hearing.

(3) This subsection applies to the accused if—

(a) he is in police detention at a police station in connection with the offence; and

(b) it appears to the court that he is likely to remain at that station in police detention until the beginning of the preliminary hearing.

(4) This subsection applies to the accused if he is at a police station in answer to live link bail in connection with the offence.

(5) A live link direction under this section is a direction requiring the accused to attend the preliminary hearing through a live link from the police station.

(6) But a direction given in relation to an accused to whom subsection (3) applies has no effect if he does not remain in police detention at the police station until the beginning of the preliminary hearing.

(6A) A live link direction under this section may not be given unless the court is satisfied that it is not contrary to the interests of justice to give the direction.

(7) (Repealed).

(8) A magistrates' court may rescind a live link direction under this section at any time during a hearing to which it relates.

(9) A magistrates' court may require or permit—

(a) (repealed)

(b) any party to the proceedings who wishes to make representations in relation to the giving or rescission of a live link direction under this section to do so through a live link.

(10) Where a live link direction under this section is given in relation to an accused person who is answering to live link bail he is to be treated as having surrendered to the custody of the court (as from the time when the direction is given).

(11) In this section, "live link bail" means bail granted under Part IV of the *Police and Criminal Evidence Act* 1984 subject to the duty mentioned in section 47(3)(b) of that Act.

[This section is printed as amended by the *Coroners and Justice Act* 2009, s.106(3). The amendment was brought into force on December 14, 2009, in limited pilot local justice areas (see post, § 7-135a); but has no effect in relation to a preliminary hearing where the court had power to give a live link direction under s.57C(2) because s.57C(4) applied to the accused and the accused was at a police station on or after December 14, 2009, to answer live link bail granted before that date: *Coroners and Justice Act 2009 (Commencement No. 1 and Transitional Provisions) Order* 2009 (S.I. 2009 No. 3253)].

Piloting of s.57C in courts sitting at specified locations

Whereas the insertion of s.57C in the 1998 Act by the *Police and Justice Act* 2006　**7–135a** has been brought into force only in a limited number of local justices for the purposes of a pilot scheme (see the main work), the amendments to that section made by the *Coroners and Justice Act* 2009 have been brought into force only in the same pilot local justice areas: *Coroners and Justice Act 2009 (Commencement No. 1 and Transitional Provisions) Order* 2009 (S.I. 2009 No. 3253).

(5) Live link sentencing hearing continuing after conviction of accused at live link preliminary hearing from custody or the police station

Crime and Disorder Act 1998, s.57D

Continued use of live link for sentencing hearing following a preliminary hearing

57D.—(1) Subsection (2) applies where—　　　　　　　　　　　　　　　**7–136**

(a) a live link direction under section 57B or 57C is in force;

(b) the accused is attending a preliminary hearing through a live link by virtue of the direction;

(c) the court convicts him of the offence in the course of that hearing (whether by virtue of a guilty plea or an indication of an intention to plead guilty); and

(d) the court proposes to continue the hearing as a sentencing hearing in relation to the offence.

(2) The accused may continue to attend through the live link by virtue of the direction if—

(a) the hearing is continued as a sentencing hearing in relation to the offence;

(b) (repealed); and

(c) the court is satisfied that the accused continuing to attend through the live link is not contrary to the interests of justice.

(3) But the accused may not give oral evidence through the live link during a continued hearing under subsection (2) unless—

(a) (repealed)

(b) the court is satisfied that it is not contrary to the interests of justice for him to give it in that way.

[This section is printed as amended by the *Coroners and Justice Act* 2009, s.106(4). The amendments have effect as from December 14, 2009: *Coroners and Justice Act 2009 (Commencement No. 1 and Transitional Provisions) Order* 2009 (S.I. 2009 No. 3253)].

(6) Live link sentencing hearing where accused convicted at other hearings

Crime and Disorder Act 1998, s.57E

Use of live link in sentencing hearings

7–137   **57E.**—(1) This section applies where the accused is convicted of the offence.

(2) If it appears to the court by or before which the accused is convicted that it is likely that he will be held in custody during any sentencing hearing for the offence, the court may give a live link direction under this section in relation to that hearing.

(3) A live link direction under this section is a direction requiring the accused, if he is being held in custody during the hearing, to attend it through a live link from the place at which he is being held.

(4) Such a direction—

(a) may be given by the court of its own motion or on an application by a party; and

(b) may be given in relation to all subsequent sentencing hearings before the court or to such hearing or hearings as may be specified or described in the direction.

(5) The court may not give such a direction unless—

(a) (repealed)

(b) the court is satisfied that it is not contrary to the interests of justice to give the direction.

(6) The court may rescind such a direction at any time before or during a hearing to which it relates if it appears to the court to be in the interests of justice to do so (but this does not affect the court's power to give a further live link direction in relation to the offender).

The court may exercise this power of its own motion or on an application by a party.

(7) The offender may not give oral evidence while attending a hearing through a live link by virtue of this section unless—

(a) (repealed)

(b) the court is satisfied that it is not contrary to the interests of justice for him to give it in that way.

(8) The court must—

(a) state in open court its reasons for refusing an application for, or for the rescission of, a live link direction under this section; and

(b) if it is a magistrates' court, cause those reasons to be entered in the register of its proceedings.

[This section is printed as amended by the *Coroners and Justice Act* 2009, s.106(5). The amendment was brought into force on December 14, 2009; but has no effect in relation to a live link direction given before that date: *Coroners and Justice Act 2009 (Commencement No. 1 and Transitional Provisions) Order* 2009 (S.I. 2009 No. 3253)].

(7) Use of live link in certain enforcement hearings

Crime and Disorder Act 1998, s.57F

Use of live link in certain enforcement hearings

7–137a   **57F.**—(1) This section applies where—

(a) a confiscation order is made against a person; and

    (b) the amount required to be paid under the order is not paid when it is required to be paid.

    (2) If it appears to the court before which an enforcement hearing relating to the confiscation order is to take place that it is likely that the person will be held in custody at the time of the hearing, the court may give a live link direction under this section in relation to that hearing.

    (3) A live link direction under this section is a direction requiring the person, if the person is being held in custody at the time of the hearing, to attend it through a live link from the place at which the person is being held.

    (4) Such a direction—
        (a) may be given by the court of its own motion or on an application by a party; and
        (b) may be given in relation to all subsequent enforcement hearings before the court or to such hearing or hearings as may be specified or described in the direction.

    (5) The court may rescind a live link direction under this section at any time before or during a hearing to which it relates.

    (6) The court may not give or rescind a live link direction under this section (whether at a hearing or otherwise) unless the parties to the proceedings have been given the opportunity to make representations.

    (7) If a hearing takes place in relation to the giving or rescinding of such a direction, the court may require or permit any party to the proceedings who wishes to make representations in relation to the giving or rescission of a live link direction under this section to do so through a live link.

    (8) The person may not give oral evidence while attending a hearing through a live link by virtue of this section unless the court is satisfied that it is not contrary to the interests of justice for the person to give it that way.

    (9) If in a case where it has power to do so a court decides not to give a live link direction under this section, it must—
        (a) state in open court its reasons for not doing so; and
        (b) cause those reasons to be entered in the register of its proceedings.

    (10) The following functions of a magistrates' court under this section may be discharged by a single justice—
        (a) giving a live link direction under this section;
        (b) rescinding a live link direction before a preliminary hearing begins; and
        (c) requiring or permitting a person to attend by live link a hearing about a matter within paragraph (a) or (b).

[This section was inserted by the *Coroners and Justice Act* 2009, s.109(1). It was brought into force as from December 14, 2009: *Coroners and Justice Act 2009 (Commencement No. 1 and Transitional Provisions) Order* 2009 (S.I. 2009 No. 3253)].

(8) Live link in extradition hearings

Policing and Crime Act 2009, s.78, inserted new sections 206A to 206C in the *Extradition Act* 2003, which make provision for the use of live link in certain hearings under Parts 1 and 2 of the 2003 Act. The provisions have effect as from January 25, 2010: *Policing and Crime Act 2009 (Commencement No. 1 and Transitional and Saving Provisions) Order* 2009 (S.I. 2009 No. 3096).   **7–137b**

D. Adjournments

(6) Adjournment of trial

(b) *General principles*

Notwithstanding the width of the discretion when deciding whether to adjourn a trial, a refusal to adjourn would be flawed where the only factor considered was the need for proceedings to be conducted expeditiously, without enquiring as to the next available trial date and without considering the history of the matter, the extent to which the trial would be delayed and the extent to which that would prejudice the other party: *R. (Nadour) v. Chester Magistrates' Court*, unreported, June 11, 2009, DC ([2009] EWHC 1505 (Admin.)).   **7–147**

(c) *Adequate time and facilities for preparation of defence case*

7–148   Where on the day of trial there is a late amendment of the charge or charges arising out of the same or substantially the same facts as the original case, the defendant must be given time to consider his position; but that time should be measured in minutes and there should not be an adjournment to another day, unless there were compelling reasons: *Williams v. DPP* , unreported, July 24, 2009, DC ([2009] EWHC 2354 (Admin)).

(f) *Non-attendance of prosecution witnesses*

7–151   See *R. (Visvaratnam) v. Brent Magistrates' Court* , unreported, October 28, 2009, DC (overturning a decision to adjourn) for a robust observation that the sooner the prosecution realised that they could not rely on their own serious failures to warn witnesses of trial dates, the sooner efficiency in the magistrates' courts would be improved.

(k) *"Ambush defences"*

7–156   The principle that trials by ambush were no longer to take place applies as much to the prosecution as it does to the defence: *Williams v. DPP,* unreported, July 24, 2009, DC ([2009] EWHC 2354 (Admin)).

E. Proceeding where a Party Fails to Appear

(2) The accused

(b) *General principles*

7–162   A decision to proceed in the absence of the accused was flawed where no enquiry was made as to the accused's absence and no consideration was given to whether the matter should be adjourned: see *James v. Tower Bridge Magistrates' Court,* unreported, June 9, 2009, DC ([2009] EWHC 1500(Admin.)).

(g) *Duties of defence advocate where trial proceeds in absence of defendant*

7–165a   Where an defendant has absconded but remains in contact with his lawyers and is then tried in his absence in circumstances where his advocate has not withdrawn, the advocate is not limited to acting on instructions received before the date when the defendant absconded; if there were to be a principle that the advocate were not permitted to take into account fresh instructions received from the absent defendant, it would increase unnecessarily the possibility of error or oversight against which legal representation provided a valuable safeguard; and it could also prevent the advocate from being able to deal effectively with new evidence or new issues, even where the absent defendant had valid points to make in relation to them; but it would always be important for the judge to keep an eye on the overall fairness of the proceedings and to exercise his discretion appropriately to prevent any unfair manipulation of the process by an absent defendant, particularly to the disadvantage of any co-defendants: *R. v. Pomfrett* , unreported, October 8, 2009, CA ([2009] EWCA Crim. 1939).

Part II

Summary Trial

Chapter 8

SUMMARY TRIAL

I. HEARING IN A OPEN COURT

D. Publicity

The new edition of the Guide to Reporting Restrictions in the Criminal Courts, a **8–18** joint production by the Judicial Studies Board, Newspaper Society, Society of Editors and The Times has been published. It can be found on *www.jsboard.co.uk.*. It endorses the open justice principle and states that fair, accurate and contemporaneous media reporting of judicial proceedings should not be prevented by any action of the court unless strictly necessary. It gives guidance on the recommended approach to follow when making decisions to exclude the media or prevent them from reporting proceedings. It states that, unless there are exceptional circumstances laid down by statute and/or common law, a court must not:

- Order or allow the exclusion of the press or public from court for any part of the proceedings
- Permit the withholding of information from the open court proceedings
- Impose permanent or temporary bans on reporting of the proceedings or any part of them including anything that prevents the proper identification, by name and address, of those appearing or mentioned in the course of the proceedings.

A magistrates' court must

- Check the legal basis for any proposed restriction
- Ask whether the action is necessary in the interests of justice – is there evidence to assess this
- If restrictions are necessary, decide how far they should go i.e. are they proportionate
- Invite oral or written media representations
- Hear legal submissions
- Where an order is made reduce it to writing as soon as possible and it should be in precise terms, give the legal basis, the precise scope, the duration and when it will cease to have effect if appropriate
- Notify the media

Where automatic reporting restrictions provide protection it is generally not necessary to impose additional discretionary restrictions. It also lays down that court lists comprising a defendant's name, age, address and, where known, his occupation and alleged offence should be made available to the media.

In *Re British Broadcasting Corporation: Att.-Gen.'s Reference (No.3 of 1999)* **8–19** [2009] 3 W.L.R. 142 the BBC had applied to set aside a reporting restriction imposed in relation to the identity of a defendant acquitted of rape. It was commissioning a series of programmes considering controversial acquittals and submitted that it was in the public interest to identify the defendant in the context of the double jeopardy rule . The House of Lords had to balance the respondent's Art. 8 rights against the BBC's Art. 10 rights over the publication of the fact that retained DNA samples had linked the respondent with a crime where indiscriminate retention of DNA samples had been held to be incompatible with Art. 8. It was held that the Art. 10 rights of freedom of expression meant that this subject was in the public interest and therefore the interference with the Art. 8 right was proportionate

IV. PLEA

A. General

8-74   In December 2009 the Senior Presiding Judge issued a reminder to all members of the judiciary that the word "must" in the Criminal Procedure Rules 2010 R3.8 means must and that exceptions to the rule requiring the pleas to be taken are rare and must be strictly justified. This obligation does not depend on the extent of advance information, service of evidence, disclosure of unused material or the grant of legal aid. The court should also pass sentence the same day if at all possible.

D. Plea of Not Guilty

8-85   The Senior Presiding Judge has emphasised the need for the explicit identification of disputed issues, a timetable for the progress of the case and that only those witnesses who are really needed in relation to genuinely disputed, relevant issues should be required to attend the trial.

V. PRELIMINARY ISSUES

B. Fitness to Plead

8-91   There is no presumption of law that a person suffering from delusions is thereby necessarily unfit to plead: *R.. v. Moyle* [2009] Crim L.R. 586, CA.

D. Abuse of Process

8-95   In determining abuse of process, magistrates must apply the test of *Wednesbury* unreasonableness and must not take into account evidence which was not available to the prosecutor when the information was laid; in a case relating to a local authority's enforcement options for a breach under the *Environmental Protection Act* 1990 it is not reasonable to expect the authority to give an explanation for rejecting alternative options: *London Borough of Wandsworth v. Rashid* (2009) 173 J.P. 547.

8-105   It is not an abuse to institute proceedings for a more serious offence arising out of an incident, where a person has been issued with a fixed penalty notice under the *Criminal Justice and Police Act* 2001 s.2, and has paid the penalty: *R. v. Gore and Maher*, [2009] 2 Cr.App.R. 27.

It is an abuse of process to prosecute someone for related money laundering offences where, arising from the same circumstances, he has been convicted of conspiracy to supply drugs based upon a detailed plea of guilty agreed between the prosecution and defence, and approved by the court, firstly for the purpose of giving an indication of sentence and secondly for sentence itself and where the evidence had been available at the first trial: *CPS v. Mattu* [2009] EWCA Crim 1483.

In the case of *R. (on the application of the Environment Agency) v. Drake* [2010] Env.L.R. 3 it was said that it is a matter for the Agency to determine how it presents the cases it prosecutes. A court, in determining abuse, may take into account the destruction of evidence. If it is evidence upon which the case hangs, a prosecution would inevitably be precluded. If it is evidence which corroborates other evidence its destruction is not fatal and then a court must question whether it has been destroyed deliberately. Where it becomes apparent that evidence fails to corroborate or even contradict other evidence and the Agency is under a duty to disclose that evidence, deliberate destruction after that event and failure to disclose, would amount to abuse.

E. PUBLIC INTEREST IMMUNITY

Where the government is a party to litigation, it has a high duty to assist the court **8–109** with full and accurate explanations of all the facts relevant to the issue that the court must decide; the complete integrity of PII certificates and the schedules attached to them, signed by ministers of the Crown, is essential as the courts must be able to have complete confidence in their credibility and reliability. Where it appears that a court has been misled or may have been misled, it should be notified immediately that there is a possible problem and the matter is under investigation: *R. (Al-Sweady and others) v. Secretary of State for Defence*, [2009] EWHC 1687 (Admin). This PII judgement, given following a stay of judicial review proceedings, warned courts to approach the content of PII certificates and schedules issued by the Ministry of Defence with caution until such time as the Ministry could demonstrate that its procedures had eliminated the risk of the kind of errors occurring that happened in this case.

VII. THE DEFENCE CASE

B. SEQUENCE OF THE DEFENCE EVIDENCE

A defendant has the right to explain his story, however improbable, without being **8–125** subjected to the bench's unnecessary interruptions, sarcasm or hostility; magistrates may clarify ambiguities and the answers given but must not cross-examine, especially during examination-in-chief, nor comment on evidence while it is being given: *Michel v. R.*, *The Times*, November 9, 2009.

C. ROLE OF LEGAL REPRESENTATIVES

Care is needed, where the defendant makes a statement which is not evidence but is **8–131** merely an aid to the legal adviser in assisting to draft questions; magistrates must not make a finding of fact on such a statement or admission made: *Haringey LBC v. Tshilumbe*, [2009] EWHC 2820 (Admin).

F. VIEWING THE SCENE OF THE CRIME

Where a court has decided that an organised view would be impracticable it is not **8–135** appropriate for a magistrate to conduct a private view, take photographs of the site or carry out experiments in relation to the site: *R.. on the application of (Broxbourne Borough Council) v. North and East Hertfordshire Magistrates' Court* [2009] N.P.C. 60.

CHAPTER 9

WITNESSES

IV. THE PROTECTION OF WITNESSES

A. GENERAL

Coroners and Justice Act 2009 ss.88–93

Witness Anonymity Orders are now governed by the *Coroners and Justice Act* 2009 **9–27** Pt 3 Ch. 2 ss.88 -93 which came into force on January 1, 2010.

Conditions for making order

88.—(1) This section applies where an application is made for a witness anonymity order to be made in relation to a witness in criminal proceedings.

(2) The court may make such an order only if it is satisfied that Conditions A to C below are met.

(3) Condition A is that the proposed order is necessary—

(a) in order to protect the safety of the witness or another person or to prevent any serious damage to property, or

(b) in order to prevent real harm to the public interest (whether affecting the carrying on of any activities in the public interest or the safety of a person involved in carrying on such activities, or otherwise).

(4) Condition B is that, having regard to all the circumstances, the effect of the proposed order would be consistent with the defendant receiving a fair trial.

(5) Condition C is that the importance of the witness's testimony is such that in the interests of justice the witness ought to testify and—

(a) the witness would not testify if the proposed order were not made, or

(b) there would be real harm to the public interest if the witness were to testify without the proposed order being made.

(6) In determining whether the proposed order is necessary for the purpose mentioned in subsection (3)(a), the court must have regard (in particular) to any reasonable fear on the part of the witness—

(a) that the witness or another person would suffer death or injury, or

(b) that there would be serious damage to property, if the witness were to be identified.

Relevant considerations Show

89.—(1) When deciding whether Conditions A to C in section 88 are met in the case of an application for a witness anonymity order, the court must have regard to—

(a) the considerations mentioned in subsection (2) below, and

(b) such other matters as the court considers relevant.

(2) The considerations are—

(a) the general right of a defendant in criminal proceedings to know the identity of a witness in the proceedings;

(b) the extent to which the credibility of the witness concerned would be a relevant factor when the weight of his or her evidence comes to be assessed;

(c) whether evidence given by the witness might be the sole or decisive evidence implicating the defendant;

(d) whether the witness's evidence could be properly tested (whether on grounds of credibility or otherwise) without his or her identity being disclosed;

(e) whether there is any reason to believe that the witness—

(i) has a tendency to be dishonest, or

(ii) has any motive to be dishonest in the circumstances of the case, having regard (in particular) to any previous convictions of the witness and to any relationship between the witness and the defendant or any associates of the defendant;

(f) whether it would be reasonably practicable to protect the witness by any means other than by making a witness anonymity order specifying the measures that are under consideration by the court

Warning to jury

90.—(1) Subsection (2) applies where, on a trial on indictment with a jury, any evidence has been given by a witness at a time when a witness anonymity order applied to the witness.

(2) The judge must give the jury such warning as the judge considers appropriate to ensure that the fact that the order was made in relation to the witness does not prejudice the defendant.

Discharge or variation of order

91.—(1) A court that has made a witness anonymity order in relation to any criminal proceedings may in those proceedings subsequently discharge or vary (or further vary) the order if it appears to the court to be appropriate to do so in view of the provisions of sections 88 and 89 that apply to the making of an order.

(2) The court may do so—

(a) on an application made by a party to the proceedings if there has been a material change of circumstances since the relevant time, or

(b) on its own initiative.

(3) The court must give every party to the proceedings the opportunity to be heard—

(a) before determining an application made to it under subsection (2);

(b) before discharging or varying the order on its own initiative.

(4) But subsection (3) does not prevent the court hearing one or more of the parties to the proceedings in the absence of a defendant in the proceedings and his or her legal representatives, if it appears to the court to be appropriate to do so in the circumstances of the case.

(5) "The relevant time" means—

(a) the time when the order was made, or

(b) if a previous application has been made under subsection (2), the time when the application (or the last application) was made.

Discharge or variation after proceedings

92.—(1) This section applies if—

(a) a court has made a witness anonymity order in relation to a witness in criminal proceedings ("the old proceedings"), and

(b) the old proceedings have come to an end.

(2) The court that made the order may discharge or vary (or further vary) the order if it appears to the court to be appropriate to do so in view of—

(a) the provisions of sections 88 and 89 that apply to the making of a witness anonymity order, and

(b) such other matters as the court considers relevant.

(3) The court may do so—

(a) on an application made by a party to the old proceedings if there has been a material change of circumstances since the relevant time, or

(b) on an application made by the witness if there has been a material change of circumstances since the relevant time.

(4) The court may not determine an application made to it under subsection (3) unless in the case of each of the parties to the old proceedings and the witness—

(a) it has given the person the opportunity to be heard, or

(b) it is satisfied that it is not reasonably practicable to communicate with the person.

(5) Subsection (4) does not prevent the court hearing one or more of the persons mentioned in that subsection in the absence of a person who was a defendant in the old proceedings and that person's legal representatives, if it appears to the court to be appropriate to do so in the circumstances of the case.

(6) "The relevant time" means—

> (a) the time when the old proceedings came to an end, or
> (b) if a previous application has been made under subsection (3), the time when the application (or the last application) was made.

Discharge or variation by appeal court

93.—(1) This section applies if—

> (a) a court has made a witness anonymity order in relation to a witness in criminal proceedings ("the trial proceedings"), and
> (b) a defendant in the trial proceedings has in those proceedings—
>> (i) been convicted,
>> (ii) been found not guilty by reason of insanity, or
>> (iii) been found to be under a disability and to have done the act charged in respect of an offence.

(2) The appeal court may in proceedings on or in connection with an appeal by the defendant from the trial proceedings discharge or vary (or further vary) the order if it appears to the court to be appropriate to do so in view of—

> (a) the provisions of sections 88 and 89 that apply to the making of a witness anonymity order, and
> (b) such other matters as the court considers relevant.

(3) The appeal court may not discharge or vary the order unless in the case of each party to the trial proceedings—

> (a) it has given the person the opportunity to be heard, or
> (b) it is satisfied that it is not reasonably practicable to communicate with the person.

(4) But subsection (3) does not prevent the appeal court hearing one or more of the parties to the trial proceedings in the absence of a person who was a defendant in the trial proceedings and that person's legal representatives, if it appears to the court to be appropriate to do so in the circumstances of the case.

(5) In this section a reference to the doing of an act includes a reference to a failure to act.

(6) "Appeal court" means—

> (a) the Court of Appeal,
> (b) the Court of Appeal in Northern Ireland, or
> (c) the Court Martial Appeal Court.

Where an application has been made before January 1st and falls to be heard on or after that date, it is to be treated as an application under the 2009 Act: Sched. 22 para. 16. The 2009 Act will also apply to applications to vary or discharge orders made before December 31, 2008.

Section 98*Coroners and Justice Act* 2009raises the upper age limit of a "child wit- **9–28** ness" from 17 to 18 and extends the use of intermediaries to the examination of defendants. These provisions are not yet in force.

C. WITNESS ANONYMITY

It is important that eye witnesses should testify and whilst the calling of anonymous **9–56A** witnesses must not become a routine event, witness anonymity orders should not be confined to cases of terrorism or gangland killings. The intimidation of witnesses has become a feature of contemporary life: *R. v. Powar* [2009] 2 Cr.App.R. 8.

VII. EXAMINATION IN CHIEF

F. UNFAVOURABLE AND HOSTILE WITNESSES

Criminal Procedure Act 1865, s.3

Once a witness has been treated as hostile, his evidence must be approached with **9–86** caution, even if, in the event he does not prove hostile because he adopts his previous statement: *R. v. Greene*, [2009] EWCA Crim 2282.

CHAPTER 10

EVIDENCE

I. INTRODUCTION

Facts in Issue

While a magistrates' court is entitled to examine all the evidence before it, it has to **10–3**
make clear what the evidential bases to be considered by it are: *Bull v. Northampton
Justices* [2009] EWHC 1768 (Admin).

II. BURDEN AND STANDARD OF PROOF

It is better to describe the criminal standard of proof as being sure of a defendant's **10–6**
guilt; beyond reasonable doubt can lead to confusion: *R. v. Majid* [2009] EWCA Crim
2563.

The burden of proving that a defendant has not acted with reasonable excuse when
breaching an Anti Social Behaviour Order rests on the prosecution: *R.. v. Charles*
[2009] EWCA Crim 1570.

IV. DOCUMENTARY EVIDENCE

B. PUBLIC DOCUMENTS

Evidence of a co-accused's conviction should not be admitted for the purpose of **10–33**
proving that he had committed the offence where his conviction was based on a plea of
guilty entered on a limited basis, if proof of the conviction might found an inference
that his role was greater than admitted in his plea: *R. v. Girma* [2009] EWCA Crim
912.

VII. HEARSAY

C. ADMISSIBILITY

The interests of justice, under s.114 (1) (d) include the public interest in crimes being **10–70**
tried as well as the interests of the accused; where at a retrial, a witness, who was
paralysed, incapable of facial expression, and had at the first trial given his evidence by
pointing to letters on an alphabet board, refused to attend, the record of his evidence at
the first trial was properly admitted: *R. v. Sadiq and Hussein* (2009)173 J P 471.

Text messages from two unidentified sources, stored on mobile telephones found in
the possession of the defendant, are statements defined by s.115; they are inadmissible
unless they can be brought within one of the exceptions in s.114 (1) (a) to (d): *obiter*
remarks in *R. v. Leonard* (2009) 173 J P 366.

Where a conviction is based solely or to a decisive extent on the statement of an
absent witness it does not breach ECHR, provided that the provisions of the *Criminal
Justice Act* 2003 are observed; the sole or decisive rule was introduced into Strasbourg
jurisprudence, largely in relation to civil cases, without discussion of its underlying
principles and without full consideration of whether there was justification for imposing
the rule as an overriding principle applicable equally to both continental and common
law jurisdictions: *R. v. Horncastle* [2010] 2 W.L.R. 47.

If a witness does not attend, the court should look first at s.116. If that does not allow **10–73** the evidence in, the rule in s.114(1)(d) should not be used to circumvent that section. Section 114 (1) (d) should not be used just because a witness is unwilling to give evidence; the question is whether he is unable to give evidence: *R. v Z* [2009] 3 All E.R. 1015.

10–74 The right to confrontation is a long standing right of common law, subsequently recognised by ECHR Art. 6 and must only be departed from in the limited circumstances prescribed by the *Criminal Justice Act*. All possible efforts must be made to get a witness to court and this must start with a witness being given all possible support and being made to understand the importance of the citizen's duty to give evidence: *R. v. T* (2009) 173 J.P. 425. This was a case under s.116(2)(e) where the witness was afraid. The principles laid down however are equally applicable to applications under (d) i.e. that in order to consider an application there must either be an agreed statement of the facts or there must be a finding upon evidence of the steps taken to find the witness. It is then that the court can establish whether steps such as are reasonably practicable have been taken.

VIII. IDENTIFICATION EVIDENCE

A. GENERAL

DNA profiles

10–96 Low template DNA can be used to obtain profiles capable of reliable interpretation if the quantity of DNA that can be analysed is above the stochastic threshold: *R. v. Reed* [2009] EWCA Crim 2698.

B. OPINION

(3) Expert opinion

10–100 It is inappropriate to rule an expert's evidence inadmissible simply because he has some connection with the party intending to call him as a witness; the association might reflect on the weight to be given to the evidence:*Leo Sawrij v. North Cumbria Magistrates' Court*, [2009] EWHC 2823 (Admin).

Where photographic comparison experts give evidence of similarities or dissimilarities between a questioned photograph and a known person, an expert may express a conclusion as to the significance of his findings and can do so by the use of conventional expressions arranged in a hierarchy e.g. "lends support/lends powerful support" but not numbers lest they give the impression of an established, measurable scale: *R.. v. Atkins* (2009) 173 J.P. 529.

The fact that an expert witness may have been discredited (having been convicted of perjury in relation to qualifications) goes to the weight of the evidence, not its admissibility: *Bates v. Chief Constable of Avon and Somerset Police and Bristol Magistrates' Court*, (2009) 173 JP 313.

IX. CHARACTER

B. BAD CHARACTER

Criminal Justice Act 2003, s.98

10–108 Where the defendant is charged with driving while disqualified, evidence of his having been disqualified at the material time falls within the exclusion in s.98:*Director of Public Prosecutions v. Agyemang* (2009) 173 J.P. 487.

10–112 The word "substantial" in the context of s.100 means that the evidence concerned has something more than trivial probative value but not necessarily conclusive probative value: *R. v. S* [2009] EWCA Crim 2457.

A court must be aware of the risk that a trial will lose focus, where an application is **10–116** made to admit bad character evidence and the parties may become embroiled in complex satellite litigation; the risk is greater where there has been no conviction in relation to the conduct alleged, where it is ancient and where it is disputed: *R. v. O'Dowd* [2009] 2 Cr.App.R. 16.

In sexual offences, a previous conviction is admissible for the purposes of showing **10–123** propensity only if the circumstances were such that it has some probative force by reason of similarity to the offence charged: *R. v. Clements, The Times,* December 4 2009.

The Vehicle and Operator Service Agency can introduce an employer's records relating to his checking of employees' completion of tachograph records in a charge of permitting a driver to fail to make those records to show there were previous purported oversights and that it was pertinent background information; it is to do with the offence alleged: *Vehicle and Operator Service Agency v. Ace Crane and Transport Ltd.,* January 19, 2010 unreported.

Where a defendant is charged with sexual activity with a child and says that it was ac- **10–125** cidental evidence of one similar incident 11 years previously is evidence capable of being found to be evidence of propensity: *R. v. Woodhouse* (2009) 173 JP 337 CA.

Propensity is not the only issue to which evidence may go under s.101(1) (d): *R. v. K* [2009] Crim L R 517,CA. Section 103(1) provides that evidence in issue between the defendant and the prosecution "may include" propensity. There will be other issues e.g. *mens rea*, accident, mistake, automatism.

Only prosecution evidence may be admitted under (f) and (g); the mere fact that the **10–128** material is contained in a statement made by a prosecution witness does not make it prosecution evidence: *R. v. Assani* [2009] Crim.L.R.514, CA. In that case it was also decided that where a defendant has elicited evidence of a non violent character it is wrong to allow cross-examination on a 13 year old incident where it was alleged that the defendant, then aged 14, had been violent: 1(e)

A court may allow evidence of a defendant's previous convictions for possession of a **10–131** bladed article where he attacks the character of the victims by suggesting that they had started the violence and colluded in their accounts: *R.. v. O* [2009] EWCA Crim 2235.

X. UNFAIRLY OR ILLEGALLY OBTAINED EVIDENCE

B. UNFAIR EVIDENCE

The prosecution may rely on intercepts and recordings made in a country outside **10–141** the UK but fairness demands that a defendant must be given an opportunity to challenge the use and admission in evidence of material which was said to have been unlawfully obtained: *R.. v. Austin* [2009] EWCA Crim 1527.

Before a court admits statements made during compulsory disclosure in divorce proceedings, it must determine whether their admission would render the trial unfair and, in so doing, it must consider the nature of the compulsion applied, the nature of the evidence obtained by means of it, the social need which the admission is intended to meet and whether the admission is proportionate; the public interest in prosecuting crime is sufficient to outweigh the public interest in the settlement of disputes and it follows that admissions made in the course of "without prejudice" negotiations will not be inadmissible simply by virtue of the fact that they were made during such negotiations: *R. v. K* [2010] 1 Cr.App.R. 3.

XIII. CORROBORATION

Where a laser speed detection device is used, the primary evidence is that of the **10–168** operator; evidence from the device as to the speed at which a motorist is travelling is secondary corroborative evidence and the fact that the device has not been calibrated in accordance with the manufacturer's instructions does not mean that it is no longer of an approved type: *R. (on the application of Bray) v Bristol Crown Court*, [2009] EWHC 3018 (Admin).

CHAPTER 11

CHALLENGING DECISIONS

II. APPEAL TO THE CROWN COURT

B. AGAINST CONVICTION

Only an authority which establishes a principle should be cited; reference should not **11–10** be made to authorities which do no more than either (a) illustrate the principle or (b) restate it: *R. v Erskine, R. v Williams* (2009) 2 Cr.App.R. 29.

III. APPEAL BY WAY OF CASE STATED

A. APPLICATIONS TO STATE CASE

It is highly probable that the High Court does not have power to extend the twenty **11–29** one day limit within which a party must apply to the court to state a case: *Chief Constable of Cleveland v. Vaughan*, [2009] EWHC 2831 (Admin).

A court requested to state a case should not speculate on what may be behind the ap- **11–30** plication nor should it point out to an applicant that he could have appealed to the Crown Court; there is a high threshold required to refuse to state a case as frivolous; time limits do not run until sentence has been concluded; a case must identify the question of law and that question might be whether there was sufficient evidence for the court to be entitled to find the applicant guilty; to ask a discrete series of evidential questions is incorrect:*R. (on the application of McCombie) v. Liverpool City Magistrates' Court,* [2009] EWHC 2881 (Admin).

IV. JUDICIAL REVIEW

A. GENERAL

Oral evidence is not normally given, and in so far as there is a factual dispute be- **11–41** tween the parties, the court is ordinarily obliged to resolve them in favour of the defendant; human rights cases, however, tend to be fact specific and cross-examination is appropriate where there are "hard-edged" questions of fact to resolve and in such cases proper disclosure must be made: *R. (on the application of Al-Sweady) v. Secretary of State for Defence* [2009] EWHC 2387 (Admin).

Part III

Specific Offences

CHAPTER 13

OFFENCES OF VIOLENCE

II. ASSAULT

B. ASSAULT OCCASIONING ACTUAL BODILY HARM

(3) Sentence

In *Southworth* [2009] EWCA Crim 147, CA, the appellant pleaded guilty to a charge **13–15** of assault occasioning actual bodily harm and was sentenced to 12 months' imprisonment. The appellant had punched his partner following a domestic argument, knocking her to the floor and knocking out two of her teeth. Dismissing his appeal against sentence, the Court held that even on the basis that the appellant had acted recklessly, the sentence was not manifestly excessive.

C. WOUNDING OR INFLICTING GRIEVOUS BODILY HARM

(4) Sentence

In *Shannon* [2008] EWCA Crim 2131, CA, the appellant had pleaded guilty to **13–21** inflicting grievous bodily harm and was sentenced to 12 months' imprisonment. Both the appellant and victim were in a bar and had both been drinking. The appellant punched the victim without any provocation, causing a broken jaw and a cracked tooth needing surgery. Substituting a sentence of eight months' imprisonment, the Court stated that although by the standard of offences of grievous bodily harm generally, the injury caused was not particularly grave, it did not follow that the case fell into the lowest category of the guidelines. The case was within the category of "premeditated assault where no weapon has been used". The appropriate starting point after a full trial would have been about 12 months' imprisonment. As the appellant pleaded guilty at the earliest opportunity the appropriate sentence would be eight months' imprisonment.

In *Howard* [2009] EWCA Crim 1984, CA, the Court discussed the meaning of 'particularly grave injury' in the context of the Sentencing Guidelines Council guideline on sentencing offences under section 20 of the *Offences Against the Person Act* 1861. The appellant had been convicted of inflicting grievous bodily harm and was sentenced to 18 months' imprisonment. The appellant had twice pushed the victim, who had attempted to intervene in an argument in a pub. The latter push caused the victim to fall through some patio doors and break his hip. The Court of Appeal stated that although the broken hip was a serious injury, it could not be described as particularly serious by the standards of grievous bodily harm generally. The appropriate starting point for the offence would therefore be six months' imprisonment. The aggravating factors (namely the fact that the victim was entirely innocent, that he was pushed twice with considerable violence, and that the second push resulted in a serious injury to a man of 63) made a sentence of nine months' imprisonment, the maximum recommended by the guideline, appropriate.

III. OFFENCES INVOLVING CHILDREN

B. Child Cruelty

(3) Elements of the Offence

13–57   In *Z* [2008] EWCA Crim 2847, CA, the appellant appealed against a sentence of 26 weeks' imprisonment, suspended for one year, imposed for cruelty to a person under 16. The appellant was a devout Shia Muslim. Whilst attending a religious festival he permitted his sons, aged 15 and 13, to use a zanjeer (a wooden handled instrument with lightweight curved blades) resulting in them sustaining cuts to their backs. The manager of the mosque had ruled that those under 16 were not allowed to use the zanjeer. Dismissing the appeal, the Court held that the judge was faced with a notoriously difficult sentencing exercise and reached a conclusion that could not be faulted. The appellant had ignored advice from mosque elders and his sons caused damage to themselves whilst under his supervision. Those circumstances did pass the custody threshold.

(4) Sentence

13–58   In *Hallmark* [2009] EWCA Crim 1180, CA, the Attorney General referred as unduly lenient a community order made up of a two-year supervision requirement, a prohibited activity requirement and a 250-hour unpaid work requirement imposed on the offender for assault and child cruelty. The offender had committed habitual acts of violence against two of his children and his stepdaughter. The offender pleaded guilty to the offences on a limited basis and received the full discount for his plea. The Attorney General argued that the judge erred in not imposing an immediate term of imprisonment. The Court held that the sentence was unduly lenient but it was not varied. The offences involved chastisement rather than sadism, or violence for its own sake, and there was no serious cruelty. However, the offences were not isolated and were attributable to the offender's repeated loss of temper. A starting point of immediate custody would be appropriate. The sentence was therefore wrong. However, as the sentence had been designed to engage the offender and encourage different behaviour and was working, it was not in the public interest to pass a different sentence.

V. OFFENCES CONNECTED WITH OFFENSIVE WEAPONS

F. Failure to Comply with Condition of Firearm or Shotgun Certificate

(4) Sentence

13–120   In *McCabe* [2009] EWCA Crim 1007, CA, the appellant had been sentenced to a term of 30 months' imprisonment for possession of an imitation firearm in a public place. He had entered a supermarket, under the influence of drink or drugs or both. While he was buying cigarettes, he produced what appeared to be a black handgun and placed it onto the supermarket counter. He did not use the gun in any way and paid for his cigarettes. However, witnesses were extremely frightened. Allowing his appeal, the Court had regard to the fact that the offence was a frightening one for members of the public who were present and did not know the firearm was an imitation. The appellant also had a very significant criminal record. Mitigating factors were the fact that he did not use the gun for any unlawful purpose, and his early guilty plea. The appropriate sentence after a trial in this case would have been nine months' imprisonment, therefore allowing for the appellant's guilty plea, a sentence of six months' imprisonment would be appropriate.

I. Having a Bladed Article in a Public Place

(3) Elements of the offence

An individual may have good reason for carrying a knife if they are carrying a knife **13–127** for their own protection and they can show on the balance of probabilities that they were in fear of an imminent attack: *McAuley* [2009] EWCA Crim 2130, CA.

CHAPTER 15

PROPERTY OFFENCES

I. OFFENCES UNDER THE THEFT ACTS 1968 AND 1978

A. THEFT

(4) Sentence

In *Kinloch* [2009] EWCA Crim 1356, CA, the appellant had pleaded guilty to theft, **15-17** and was sentenced to 16 months' imprisonment. He had worked for his employer, which ran public houses, for several years, and confessed to having stolen more than £20,000 from the company in the space of a fortnight. He told the police that he had gone away for a few days and on his return £2,400 was missing. The appellant had previously been in trouble for taking money from the company, and he was thus worried about his position. He decided to use the money still in the public house to gamble, aiming to recoup the missing £2,400. Using online facilities he gambled, and lost, all this money. Substituting a sentence of nine months' imprisonment, the Court of Appeal referred to the Sentencing Guidelines Council's guideline on theft in breach of trust and stated that the appellant would not fall into the category of theft involving breach of a high degree of trust. The case fell within the category of theft of £2,000 to £20,000.

In *Graham* [2009] EWCA Crim 611, CA, the appellant had pleaded guilty to three offences of theft and been sentenced to eight months' imprisonment on each concurrent with two offences of theft taken into consideration. As part of his job, the appellant had access to sites where there were large quantities of old rail. The appellant had offered this old rail to someone from a haulage company on the understanding that the proceeds from sale of the old rail could be split. The value of the stolen metal amounted to somewhere in the region of £18,300. Substituting a sentence of six months' imprisonment for each offence, to run concurrently, the Court had regard to the aggravating features of the case (namely the abuse of a position of trust, the fact that the offences were the appellant's idea, the fact that the thefts were organised by him and that he profited significantly from them). However, the appellant was entitled to full discount for his pleas of guilty and his acceptance of guilt at an early stage, and there was substantial mitigation in the context of previous good character of a very positive kind.

In *De Weever* [2009] EWCA Crim 803, CA, the appellant had pleaded guilty to an offence of theft, and sentenced to 18 months' imprisonment (less 132 days spent in custody on remand). The appellant had stolen the victim's purse from her bag after pushing her as she boarded a train. Substituting a sentence of 10 months' imprisonment, the Court had regard to the Sentencing Guidelines Council guideline on sentencing offences of theft from the person and held that the sentencing judge's decision to consider the victim to be a vulnerable person was wrong. The victim had been targeted because she was carrying a bag which enabled the appellant to steal without her realising in time, not because she was of an age, or suffering from a disability, that made her unlikely or unable to resist the theft. The appropriate starting point would therefore be a medium level community order with a range from a fine to 18 weeks in custody. The Court went on to identify aggravating features of the offence (namely, the offence was clearly planned and, as the photographs from the CCTV footage show, carried out in a highly professional manner; it involved the use of force (the push) short of robbery; it involved a high level of inconvenience to the victim, who lost, amongst other things, a credit card and a debit card; the appellant had a number of previous convictions for theft and attempted theft from the person, albeit their aggravation is tempered by the fact that they were committed many years ago and more importantly, the appellant had plainly failed to respond to his most recent sentences). These aggravating factors took the sentence out of the lower bracket in the sentencing guideline and into the bracket above it, which gave a starting point of 12 months' imprisonment. The only mitigation was the appellant's last minute guilty plea, which made a total sentence of 10 months' imprisonment (less the 132 days spent on remand) appropriate.

B. Burglary

(4) Sentence

15–27　　Whilst the decision in *Saw* [2009] EWCA Crim 1, CA, stressed the impact of burglary on home-owners, the courts may, in certain circumstances, take a lenient approach to sentence, especially in the case of a young offender or a first offender, or an offender who had reached a critical stage in his life with a real prospect of turning his back on crime: *Martin* [2009] EWCA Crim 1963, CA. In this case, the appellant appealed against a sentence of 16 months' detention in a young offender institution following his guilty plea to an offence of burglary. The appellant had burgled an isolated family home, taking property worth approximately £12,000. Prior to his conviction for that offence, he had received a suspended sentence order for two other burglaries, with eight matters of burglary or attempted burglary taken into consideration, but the appellant had not requested that this burglary be taken into consideration. He had no previous convictions prior to the suspended sentence order. Allowing his appeal, the Court held that the appellant's genuine attempt to break the cycle of offending was a factor which the court should take into account, set against the aggravating features of the case. The appellant was 19 years old, in good employment, had very favourable references, had complied with the suspended sentence order and had a very low risk of reoffending. The sentence was quashed and a sentence of six months' detention in a young offender institution was substituted. The revocation of the suspended sentence order was confirmed.

H. False Accounting

(4) Sentence

15–61　　The Sentencing Guidelines Council guideline on *Sentencing for Fraud – statutory offences*, issued on October 13, 2009, states that false accounting under s.17 of the *Theft Act* 1968 may be sentenced as a type of confidence fraud; as fraud involving banking and insurance fraud; as obtaining credit through fraud; as benefit fraud or as revenue fraud (against HM Revenue and Customs). The Sentencing Guidelines Council's guideline on these types of fraud is considered at 15-109, below.

II. OFFENCES UNDER THE FRAUD ACT 2006

A. General

Introduction

15–102　　On October 13, 2009, the Sentencing Guidelines Council published a Final Guideline on *Sentencing for Fraud – statutory offences*. For the guideline in full, see *http://www.sentencing-guidelines.gov.uk/docs/sentencing_for_fraud_statutory_offences.pdf.*

The introduction to the guideline states that since many of the fraud offences are defined broadly (in order to encapsulate a wide range of behaviour), some types of fraudulent activity are capable of leading to conviction for more than one offence; accordingly, the guidelines focus on the type of fraud, rather than the specific conviction offence, in order to establish appropriate sentence levels which take account of the inter-relationship between the offences. The offences are grouped by type as follows:

Confidence fraud
Fraud Act 2006, s.1
Theft Act 1968, s.17
Possessing, making or supplying articles for use in fraud
Fraud Act 2006, ss.1, 6 and 7
Banking and insurance fraud, and obtaining credit through fraud
Fraud Act 2006, s.1
Theft Act 1968, s.17
Benefit fraud
Fraud Act 2006, s.1
Theft Act 1968, s.17
Tax Credits Act 2002, s.35
Social Security Administration Act 1992, ss.111A(1), 111(1A), 111(1B), 111(1D) and 111(1E)
Revenue fraud (against HM Revenue and Customs)
Fraud Act 2006, s.1
Theft Act 1968, s.17
Value Added Tax Act 1994, ss.72(1), 72(3), and 72(8)
Finance Act 2000, s.144
Customs and Excise Management Act 1979, ss.170(1)(a)(i) and (ii), 170(1)(b), 170(2)(a), 170B, 50(1)(a), and 50(2)*

The guideline states that the offence of obtaining services dishonestly (contrary to s.11 of the *Fraud Act* 2006) may be committed in circumstances that otherwise could be charged as an offence contrary to s.1 of the Act or may be more akin to the offence under the *Theft Act*. For this reason, it has not been included specifically within any of these guidelines, and one of the following approaches should be used:

1. Where it involves conduct which can be characterised as a fraud offence (such as obtaining credit through fraud or payment card fraud), the court should apply the guideline for the relevant type of fraud; or

2. Where the conduct could be characterised as *making off without payment* (that is, where an offender, knowing that payment on the spot for any goods supplied or service done is required or expected, dishonestly makes off without having paid and with intent to avoid payment), the guideline for that offence in the *Magistrates' Court Sentencing Guidelines* (2008) should be used.

The guideline states that the primary consideration when sentencing fraud offences is the seriousness of the offending behaviour. Sentencers must also have regard to the five purposes of sentencing set out in s.142(1) of the *Criminal Justice Act* 2003; as a general principle, the approach to sentencing types of fraud offence should be the same, regardless of the context within which the offence was committed.

The approach to sentencing, starting points and ranges takes account of the other sanctions and ancillary orders likely to be applied (some of which are mandatory and others discretionary), which may have a significant impact on an offender. The guideline applies to the sentencing of adult offenders only; separate legislative provisions and sentencing principles apply to young offenders.

Assessing seriousness
The court must consider the offender's culpability in committing the offence and any harm that the offence caused, was intended to cause, or might foreseeably have caused. Key considerations are the degree of planning, the determination with which the offender carried out the offence and the value of the money or property involved.

Culpability and harm
The guideline refers to the four levels of culpability set out in the *Overarching Principles: Seriousness* guideline and states that it is a general feature of fraud offences

that an offender intended to bring about a gain (whether for the offender or for another person) or to cause a loss, or risk of loss, to another (except VAT fraud, which can be committed recklessly). Fraud offences will therefore generally involve the highest level of culpability. Within that level, culpability will vary according to the offender's motivation, whether the offence was planned or spontaneous and whether the offender was in a position of trust.

Where the offending involves a number of people acting co-operatively, the offence of fraud will be aggravated as it indicates planning or professional activity; it may also increase the degree of loss caused or intended. As a result, it is likely to cause an offence to be in a higher level of seriousness. The role of each offender will therefore be important in determining movement above or below the starting point within the range applicable to that level (see aggravating and mitigating factors below).

The guideline states that fraud is not a victimless crime.

In assessing the harm caused by fraud offences, the primary consideration is the loss to the victim or to the community at large. In some fraud cases, the harm that results from an offence may be greater than the harm intended by the offender. In others, the offender may have intended more harm than actually results. In these situations, the harm caused by the offence should be judged in light of the offender's culpability.

In general terms, the greater the loss, the more serious will be the offence. However, the financial value of the loss may not reflect the full extent of the harm caused by the offence. The court should also take into account:

(a) The impact of the offence on the victim

(b) Harm to persons other than the direct victim

(c) Erosion of public confidence

(d) Any physical harm or risk of physical harm to the direct victim or another person

(e) Difference between loss intended and resulting

(f) Legitimate entitlement to part or all of the amount obtained

Aggravating factors

Factors indicating higher culpability

Planning of an offence

An intention to commit more serious harm than actually resulted from the offence (including any physical harm or risk of physical harm)

Offenders operating in groups or gangs

'Professional offending'

High level of profit from the offence

An attempt to conceal or dispose of evidence

Deliberate targeting of vulnerable victim(s)

Abuse of a position of trust

Factors indicating a more than usually serious degree of harm

Multiple victims

Victim is particularly vulnerable

High value (including sentimental value) of property to the victim, or substantial consequential loss

The Council identified four factors that are particularly relevant to this type of offending behaviour:

(a) *Number involved in the offence and role of offender*

(b) *Offending carried out over a significant period of time*

(c) *Use of another person's identity*

(d) *Offence has a lasting effect on the victim*

Mitigating factors

Factors indicating significantly lower culpability:

Mental illness or disability

Youth or age, where it affects the responsibility of the individual defendant

The fact that the offender played only a minor role in the offence

The Council identified three mitigating factors that are particularly relevant to this type of offending:

(a) *Peripheral involvement*

(b) *Behaviour not fraudulent from the outset*

(c) *Misleading or incomplete advice*

Personal mitigation

(a) *Voluntary cessation of offending*

(b) *Complete and unprompted disclosure of the extent of the fraud*

(c) *Voluntary restitution*

(d) *Financial pressure*

Combining custodial sentences and fines

The guideline states that the issue of whether to impose a fine alongside a custodial sentence may arise when sentencing for fraud offences. If a fine is imposed, further issues arise concerning the impact of the fine on the length of the custodial sentence. In the light of additional powers relating to confiscation and to seizure of assets and the proceeds of crime, a court normally should not impose a fine alongside a custodial sentence. However, exceptionally, it may be appropriate to impose a fine in addition to a custodial sentence where:

(i) a confiscation order is not being contemplated; and

(ii) there is no obvious victim to whom compensation can be awarded; and

(iii) the offender has, or will have, resources from which a fine can be paid.

A court must ensure that the overall sentence remains commensurate with the seriousness of the offence and that the size of the fine does not enable wealthier offenders to 'buy themselves out of custody'.

Ancillary and other orders

Orders relating to property that either must be considered or are most likely to be imposed in relation to fraud offences are:

(i) Compensation order

(ii) Confiscation order

(iii) Deprivation order

(iv) Restitution order

(v) Disqualification from acting as a company director

(vi) Disqualification from driving

(vii) Financial reporting order

(viii) Serious crime prevention order

Guidelines and approach to sentencing

The guidelines are based on types of conduct reflecting common fraudulent behaviour. Confidence frauds are dealt with as a separate category as is the possession, making or supply of articles for use in fraud.

A further group includes those offences committed against an organisation in either the private or public sector; most commonly, in the public sector these will arise in relation to the tax and benefit system and, in the private sector, in relation to banking and insurance.

Although not intended to be exclusive, each guideline includes examples of the fraudulent activity likely to have taken place. In addition, the guideline refers to the offences under which the activity might be charged and the related legislative provisions.

The starting points and sentencing ranges for banking and insurance fraud, for benefit fraud, and for fraud against HM Revenue and Customs (revenue fraud) are the same since the seriousness of all offences of organisational fraud derives from the extent of the fraudulent activity (culpability) and the financial loss caused or likely to be caused (harm).

Separate guidelines are provided for banking, insurance and credit fraud, benefit fraud and revenue fraud, allowing greater detail of the types of activity and the aggravating or mitigating factors likely to be particularly relevant to be included.

In relation to these types of fraud, the Council considers that there will be few cases where £100,000 or more is obtained in a single fraudulent transaction. Similarly, it is likely that there will be few cases where less than £20,000 is obtained in a professionally planned fraud carried out over a significant period of time or multiple professionally planned frauds. Accordingly, the Council has not proposed starting points and ranges for such frauds. In this chapter, the guidelines on each type of fraud will be considered alongside the individual offences to which they relate.

(4) Sentence

15–109　　The Sentencing Guidelines Council guideline on *Sentencing for Fraud – statutory offences* states that frauds under s.1 of the *Fraud Act* 2006 may be sentenced as confidence frauds; frauds involving the possession, making or supplying articles for use in fraud; banking and insurance fraud, and obtaining credit through fraud; benefit fraud and revenue fraud.

CONFIDENCE FRAUD

Factors to take into consideration

This type of offending involves a victim transferring money and/or property as a result of being deceived or misled by the offender. An example of a simple confidence fraud is a person claiming to be collecting money for charity when, in fact, he or she intends to keep the money. Other examples of common confidence frauds are:

> *Advance fee frauds*—Common advance fee frauds include *lottery/prize draw scams* and *foreign money-making frauds*.
>
> *Fraudulent sales of goods and services*—These include goods that are never received by the purchaser or are worth less than the seller represents; services that are unnecessary, overpriced or not performed; and investments that are never obtained for the investor or are worth less than the seller represents.

A factor common to many confidence frauds is that the offender targets a vulnerable victim; it is therefore a determinant of seriousness for this type of fraud. An offender is more culpable if he or she deliberately targets a victim who is vulnerable as a result of old age, youth or disability and there is a more than usually serious degree of harm where the victim is particularly vulnerable.

Some victims of advance fee frauds may have personalities which make them 'vulnerable in a way and to a degree not typical of the general population' because they fall for scams many times. It is a feature of some advance fee frauds that victims are targeted using 'sucker lists' of people who have previously fallen victim to scams. An offender who uses a 'sucker list' will have planned the offence and deliberately targeted vulnerable victims; therefore he or she has a higher level of culpability.

As the determinants of seriousness include the "value of property or consequential loss involved", the table provides both a fixed amount (on which the starting point is based) and a band (on which the sentencing range is based). Where the value is larger or smaller than the amount on which the starting point is based, this should lead to upward or downward movement as appropriate. Where the amount the offender intended to obtain cannot be established, the appropriate measure will be the amount that was likely to be achieved in all the circumstances.

A further determinant of seriousness is whether the fraud was a single fraudulent transaction or a multiple fraud. Most confidence frauds will by their nature involve many actual or potential victims and multiple transactions and should be regarded as multiple fraud.

Confidence fraud

Fraud: *Fraud Act* 2006 (s.1)
False accounting: *Theft Act* 1968 (s.17)
Maximum penalty: Fraud, 10 years custody
False accounting, 7 years custody

Nature of offence	Value of property or consequential loss			
	£500,000 or more Starting point based on: £750,000*	£100000 or more and less than £500,000 Starting point based on: £300,000*	£20,000 or more and less than £100,000 Starting point based on: £60,000*	Less than £20,000 Starting point based on: £10,000*
Large scale advance fee fraud **or** other confidence fraud involving the deliberate targeting of a large number of vulnerable victims	**Starting point:** 6 years custody **Range:** 5-8 years custody	Starting point: 5 years custody **Range** : 4-7 years Custody	**Starting point:** 4 years custody **Range:** 3-6 years custody	**Starting point:** 3 years custody **Range:** 2-5 years custody
Lower scale advance fee fraud **or** other confidence fraud characterised by a degree of planning and/or multiple transactions	**Starting point:** 5 years custody **Range** : 4-7 years custody	**Starting point:** 4 years custody **Range:** 3-6 years custody	**Starting point:** 3 years custody **Range:** 2-5 years custody	**Starting point:** 18 months custody **Range:** 26 weeks-3 years Custody
Single fraudulent transaction confidence fraud involving targeting of a vulnerable victim			**Starting point:** 26 weeks custody **Range:** Community order (HIGH)-18 months custody	**Starting point:** 6 weeks custody **Range:** Community order (MEDIUM)-26 weeks custody

Single fraudulent transaction confidence fraud not targeting a vulnerable victim, and involving no or limited planning			**Starting point:** 12 weeks custody **Range**: Community order (MEDIUM)-36 weeks custody	**Starting point:** Community order (MEDIUM) Range:Fine-6 weeks custody

* Where the actual amount is greater or smaller than the figure on which the starting point is based, that is likely to be one of the factors that will move the sentence within the range.

Additional aggravating factors	Additional mitigating factors
1. Number involved in the offence and role of the offender	1. Peripheral involvement
2. Offending carried out over a significant period of time	2. Behaviour not fraudulent from the outset
3. Use of another person's identity	3. Misleading or inaccurate advice
4. Offence has a lasting effect on the victim	

The presence of one or more aggravating factors may indicate a more severe sentence within the suggested range while the presence of one or more mitigating factors may indicate a less severe sentence within the suggested range.

The presence of aggravating or mitigating factors of exceptional significance may indicate that the case should move to a higher or lower level of seriousness.

POSSESSING, MAKING OR SUPPLYING ARTICLES FOR USE IN FRAUD

There are many ways in which offenders may commit this group of offences. 'Articles' will include any electronic programs or data stored electronically.

As lists of credit card and bank account details constitute 'articles', the making of such lists through certain electronic programmes, which contravenes s.1 of the *Fraud Act* 2006, is also criminalised by s.7 of the same Act. The Council considers that carrying out the following activities should be treated as making articles for use in fraud and sentenced using this guideline, regardless of whether the offence is charged under s.1 or s.7:

> *Phishing* —where an offender sends an email purporting to come from a financial institution, which asks victims to follow a hyperlink to a (false) website and induces them to enter their card or account details;
>
> *Vishing* —where an offender uses an automated telephone system, purporting to be the telephone system of a financial institution, to induce victims to disclose their card or account details;
>
> *Pharming* —where victims intend to visit a financial institution's website but are redirected to the offender's website (which purports to be the financial institution's website) and induced to enter their card or account details; and
>
> *Use of a 'Trojan'*—where an offender installs a virus on victims' computers to gain access to their card or account details. Often the offender will send an email inducing victims to visit a website, where the virus is automatically downloaded onto their computers.

Making, adapting, supplying or offering to supply computer programmes, emails or websites for the above activities amounts to an offence under s.7 of the *Fraud Act* 2006.

Offenders who possess, make or supply articles for use in fraud intend their actions to lead to a fraud. Such offenders therefore have the highest level of culpability.

There are three types of activity relating to articles for use in fraud: making or adapting, supplying or offering to supply and possession. The guideline does not distinguish between the first two categories; they carry the same maximum penalty and, depending on the sophistication and planning involved and the harm resulting from an offence, they may be equally serious.

The three offences in this group all involve an element of planning (whether by the offender or by another person); the planning of an offence has been identified by the Council as a factor indicating a higher level of culpability and the proposed starting points incorporate this aggravating factor.

In relation to harm, the value of the fraud (either that intended by the offender where that can be ascertained, or that which was likely to be achieved) is not a determinant of seriousness for these offences in the way that it is for other offences of fraud. However, it is a factor that should be taken into account in determining the appropriate sentence within the sentencing range.

Possessing, making or supplying articles for use in fraud

Possession of articles for use in frauds: *Fraud Act* 2006 (s.6)
Making or supplying articles for use in frauds: *Fraud Act* 2006 (s.7)
Fraud: *Fraud Act* 2006 (s.1)

Maximum penalty: Possession of articles for use in frauds, 5 years custody. For both other offences, 10 years custody

	Type of offence	
Nature of offence	Making or adapting (ss.1 or 7) **or** Supplying or offering to supply (s.7)	Possessing (s.6)
Article(s) intended for use in an extensive and skilfully planned fraud	**Starting point:** 4 years custody **Range:** 2-7 years custody	**Starting point:** 36 weeks custody **Range:** 6 weeks–2 years custody
Article(s) intended for use in a less extensive and less skilfully planned fraud	**Starting point:** 26 weeks custody **Range:** Community order (HIGH)-2 years custody	**Starting point:** Community order (MEDIUM) **Range:** Community order (LOW)-26 weeks custody

Additional aggravating factors	Additional mitigating factors
1. Number involved in the offence and role of the offender	1. Peripheral involvement
2. Offending carried out over a significant period of time	
3. Use of another person's identity	
4. Offence has a lasting effect on the victim	

The presence of one or more aggravating factors may indicate a more severe sentence within the suggested range while the presence of one or more mitigating factors may indicate a less severe sentence within the suggested range.

The presence of aggravating or mitigating factors of exceptional significance may indicate that the case should move to a higher or lower level of seriousness.

BANKING AND INSURANCE FRAUD, AND OBTAINING CREDIT THROUGH FRAUD

Types of offending behaviour include:

Payment card and bank account fraud—Frauds involving the use of payment cards and bank accounts include use of another person's card, cloning another person's card, taking over or sending instructions relating to another person's bank or card account, and use of another person's cheque.

Insurance fraud —Fraudulent claims by or against the insurer (claims that are entirely fraudulent and those that are exaggerated through either claiming for injury, loss or damage that did not occur or increasing the value of a genuine claim for injury, loss or damage) and supplier fraud (whereby builders, motor repairers and other trades-people engaged by insurers to repair insured property charge for work that they have not done or inflate the cost of their work).

Obtaining credit through fraud —Obtaining credit through fraud includes the fraudulent obtaining of mortgages, loans, interest free credit, in-store credit, goods or services on a 'buy now pay later' basis, car finance, credit cards, store cards, and bank accounts (with overdrafts).

A payment card or bank account fraud is unlikely to be committed in circumstances where the offender's intention was not fraudulent from the outset.

As the determinants of seriousness include the "value of property or consequential loss involved", the table provides both a fixed amount (on which the starting point is based) and a band (on which the sentencing range is based). Where the value is larger or smaller than the amount on which the starting point is based, this should lead to upward or downward movement as appropriate. Where the amount the offender intended to obtain cannot be established, the appropriate measure will be the amount that was likely to be achieved in all the circumstances.

A further determinant of seriousness is whether the fraud was a single fraudulent transaction or a multiple fraud. Where one false declaration or a failure to disclose a change in circumstances results in multiple payments, this should be regarded as multiple fraud.

The maximum penalty for most of the offences covered by this guideline is seven years imprisonment. Where fraud under the 2006 Act is charged and the maximum penalty is 10 years, the proposed sentencing ranges leave headroom for offences involving the most serious frauds to be sentenced outside the range and up to the maximum.

Banking and insurance fraud, and obtaining credit through fraud

Maximum penalty: Fraud (prosecuted under the *Fraud Act* 2006), 10 years custody. For all other offences, seven years custody.

	Amount obtained or intended to be obtained				
Nature of offence	**£500,000 or more Starting point based on: £750,000***	**£100,000 or more and less than £500,000 Starting point based on: £300,000***	**£20,000 or more and less than £100,000 Starting point based on: £60,000***	**£5,000 or more and less than £20,000 Starting point based on: £12,500***	**Less than £5,000 Starting point based on: £2,500***
Fraudulent from the outset, professionally planned **and either** fraud carried out over a significant period of time **or** multiple frauds	**Starting point**: 5 years custody **Range:** 4-7 years custody	**Starting point**: 4 years custody **Range:** 3-5 years custody	**Starting point**: 2 years custody **Range:** 18 months- 3 years custody		
Fraudulent from the outset **and either** fraud carried out over a significant period of time **or** multiple frauds	**Starting point**: 4 years custody **Range:** 3-7 years custody	**Starting point**: 3 years custody **Range:** 2-4 years custody	**Starting point**: 15 months custody **Range:** 18 weeks-30 months custody	**Starting point**: 12 weeks custody **Range:** Community order (HIGH)-12 months custody	**Starting point:** Community order (HIGH) **Range:** Community order (LOW)-6 weeks custody
Not fraudulent from the outset **and either** fraud carried out over a significant period of time **or** multiple frauds	**Starting point**: 3 years custody **Range:** 2-6 years custody	**Starting point**: 2 years custody **Range:** 12 months-3 years custody	**Starting point**: 36 weeks custody **Range:** 12 weeks-18 months custody	**Starting point**: 6 weeks custody **Range:** Community order (MEDIUM)- 26 weeks custody	**Starting point:** Community order (MEDIUM) **Range:** Fine-Community order (HIGH)

Single fraudulent transaction, fraudulent from the outset			**Starting point:**26 weeks custody **Range:** 6 weeks-12 months custody	**Starting point:** Community order (HIGH) **Range:** Fine-18 weeks custody	**Starting point:** Community order (LOW) **Range:** Fine-Community order (MEDIUM)
Single fraudulent transaction, not fraudulent from the outset			**Starting point:** 12 weeks custody Range: Community order (MEDIUM)-36weeks weeks custody	**Starting point:** Community order (MEDIUM) **Range:** Fine-6 weeks custody	**Starting point:** Fine **Range:** Fine-Community order (LOW)

* Where the actual amount is greater or smaller than the figure on which the starting point is based, that is likely to be one of the factors that will move the sentence within the range.

Additional aggravating factors	Additional mitigating factors
1. Number involved in the offence and role of the offender	1. Peripheral involvement
2. Use of another person's identity	2. Misleading or incomplete advice

The presence of one or more aggravating factors may indicate a more severe sentence within the suggested range while the presence of one or more mitigating factors may indicate a less severe sentence within the suggested range.

The presence of aggravating or mitigating factors of exceptional significance may indicate that the case should move to a higher or lower level of seriousness.

BENEFIT FRAUD

This guideline is based on an understanding that the prosecutor will generally seek summary trial for appropriate benefit fraud cases involving sums up to £35,000; the Council does not consider that the starting points proposed would interfere with that practice.

The Council's proposals are governed by bands based on amounts of money. The starting point defined at the top of each column relates to the midpoint of each financial band.

As the determinants of seriousness include the "value of property or consequential loss involved", the table provides both a fixed amount (on which the starting point is based) and a band (on which the sentencing range is based). Where the value is larger or smaller than the amount on which the starting point is based, this should lead to upward or downward movement as appropriate. Where the amount the offender intended to obtain cannot be established, the appropriate measure will be the amount that was likely to be achieved in all the circumstances.

A further determinant of seriousness is whether the fraud was a single fraudulent transaction or a multiple fraud. Where one false declaration or a failure to disclose a change in circumstances results in multiple payments, this should be regarded as multiple fraud.

The Council considers it unlikely that more than £100,000 could be obtained in a benefit fraud, unless the offence was professionally planned and either carried out over a significant period of time or through multiple frauds. In addition, it is unlikely that more than £20,000 could be obtained in a single fraudulent transaction benefit fraud. Consequently, the guideline does not provide separately for such circumstances.

The maximum penalty for most of the offences covered by this guideline is seven years imprisonment. Where fraud under the 2006 Act is charged and the maximum penalty is 10 years, the proposed sentencing ranges leave headroom for offences involving the largest scale frauds to be sentenced outside the range and up to the maximum.

Benefit Fraud

Maximum penalty: Fraud (prosecuted under the *Fraud Act* 2006), 10 years custody. For all other offences, seven years custody

	Amount obtained or intended to be obtained				
Nature of offence	£500,000 or more **Starting point based on:** £750,000*	£100,000 or more and less than £500,000 **Starting point based on:** £300,000*	£20,000 or more and less than £100,000 **Starting point based on:** £60,000*	£5,000 or more and less than £20,000 **Starting point based on:** £12,500*	Less than £5,000 **Starting point based on:** £2,500*
Fraudulent from the outset, professionally planned **and either** fraud carried out over a significant period of time **or** multiple frauds	**Starting point:** 5 years custody **Range:** 4-7 years custody	**Starting point:** 4 years custody **Range:** 3-5 years custody	**Starting point:** 2 years custody **Range:** 18 months-3 years custody		

Fraudulent from the outset **and either** fraud carried out over a significant period of time **or** multiple frauds	**Starting point:** 4 years custody **Range:** 3-7 years custody	**Starting point:** 3 years custody **Range:** 2-4 years custody	**Starting point:** 15 months custody **Range:** 18 weeks-30 months custody	**Starting point:** 12 weeks custody **Range:** Community order (HIGH)-12 months custody	**Starting point:** Community order (HIGH) **Range:** Community order (LOW)-6 weeks custody
Not fraudulent from the outset **and either** fraud carried out over a significant period of time **or** multiple frauds	**Starting point:** 3 years custody **Range:** 2-6 years custody	Starting point: 2 years custody **Range:** 12 months-3 years custody	**Starting point:** 36 weeks custody **Range:** 12 weeks-18 months custody	**Starting point:** 6 weeks custody **Range:** Community order (MEDIUM)-26 weeks custody	**Starting point:** Community order (MEDIUM) **Range:** Fine-Community order (HIGH)
Single fraudulent transaction, fraudulent from the outset			**Starting point:** 26 weeks custody **Range:** 6 weeks-12 months custody	**Starting point:** Community order (HIGH) **Range:** Fine-18 weeks custody	**Starting point:** Community order (LOW) **Range:** Fine-Community order (MEDIUM)
Single fraudulent transaction, not fraudulent from the outset			**Starting point:** 12 weeks custody **Range:** Community order (MEDIUM)-36 weeks custody	**Starting point:** Community order (MEDIUM) **Range:** Fine-6 weeks custody	**Starting point:** Fine **Range:** Fine-Community order (LOW)

* Where the actual amount is greater or smaller than the figure on which the starting point is based, that is likely to be one of the factors that will move the sentence within the range.

Additional aggravating factors	Additional mitigating factors
1. Number involved in the offence and role of the offender	1. Peripheral involvement
2. Use of another person's identity	2. Misleading or incomplete advice

The presence of one or more aggravating factors may indicate a more severe sentence within the suggested range while the presence of one or more mitigating factors may indicate a less severe sentence within the suggested range.

The presence of aggravating or mitigating factors of exceptional significance may indicate that the case should move to a higher or lower level of seriousness.

REVENUE FRAUD (AGAINST HM REVENUE AND CUSTOMS (HMRC))

This type of offending may take many forms, including:

Fraudulent evasion of VAT—this includes situations where a trader does not charge VAT to the customer, situations where a customer pays VAT to the trader but the trader does not pay it to HM Revenue and Customs (HMRC), and so-called 'Missing Trader Intra-Community Frauds' (MTIC Frauds) or 'Carousel Frauds'.

MTIC Frauds— involve traders importing goods from the European Union free from VAT, charging VAT when they sell the goods and then keeping the money rather than paying it to HMRC. Carousel Frauds are MTIC Frauds where the trader sells the goods to another trader who re-exports them and claims back the VAT paid to the first trader from HMRC. Usually the goods are passed along a chain of traders between the missing trader and the broker known as 'buffers', in order to disguise the fraudulent nature of the activity. Having been exported by the broker, the goods are typically re-imported by the missing trader and pass through the same circle of transactions again and again in rapid succession

Fraudulent evasion of income tax—this may be committed by failing to declare earnings in a tax return or by an employer keeping the tax collected from employees rather than paying it to HMRC.

Fraudulent evasion of excise duty—this includes alcohol and tobacco smuggling and the laundering of 'red diesel' into diesel engine road fuel.

The Council considers it unlikely that more than £20,000 could be obtained in a single fraudulent transaction against HMRC in circumstances where the offender's intention was not fraudulent from the outset or where the claim was exaggerated. In addition, it is unlikely that more than £100,000 could be obtained in a fraud against HMRC in circumstances where the offender's intention was not fraudulent from the outset.

As in other types of fraud, the fact that the behaviour was not fraudulent from the outset may be a mitigating factor. Although the type of harm is the same since both lead to a loss to HMRC, where payment is sought from HMRC in such circumstances, culpability is likely to be higher. Such offences are therefore likely to be regarded as more serious.

As the determinants of seriousness include the "value of property or consequential loss involved", the table provides both a fixed amount (on which the starting point is based) and a band (on which the sentencing range is based). Where the value is larger or smaller than the amount on which the starting point is based, this should lead to upward or downward movement as appropriate. Where the amount the offender intended to obtain cannot be established, the appropriate measure will be the amount that was likely to be achieved in all the circumstances.

A further determinant of seriousness is whether the fraud was a single fraudulent transaction or a multiple fraud. Where one false declaration or a failure to disclose a change in circumstances results in multiple payments, this should be regarded as multiple fraud.

The maximum penalty for most of the offences covered by this guideline is seven years' imprisonment. Where fraud under the 2006 Act is charged and the maximum penalty is 10 years, the proposed sentencing ranges leave headroom for offences involving multi-million pound frauds to be sentenced outside the range and up to the maximum.

	Amount obtained or intended to be obtained				
Nature of offence	**£500,000 or more Starting point based on: £750,000***	**£100,000 or more and less than £500,000 Starting point based on: £300,000***	**£20,000 or more and less than £100,000 Starting point based on: £60,000***	**£5,000 or more and less than £20,000 Starting point based on: £12,500***	**Less than £5,000 Starting point based on: £2,500***
Fraudulent from the outset, professionally planned **and either** fraud carried out over a significant period of time **or** multiple frauds	**Starting point:** 5 years custody **Range:** 4-7 years custody	**Starting point:** 4 years custody **Range:** 3-5 years custody	**Starting point:** 2 years custody **Range:** 18 months-3 years custody		
Fraudulent from the outset **and either** fraud carried out over a significant period of time **or** multiple frauds	**Starting point:** 4 years custody **Range:** 3-7 years custody	**Starting point:** 3 years custody **Range:** 2-4 years custody	**Starting point:** 15 months custody **Range:** 18 weeks-30 months custody	Starting point: 12 weeks custody **Range:** Community order (HIGH)-12 months custody	**Starting point:** Community order (HIGH) **Range:** Community order (LOW)-6 weeks custody

Not fraudulent from the outset **and either** fraud carried out over a significant period of time **or** multiple frauds	**Starting point: 3** years custody **Range:**2-6 years custody	**Starting point: 2** years custody **Range:**12 months-3 years custody	**Starting point: 36** weeks custody **Range: 12** weeks-18 months custody	**Starting point: 6** weeks custody **Range:** Community order (MEDIUM)-26 weeks custody	**Starting point:** Community order (MEDIUM) **Range:** Fine-Community order (HIGH)
Single fraudulent transaction, fraudulent from the outset			**Starting point: 26** weeks custody **Range: 6** weeks-12 months custody	**Starting point:** Community order (HIGH) **Range:** Fine-18 weeks custody	**Starting point:** Community order (LOW) **Range:** Fine-Community order (MEDIUM)
Single fraudulent transaction, not fraudulent from the outset			**Starting point:**12 weeks custody **Range:** Community order (MEDIUM)-36 weeks custody	**Starting point:** Community order (MEDIUM) **Range:** Fine-6 weeks custody	**Starting point:** Fine **Range:** Fine-Community order (LOW)

* Where the actual amount is greater or smaller than the figure on which the starting point is based, that is likely to be one of the factors that will move the sentence within the range.

Additional aggravating factors	Additional mitigating factors
1. Number involved in the offence and role of the offender	1. Peripheral involvement
2. Use of another person's identity	2. Misleading or incomplete advice
3. Making repeated importations, particularly in the face of warnings from the authorities	
4. Dealing in goods with an additional health risk	
5. Disposing of goods to under-aged purchasers	

In *Awosika* [2009] EWCA Crim 625, CA, the appellant had pleaded guilty to an offence of fraud contrary to s.1 of the *Fraud Act* 2006, and was sentenced to 10 months' imprisonment. The appellant was sentenced before the Sentencing Guidelines Council's

Final Guideline had been issued. The appellant and a colleague sought to purchase a watch costing £11,480 and attempted to pay with an American Express card in the name of another person. Substituting a sentence of six months' imprisonment, the Court concluded that although an immediate custodial sentence was appropriate, the sentencing judge had adopted too high a starting point. The appellant did have a long record of deception-type offences. The four-year interval between this offence and her previous conviction showed, if anything, the precariousness of any change in her way of life. While there was a degree of pre-planning and the use of another person's identity, this was an attempt to commit a fairly elementary fraud. A sentence of 12 months would have marked the court's duty to honest traders and the appellant's record. Further reduction would be appropriate to reflect recent efforts at reform and the appellant's guilty plea.

In *Peacock* [2009] EWCA Crim 766, CA, the appellant had pleaded guilty to fraud contrary to ss.1 and 2 of the *Fraud Act* 2006 and sentenced to nine months' imprisonment. The appellant was one of a group of people making dishonest representations to the Department of Work and Pensions. He had changed the amount on a cheque for his incapacity benefit from £110.62 to £410.62. The Court held that the sentence of nine months' imprisonment was too long. An appropriate loss of liberty would be three months.

In *Rahman (Mohammed)* [2009] EWCA Crim 1073, CA the appellant appealed against a sentence of 40 weeks' imprisonment suspended for two years following his guilty plea to an offence of fraud. The appellant's co-defendant had been employed by a major chain store and ordered goods from the store using a customer's credit card details. The appellant collected these goods from the store using a false name. Allowing his appeal, the Court stated that the appellant's offence did not involve a breach of trust and did not have the aggravating feature often present in such cases of suspicion being cast on another employee. He had committed a short and unsuccessful act of dishonesty for which a non-custodial sentence was appropriate. The appropriate sentence was a community order with a requirement to perform 125 hours of unpaid work within 12 months.

C. FRAUD BY FAILING TO DISCLOSE INFORMATION

(4) Sentence

15–113   The Sentencing Guidelines Council guideline on Sentencing for Fraud—statutory offences states that frauds under s.1 of the *Fraud Act* 2006 may be sentenced as confidence frauds; frauds involving the possession, making or supplying articles for use in fraud; banking and insurance fraud, and obtaining credit through fraud; benefit fraud and revenue fraud. See 15-109 above, for guidance on factors that should be taken into consideration when sentencing these types of fraud.

D. FRAUD BY ABUSE OF POSITION

(4) Sentence

15–118   The Sentencing Guidelines Council guideline on *Sentencing for Fraud – statutory offences*, issued on October 13, 2009, describes fraud under s.1 of the *Fraud Act* 2006 as 'confidence fraud'. The Sentencing Guidelines Council's guideline on sentencing such frauds are considered at 15-109, above.

E. POSSESSION ETC. OF ARTICLES FOR USE IN FRAUD

(4) Sentence

15–124   The Sentencing Guidelines Council guideline on Sentencing for Fraud – statutory offences states that fraud under s.6 of the *Fraud Act* 2006 may be sentenced as frauds involving the possession, making or supplying articles for use in fraud. See 15-109, above, for guidance on factors that should be taken into consideration when sentencing this type of fraud

In *Mensah-Golo* [2009] EWCA Crim 640, CA, the appellant had pleaded guilty to possessing articles for use in frauds. He was sentenced to 18 months' imprisonment and recommended for deportation. Following a search of the car the appellant was driving when stopped by the police, the police found a bank card in the name of another person, which the appellant claimed belonged to his brother. Upon searching the appellant, the police officers found bank cards in the names of two other people. The police also found a piece of paper with the names, addresses and bank details of various people. The appellant had three previous convictions. Substituting a sentence of 12 months' imprisonment, the Court stated that the culpability of the offender depended on whether the fraud for which the articles were intended to be used was an extensive and skilfully planned one, whether the offender was involved in a professional operation, and how much money was involved. Since three different cards were involved, and the appellant had them to enable the proceeds of fraud to be transferred into those accounts, the case had all the hallmarks of professionalism and would be on the serious side of such cases. However, there was nothing to suggest that the appellant had been involved in the frauds whose proceeds he was being asked, albeit fraudulently, to transfer. The appropriate starting point in this case would be 18 months' imprisonment; as the appellant had pleaded guilty, a sentence of 12 months would be appropriate.

In *Omgbwa* [2009] EWCA Crim 1215, CA, the appellant was convicted of an offence of possessing articles for use in fraud, contrary to s.6(1) of the *Fraud Act* 2006 and sentenced to twelve months' imprisonment. The case involved what was described as a "black money" scam or a "wash wash" fraud. The appellant and his co-accused would coat a genuine bank note with glue and iodine, turning the note black. This note would be shown to a victim, who would then be shown then note being treated with a "special" chemical which washed it clean and made it legal tender. The victim would then be persuaded to buy a pile of similar bank notes and some of the "special" chemical. In reality the black notes would be pieces of blank paper and the chemical would be washing-up liquid. The appellant had been arrested and found to be in possession of some "black money", padding tissue, four bottles of an unknown liquid, some plastic goods, a vial of clear liquid, two pieces of paper cut to the size of a £20 note and a bottle of iodine. Substituting a sentence of eight months' imprisonment, the Court described the significant planning the appellant and his co-accused had engaged in to carry out the offences. However, the sums of money involved in the instant offence were small, and this offence was the appellant's first offence of anything like this nature.

F. MAKING OR SUPPLYING ARTICLES FOR USE IN FRAUDS

(4) Sentence

The Sentencing Guidelines Council guideline on *Sentencing for Fraud – statutory* **15–128**
offences states that fraud under s.7 of the *Fraud Act* 2006 may be sentenced as fraud involving the possession, making or supplying articles for use in fraud. See 15-109, above, for guidance on factors that should be taken into consideration when sentencing this type of fraud.

G. PARTICIPATING IN FRAUDULENT BUSINESS CARRIED ON BY SOLE TRADER ETC

(4) Sentence

The Sentencing Guidelines Council guideline on *Sentencing for Fraud – statutory* **15–132**
offences does not specifically refer to s.9 of the *Fraud Act* 2006. However, as the guideline states it 'aims to produce a coherent and consistent approach to sentencing all forms of fraudulent behaviour', it may be assumed that the general guidelines on sentencing offences of fraud in the guideline (see 15-109, above) may be applied to the offence under s.9 of the *Fraud Act* 2006.

H. OBTAINING SERVICES DISHONESTLY

(4) Sentence

15–136   The Sentencing Guidelines Council guideline on *Sentencing for Fraud – statutory offences* states that the offence of obtaining services dishonestly (contrary to s.11 of the *Fraud Act* 2006) may be committed in circumstances that otherwise could be charged as an offence contrary to s.1 of the Act or may be more akin to *making off without payment*. It has therefore not been specifically included in the guideline, and the guideline states that one of the following approaches should be used:

1. Where the offence involves conduct which can be characterised as a fraud offence (such as obtaining credit through fraud or payment card fraud), the court should apply the guideline for the relevant type of fraud; or
2. Where the conduct could be characterised as *making off without payment* (that is, where an offender, knowing that payment on the spot for any goods supplied or service done is required or expected, dishonestly makes off without having paid and with intent to avoid payment), the guideline for that offence in the *Magistrates' Court Sentencing Guidelines* (2008) should be used.

III. OFFENCES OF FORGERY, PERSONATION AND CHEATING

G. CUSTODY OR CONTROL OF COUNTERFEITS

(4) Sentence

15–178   In cases involving poor quality counterfeit notes and a lack of intention to use them, a community sentence may be appropriate: *Leslie* [2009] EWCA Crim 884, CA. In this case, the appellant had been sentenced to four years' imprisonment following his guilty plea to having custody or control of counterfeit currency contrary to s.16(2) of the *Forgery and Counterfeiting Act* 1981. Police officers had found 15 counterfeit £20 notes were found following a search of the appellant's car. The serial numbers on all the notes were the same and under ultra violet light there was no watermark. The appellant was initially charged under s.16(1) which involves the element of intention to pass the notes. However, the pleas were accepted to s.16(2), seemingly on the basis that the fakes were so poor that they could not have been passed for profit. Substituting a community order with a requirement for 80 hours of unpaid work, the Court held that the poor quality of the notes and lack of intention to use them made a community penalty appropriate.

IV. MISCELLANEOUS OFFENCES

A. OFFENCES UNDER THE PROCEEDS OF CRIME ACT 2002

(1) Concealing

"Criminal Property"

15–196   Lodging, receiving, retaining and withdrawing money from a bank account might all amount to a conversion: *Fazal* [2009] EWCA Crim 1697, CA. In this case, the appellant appealed against his conviction on seven counts of converting criminal property contrary to the *Proceeds of Crime Act* 2002 s.327(1)(c). Seven deposits had been made into his bank account, which were the proceeds of fraud. The appellant had given his bank details, debit card and PIN to a friend who had needed to use his account to have his wages paid into it. He stated that he did not use the account. Dismissing his appeal, the Court held that each transaction of lodging, receiving, retaining and withdrawing money from a bank account could amount to a conversion. Asking or allowing another person, who might or might not have had the required *mens rea* to make such transactions did not prevent an account owner from converting money through his account. When the money was withdrawn from the appellant's account it was transferred into cash. At each stage the property concerned was passed through the appellant's account, thereby being converted.

(3) Acquisition, use or possession of criminal property

"Adequate consideration"

If the property in question was not acquired for inadequate consideration, no offence **15–217** will be committed, and even if the person knew or suspected the property to be criminal property: *Kausar* [2009] EWCA Crim 2242, CA. In this case, the appellant appealed against a conviction of acquiring criminal property contrary to s.329 of the *Proceeds of Crime Act* 2002. The appellant had applied for a "buy to let" mortgage but the information given on the application form concerning her employment and income was false. The Court was required to determine on appeal whether the property in question had been acquired for inadequate consideration under s.329. Allowing her appeal, the Court stated that the use of 'consideration' in criminal statutes was not unusual, and it was difficult to see why Parliament should have used a legal term of art in the 2002 Act if some other meaning was intended. Section 329 made perfect sense if the word was given its normal legal meaning. Given the availability of other offences with which the appellant could have been charged, there was no reason for any unusual meaning to be given to a clearly worded statutory provision. The charge and the undertaking to repay with interest were the consideration for the advance. There was no suggestion that the interest was not at a market rate, or that in any other respect the consideration passing from the appellant was inadequate. Inadequacy of consideration was clearly a separate ingredient of the offence under s.329. The Court added that the appellant should never have been charged with an offence under s.329.

B. Offences Under the Identity Cards Act 2006

(1) Possession of false identity documents

(d) Sentence

Possession of stolen passports and the theft of passports are serious matters that must **15–255** be marked with a custodial sentence. However, there is a distinction between those who possess such documents with intent to use them and those who merely have them in their possession: *Mundirwa* [2009] EWCA Crim 521, CA. In this case, the appellants had been sentenced to 12 months' imprisonment for theft of a passport and possession of a false identity document. The first appellant had flown to the United Kingdom from South Africa and claimed asylum. His sister, the second appellant, had travelled on the same flight with her boyfriend. She admitted that she had facilitated the first appellant's entry into the UK using her boyfriend's passport, which she had stolen and given to the first appellant, who admitted having the passport and that it had permitted him to board the plane to enter the UK. The first appellant agreed that he told lies to immigration officers on arrival, but his story that he was seeking refuge from Zimbabwe was accepted and he was granted asylum. The Court of Appeal held that the sentences of 12 months' imprisonment were excessive, and substituted sentences of 6 months' imprisonment.

CHAPTER 16

PUBLIC ORDER OFFENCES

V. MISCELLANEOUS OFFENCES

E. Information About Acts of Terrorism

(1) Definition

Terrorism Act 2000, s.38B

While it is not sufficient for the prosecution to prove that the defendant closed his **16–332** eyes to the obvious in order to show an offence contrary to s.38B of the 2000 Act, evidence that he did so because he did not wish to be told the truth was capable of being evidence in support of the conclusion that he did either know or believe the matter in question: *R. v. Sherif, Mohammed, Abdurahman and Abdullahi, The Times,* February 11, 2009, CA.

CHAPTER 17

ROAD TRAFFIC OFFENCES

I. DEFINITIONS

F. ROAD OF OTHER PUBLIC PLACE

Many uses of a vehicle only become a road traffic offence when on a "road". A fur- **17–7** ther examination of the meaning of "road" for these purposes can be seen in *Barrett v. DPP* [2009] EWHC Admin 423. Again, the issue revolved around a roadway inside a caravan park. This park was situated between a main road and a beach. A public footpath existed commencing at the main road and, in part, following the line of the roadway through the park; that footpath was found to be a "highway" and so, justices found, the roadway was a "road". The defence contended that the caravan park was private and, since there was no right for vehicles to access the beach through the caravan park (and no car park at the beach), it was not a place to which the public had access. There appeared to be some confusion about what needed to be proved before the justices but the Divisional Court was clear that it was a "road"; the defendant had followed a route marked on a plan which was a tarmac roadway with defined edges, road markings and signs and in respect of which there was unchallenged evidence that it was used by members of the public as a route to the beach, including those who had no other business in the caravan park. The absence of a beach car park was not significant.

II. BAD DRIVING

C. DANGEROUS DRIVING

(4) Meaning of "dangerous driving"

Road Traffic Act 1988, s.2A

Part of the test on what type of driving is "dangerous" is that "it would be obvious to **17–21** a careful and competent driver that driving in that way would be dangerous": Road Traffic Act 1988, s.2A(1)(b). In determining what is "obvious", regard has to be had not only to circumstances of which the driver could be expected to be aware but also to those shown to have been within the driver's knowledge: s.2A(3). As reported in the main work, the Divisional Court in *Milton v. DPP* concluded that unusual driving skills might be relevant to that decision but that it was for the court to determine the weight to be given to them—that case arose from driving by an advanced police driver. That approach has, however, been found to be wrong. In a further case involving an experienced police driver, the Court of Appeal determined that the approach in *Milton* was "inconsistent with the objective test of the competent and careful driver set out in the statute": *Bannister* [2009] EWCA Crim 1571. To take account of the special skills of a driver would mean that the standard being applied is that of a driver with special skills and not, as the statute specifies, the "competent and careful driver". The special skill (or lack of skill) of a driver is an irrelevant circumstance when a court is considering whether driving is dangerous.

(6) Sentence

A number of cases have been reported in which a court has had to consider sentence **17–28** where dangerous driving had resulted in very serious injury but not death. In such circumstances, the maximum custodial is restricted to two years compared with a maximum of 14 years where death has resulted; offences of dangerous driving are triable either way but it seems clear from these cases that the Crown Court is the appropriate tribunal where serious injury has resulted. In *Grover* [2009] EWCA Crim 876 the defendant drove through red lights at 35-40mph in a 30mph zone. He struck a woman who was eight months pregnant; she suffered multiple injuries including a ruptured placenta which meant that an emergency caesarean section had to be carried out; the child survived. The mother remained in a coma for some time and was not able to see her child for some two months and so missed the bonding that would otherwise have occurred; she was unlikely to make a complete recover from her injuries. The defendant was of previous good character and asserted that he had been dazzled by the sun (a clear bright, November afternoon) and simply not seen the colour of the traffic lights. He pleaded guilty at the earliest opportunity. The Court of Appeal reduced the sentence from eight months to five months and so within the powers of a magistrates' court. In *Ball* [2009] EWCA Crim 1265 the defendant had overtaken five vehicles whilst driving up a hill. He accelerated to 50mph as he approached the brow of the hill and, as he went over the brow, he collided with another vehicle. The driver of that other vehicle suffered serious injuries with continuing mental impairment and scarring. The defendant was aged 17 at the time of the offence. Noting that there had not been a prolonged course of bad driving, the speed limit had not been exceeded and that neither drugs nor alcohol were involved, the Crown Court had been wrong to take the maximum sentence as the starting point; it should have used 18 months as the starting point. That was then reduced to 12 months on account of personal mitigation and the guilty plea. In *Byrne* [2009] EWCA Crim 1825the defendant had consumed a quantity of strong lager and brandy and then drove "as if he was on a race track". In due course, the car hit the pavement, went out of control and veered into the path of a car coming in the opposite direction; the estimated speed of the defendant's car before impact was 80mph and he fled the scene before the emergency services arrived although he was found nearby shortly afterwards. The driver of the car that was hit was a 19 year old woman who suffered severe injuries to her body, particularly severe head injuries. Although the prognosis had been poor, she had made a better than expected recovery; nonetheless the effect on her had been profound and continuing. A passenger in her car has also been injured though suffering relatively minor injuries. There had been a late guilty plea and the sentence of 20 months was upheld with the court remarking on the inadequacy of the current maximum sentence for cases such as this.

These three cases illustrate the range of situations that might occur and the degrees of injury likely to result. Although some cases may end with a sentence within the powers of a magistrates' court, it is submitted that all cases involving serious injury should be sentenced in the Crown Court since the level of sentence will only be able to be determined after full inquiry into the relevant circumstances.

E. CAUSING DEATH BY CARELESS, OR INCONSIDERATE, DRIVING

(6) Sentence

17–45   The main work noted the problems that might be caused in sentencing for this offence because of the high level of harm compared with the low level of culpability and the fact that Parliament has prescribed a maximum sentence of five years imprisonment where death results and a maximum sentence of £5000 where it does not. Cases are beginning to appear in the courts and, occasionally, in the Court of Appeal. In *Larke* [2009] EWCA Crim 870 the defendant was performing a U turn from a lay-by on an A road. She failed to see an oncoming car which swerved and avoided a collision; however, a following motorcyclist was unable to avoid a collision and both he and his passenger (his 11 year old step-daughter) were killed. The defendant was aged 74 with an unblemished driving record for 50 years; until four years before she had worked with adults with learning disabilities including driving them in a minibus. The U turn was a manoeuvre she had often undertaken successfully at this spot. She was genuinely devastated by what she had done. The Crown Court found carelessness of a high order approaching dangerousness and imposed a sentence of two years imprisonment; it was recognised that the carelessness was momentary, not continuing, but also that two deaths had been caused. The sentence was above the starting point but well below the top of the range provided in the relevant Sentencing Guidelines Council definitive guideline. The Court of Appeal did not place the offence within a different level of seriousness but noted the early guilty plea, the considerable remorse and the impeccable driving history. In all the circumstances, a custodial sentence was warranted but it could be at the lower end of the range and could be suspended; a sentence of 39 weeks suspended for 12 months was substituted. It appears that the defendant is likely to have spent almost two months in custody pending the hearing of the appeal and this may have been a factor in the decision of the Court of Appeal though not overtly referred to.

III. ALCOHOL/DRUGS RELATED OFFENCES

C. FAILURE TO SUPPLY A PRELIMINARY SPECIMEN OF BREATH

(3) What must the prosecution prove?

Where a preliminary blood test is given by a person who is in hospital, there is a pro- **17–91** hibition on the exercise of the usual power of arrest where that test indicates the presence of alcohol above the prescribed limit: s.6D(3) of the 1988 Act (see 17-84in the main work). Despite this provision, in *DPP v. Wilson* [2009] EWHC Admin 1988 a driver was arrested whilst in hospital where he had been taken after an accident. He had consented to provide a preliminary breath test and that showed a figure in excess of the legal limit. It was accepted on all sides that the arrest was unlawful; the defence argued that the subsequent sample was illegal and should be disregarded. This argument was accepted in the magistrates' court and the defendant acquitted. Allowing the prosecution appeal, the Divisional Court noted that a valid arrest is not a prerequisite for a sample and that, as all the other requisites and procedures had been properly followed, there was no justification for excluding the sample.

VI. EFFECT OF PENALTIES

C. DISQUALIFICATION

(2) Driving licences

Special reasons

In *Warring Davies v. DPP* [2009] EWHC Admin 1172, the defendant pleaded **17–207** guilty to speeding but sought to persuade the court not to endorse his licence on the grounds that he anticipated that he was becoming hypoglycaemic and decided to speed up in order to reach a safe point at which he could take glucose. This was rejected by the magistrates' court, the Crown Court and the Divisional Court. Whilst accepting that the onset of a medical condition could amount to a special reason where it caused momentary excess speed or was otherwise reasonable, here the defendant had made a conscious decision to speed up which the court had concluded was not reasonable in the circumstances. Accordingly, the decision of the Crown Court to endorse the licence was upheld.

CHAPTER 20

REGULATORY OFFENCES

II. ANIMALS

B. DANGEROUS DOGS

(5) Sentence

In *R. v. Jamal Richards* [2009] 1 Cr.App.R. (S) 48 the appellant owned two pit-bull **20–30** dogs which escaped from his yard and attacked and bit a postman who sustained deep lacerations and permanent scarring. The appeal was against a sentence of nine months custody. The appeal court recognised the need to take into account the serious consequences to the victim but in light of the young age of the defendant and his genuine remorse and pleas of guilty it was held that the sentence should be reduced to four months. However in *R. v. Joel Lee* [2009] EWCA Crim 2046 the appeal court stated that previous cases were not guideline cases setting a maximum sentence of four months as each case depended on its individual facts but where the appellants two dogs attacked and severely injured a 72 year old neighbour of the appellant the sentence was reduced from ten to six months custody.

III. CONSUMER PROTECTION

C. UNAUTHORISED USE OF TRADE MARK

(4) Defences

In *Essex Trading Standards v. Singh* [2009] EWHC 520 (Admin) the defendant **20–65** was charged with an offence of trade mark infringement. He was helping out a sick friend by working at his market stall selling trainers which bore a Nike trade mark. He said his friend was a drug addict and he had asked him if the shoes were counterfeit and he had been assured they were not. The magistrates found that the statutory defence had been made out and acquitted the defendant. On appeal by the prosecution it was held that the burden under s.92(5) was to show that there were objectively reasonable grounds to believe the goods were genuine and the defendant had to show he had acted not only honestly but also reasonably. On the facts of the case it was held that the defendant had not sought any independent evidence of the genuineness of the goods and in fact could hardly have done less to establish their genuineness and he had not acted reasonably. On that basis the decision of the magistrates was quashed as being one no reasonable bench could have reached.

XI. SOCIAL SECURITY

A. DISHONEST REPRESENTATIONS FOR OBTAINING BENEFIT

(3) Elements of the offence

In *R. v. T* [2009]EWCA Crim 1426 the defendant was charged under s.111A (1B) of **20–189** the *Social Security Administration Act* 1992 with an offence of 'allowing' another to fail to give prompt notification of a change of circumstances affecting benefit payment. His partner had continued to claim benefits when he was maintaining a common household with her and she had not notified that change of circumstances.

The interpretation of the word 'allow' in these circumstances fell to be considered. It was held that by standing by and failing to do anything the defendant did no positive act of allowing the offence to be committed so his conviction was quashed.

(4) Sentence

20–190   Offences under s.111(A) of the *Social Security Administration Act* 1992 are now covered by guidelines issued by the Sentencing Guidelines Council. The definitive guideline on offences of fraud incorporates benefit fraud. The guidelines are included in Ch. 15.

Part IV

Sentencing

CHAPTER 23

SPECIFIC SENTENCES

III. CUSTODIAL SENTENCES

B. SENTENCES OF IMPRISONMENT

(4) Time served prior to imposition of sentence

Remand in custody (Effect of Concurrent and Consecutive Sentence of Imprisonment) Rules 2005 (S.I. 2005 No. 2054)

Continuing difficulties in obtaining accurate information about qualifying periods on **23–166** remand have prompted the Court of Appeal to emphasise again the importance of using appropriate wording to minimise the risk of unnecessary appeals or re-listing of cases. The Court noted that this was even more important now that the credit can extend to certain periods on bail. In *Nnaji* [2009] EWCA Crim 468 the Court suggested wording along the following lines: "The defendant will receive full credit for the full period of time spent in custody on remand and half the time spent under curfew if the curfew qualified under the provisions of s.240. On the information before me the total period is . . . days but if this period is mistaken, this Court will order an amendment of the record for the correct period to be recorded."

The strength of the presumption in favour of allowing credit for the whole of the qualifying period was emphasised in *McGrail* [2009] EWCA Crim 1400. Following conviction for robbery in which the defendant had pleaded guilty at a late stage, the Judge declined to give credit for the 154 days spent in custody on remand. Although the reasoning was not clear for that decision, it was apparent that the Judge had little sympathy for the defendant and that the late plea may have been amongst the reasons. Allowing the appeal on this point, the Court of Appeal noted that the 2003 Act obliges a court to direct that the time should count towards the sentence unless that would be unjust; in this case, there appeared to be no reason to justify a determination that it would be unjust.

B. COMPENSATION ORDERS

(1) Purpose and effect

Powers of Criminal Courts (Sentencing) Act 2000, ss.130, 131

In the main work, increasing flexibility in determining whether compensation could **23–226a** be ordered was noted as a result of the *Magistrates' Court Sentencing Guidelines*. This trend has been continued in *Pola* [2009] EWCA Crim 655 in which serious injury was caused following breaches of obligations under health and safety legislation. It was argued that compensation orders should be confined to simple and straightforward cases where the amount of compensation can be readily and easily ascertained. The Court of Appeal rejected that approach and upheld the decision to award £90,000 noting that this was within the means of the offender (and that fines had been adjusted to ensure that it could be paid) and that the injured person would not benefit under any insurance policy, would not qualify under the criminal injuries compensation scheme, would be unlikely to succeed in civil action because of the appellant's means and was not entitled to state benefits either in this country or in his home country (Slovakia). The suggested bracket for damages was between £58,000 and £96,000 with some features suggesting a higher award could be justified. Attention was drawn to other cases in which a court had determined compensation in the face of complex issues and disputed evidence and to the growing expertise of courts developing from confiscation proceedings. Here, there was a clear causal link between the conviction and the injury, there was sufficient evidence to show that the gravity of the injury would justify an award far in excess of what the court was contemplating and there was no more convenient or practicable alternative route available to the injured person. The order was within the means of the defendant and was just and proper in the context of his culpability.

IV. ANCILLARY ORDERS

E. BINDING OVER

(1) Purpose and effect

Magistrates' Courts Act 1980, s.115

23–253   The principles and basis for making a binding over order following acquittal were considered in *Emohare v. Thames Magistrates' Court* [2009] EWHC Admin 689. The defendant had been stopped whilst driving home from hospital (following medical treatment to his shoulder and arm) and questioned about a bag snatch in the area. He was aggressive and, when a police officer took hold of his arm, he reacted by swinging his head which caught the officer's head—he was charged with assault. The court was not sure that the assault was more than an involuntary reaction to the pain caused when the police officer took hold of his arm and acquitted the defendant. Nonetheless, the court considered the defendant's conduct to be reprehensible and, having invited representations, bound him over for two years to keep the peace. This order was overturned on appeal. The Court had not considered the relevant provisions of the *Consolidated Criminal Practice Direction* (described in the main work) which emphasised the importance of the court being satisfied either that a breach of the peace involving violence (or an imminent threat of violence) had occurred or that there was a real risk of violence in the future; on the facts found, neither condition could have been satisfied. Even if the bind over had been justified, the court had not made the order in the specific terms required by the Consolidated Criminal Practice Direction, para. III.31.4.

(2) Fulfilment of criteria

23–269   The criteria for an order is that the proposed subject of the order has acted in an anti-social manner and that an order is necessary to protect other people from further anti-social acts. In *Birmingham City Council v. Dixon* [2009] EWHC Admin 761 the applicant sought to use evidence of conduct after the dates stated in the application to substantiate the evidence on which the application was based. This conduct had taken place whilst the person in respect of whom the application was made had been subject to an interim order. The District Judge ruled that the evidence was inadmissible since it was not relevant to either of the criteria on which the decision to make an order had to be based. The Divisional Court disagreed with that conclusion holding that (whilst not removing the obligation to prove the allegations specified in the complaint) such evidence might be relevant either in showing a propensity to behave in an anti-social manner or in substantiating the need for an order.

23–276   An order can be breached only if its terms are not complied with "without reasonable excuse". The question of where the burden of proof lies arose for decision in *Charles*

[2009] EWCA Crim 1570. The Court affirmed the approach set out in the *Guide for the Judiciary on Anti-Social Behaviour Orders 2007* which (at para. 6.5) states that the prosecution must prove a breach of the order to the criminal standard and that, if the defendant raises the evidential issue of reasonable excuse, that it is for the prosecution to prove lack of reasonable excuse.

CHAPTER 24

EXCLUSION, ALTERATION AND ENFORCEMENT

II. POWER TO ENFORCE FINANCIAL PENALTIES

C. IMPRISONMENT IN DEFAULT OF PAYMENT

A further reminder of the need for care in determining that a defaulter is "wilfully **24–52** refusing" to pay is seen in *Louis v. Ealing Magistrates' Court* [2009] EWHC Admin 521. Mr. Louis had been fined £1,600 by the Crown Court for eight trade mark offences. The payment rate fixed by the Crown Court was subsequently varied downwards by a magistrates' court. Although not paying at the rate specified, Mr. Louis made small, regular payments so that by the time of the hearing he had paid £600. However, finding that he had consistently failed to make regular payments and that he should have made greater efforts to obtain work, the court found "wilful refusal" and activated the period of committal in default (making no allowance for the part payment, it would appear). The Divisional Court recited the text at 24-52 in the main work and was satisfied that the court had properly considered the various options available to it. However, it allowed the appeal on the ground that the court had not properly explained the basis on which it had rejected the evidence from Mr. Louis particularly as it seemed to the Divisional Court that he had made significant efforts; if there was evidence to the contrary, the court should have highlighted it and not simply asserted that he should have made more effort.

III. ENFORCEMENT OF COMMUNITY ORDERS

A. LEGISLATIVE FRAMEWORK

(2) Breach provisions

The statutory provisions allow for a warning to be given following first breach of an **24–94** order at the discretion of the responsible officer. Where there is a second breach and proceedings initiated, the issue has been raised as to whether the breach that resulted in the warning could also be included in the information bringing the matter before the court following the second breach. In *West Yorkshire Probation Board v. Tinker, Robinson* [2009] EWHC Admin 2468 the Divisional Court affirmed that a warning did not expunge the breach in respect of which it had been given and could legitimately be included in an information following a second breach. The warning did not act as a punishment and did not deal with the breach.

IV. ENFORCEMENT OF SUSPENDED SENTENCE ORDER

(1) General

The statutory provisions allow for a warning to be given following first breach of an **24–133** order at the discretion of the responsible officer. Where there is a second breach and proceedings initiated, the issue has been raised as to whether the breach that resulted in the warning could also be included in the information bringing the matter before the court following the second breach. In *West Yorkshire Probation Board v. Tinker, Robinson* [2009] EWHC Admin 2468 the Divisional Court affirmed that a warning did not expunge the breach in respect of which it had been given and could legitimately be included in an information following a second breach. The warning did not act as a punishment and did not deal with the breach.

Part V

Youth Courts

CHAPTER 27

SENTENCING IN THE YOUTH COURT

XV. SENTENCING YOUTHS UNDER THE PROVISIONS OF THE CJIA 2008

The sentencing provisions of the *Criminal Justice and Immigration Act* 2008 affect- **27–89a** ing youths came into effect on November 30, 2009 with the *Criminal Justice and Immigration Act 2008 (Commencement No. 13 and Transitory Provision) Order* 2009 S.I. No.3074 of 2009.

The full impact of the new sentencing framework and the scaled approach to sentence will be considered in detail in the next main work once the interpretation and application of the sections has been further developed.

The Sentencing Guidelines Council has issued a definitive guideline—Overarching Principles-Sentencing Youths, to coincide with the new orders available. The Guideline applies to all defendants in the Youth Court sentenced on or after November 30, 2009. A copy of the Guidelines can be found at *www.sentencing-guidelines.gov.uk*

Part VI

Mentally Disordered Offenders

CHAPTER 28

MENTALLY DISORDERED OFFENDERS

VI. SENTENCING POWERS

A. PRE-SENTENCE REPORTS

Powers of Criminal Courts (Sentencing) Act 2000, s.11

In *R. (on the application of Varma) v. Redbridge Magistrates' Court* [2009] **28–17**
EWHC 836 (Admin), DC, the claimant applied for judicial review of a decision of the
defendant magistrates' court to convict him of an offence of driving whilst disqualified.
The appellant had initially pleaded guilty to the offence but was deemed unfit to plead
in respect of separate proceedings in the Crown Court on the basis of medical reports.
A successful application was made to withdraw his guilty plea, a not guilty plea was
entered and a trial of the issues listed. A further medical report was ordered and directions given, with a mental health disposal anticipated. However, following an application
by the Crown based on a further medical report which found that the appellant was fit
to plead, the matter proceeded to trial, despite the appellant's request for an adjournment for further consideration of the medical evidence. The appellant did not give evidence and was convicted. A report prepared after conviction concluded that the appellant was unfit to be tried. The magistrates' court and the Crown declined to sign a
consent order quashing the conviction.

Granting the application, the Court held that as the Crown had given no effective notice of its proposed course for the case, which was contrary to the directions given by the
district judge, the magistrates' court was quite wrong not to grant the adjournment
sought by the appellant to allow the medical evidence to be called. The court was also
wrong to proceed on the basis of the further report, as it was not agreed, was not in evidence and was contradicted by four other medical reports. The court should not have
embarked on a summary trial as if there was no problem with the appellant's
understanding and the court should not have acceded to the Crown's submission that
any unfairness in the trial could be corrected on appeal. The trial was not fair and the
conviction had to be quashed. The case was remitted to the magistrates' court to be
reconsidered by a different bench to determine whether the appellant committed the
acts alleged and to make appropriate orders under s.37(3) of the *Mental Health Act*
1983.

Part VII

Legal Aid and Costs

CHAPTER 29

LEGAL REPRESENTATION

I. CRIMINAL DEFENCE REPRESENTATION ORDERS

A. GENERAL

The *Criminal Defence Service (Financial Eligibility) (Amendment) Regulations* **29–1**
2009 S.I. 2009 No. 2878 extend the cases in which a person may be financially eligible
to receive publicly funded representation to proceedings where a defendant is committed from the magistrate' court to the Crown Court for sentence. This is a staged amendment which comes into force at different dates in 2010 throughout the country in accordance with the Schedule attached to the statutory instrument.

D. CRIMINAL DEFENCE SERVICE

(1) The Role of the Criminal Defence Service

Criminal Defence Service (General) (No.2) Regulations 2001, reg.3(1)–(2)

Criminal Proceedings
   3.—(1) For the purposes of this regulation, "the 1998 Act" means the *Crime and Disorder* **29–14**
Act 1998.
   (2) The following proceedings are criminal proceedings for the purposes of section
12(2)(g) of the Act:
   (a) civil proceedings in a magistrates' court arising from failure to pay a sum due or
       to obey an order of that court where such failure carries the risk of imprison-
       ment;
   (b) proceedings under sections 1, 1D and 4 of the 1998 Act relating to anti-social be-
       haviour orders;1
   (ba) proceedings under sections 1G and 1H of the 1998 Act relating to intervention
       orders, in which an application for an anti-social behaviour order has been made;
   (c) proceedings under section 8(1)(b) of the 1998 Act relating to parenting orders
       made where an anti-social behaviour order or a sex offender order is made in re-
       spect of a child;
   (d) proceedings under section 8(1)(c) of the 1998 Act relating to parenting orders
       made on the conviction of a child;
   (e) proceedings under section 9(5) of the 1998 Act to discharge or vary a parenting
       order made as mentioned in sub-paragraph (c) or (d);
   (f) proceedings under section 10 of the 1998 Act to appeal against a parenting order
       made as mentioned in sub-paragraph (c) or (d);
   (g) proceedings under sections 14B, 14D, 14G, 14H, 21B and 21D of the *Football
       Spectators Act* 1989 (banning orders and references to a court)
   (h) proceedings under section 137 of the *Financial Services and Markets Act* 2000 to
       appeal against a decision of the Financial Services and Markets Tribunal
   (i) proceedings under sections 2, 5 and 6 of the *Anti-social Behaviour Act* 2003 relat-
       ing to closure orders;
   (j) proceedings under sections 20, 22, 26 and 28 of the *Anti-Social Behaviour Act*

2003 relating to parenting orders in cases of exclusion from school and parenting orders in respect of criminal conduct and anti-social behaviour;

(k) proceedings under sections 97, 100 and 101 of the *Sexual Offences Act* 2003 relating to notification orders and interim notification orders;

(l) proceedings under sections 104, 108, 109 and 110 of the *Sexual Offences Act* 2003 relating to sexual offences prevention orders and interim sexual offences prevention orders;

(m) proceedings under sections 114, 118 and 119 of the *Sexual Offences Act* 2003 relating to foreign travel orders;

(n) proceedings under sections 123, 125, 126 and 127 of the *Sexual Offences Act* 2003 relating to risk of sexual harm orders and interim risk of sexual harm orders;

(o) proceedings under Part 1A of Schedule 1 to the *Powers of Criminal Courts (Sentencing) Act* 2000 relating to parenting orders for failure to comply with orders under section 20 of that Act

(p) proceedings before the Crown Court or the Court of Appeal relating to serious crime prevention orders and arising by virtue of section 19, 20, 21 or 24 of the *Serious Crime Act* 2007

(q) proceedings under sections 100, 101, 103, 104 and 106 of the *Criminal Justice and Immigration Act* 2008 relating to violent offender orders and interim violent offender orders

(r) proceedings under sections 3, 5, 9 and 10 of the *Violent Crime Reduction Act* 2006 relating to drinking banning orders and interim orders.

(3) Proceedings:

(a) in the Crown Court, following committal for sentence by a magistrates' court;

(b) to quash an acquittal under the *Criminal Procedure and Investigations Act* 1996; and

(c) for confiscation and forfeiture in connection with criminal proceedings under RSC Order 115 in Schedule 1 to the *Civil Procedure Rules* 1998 are to be regarded as incidental to the criminal proceedings from which they arise.

(4) Applications for judicial review or habeas corpus relating to any criminal investigations or proceedings are not to be regarded as incidental to such criminal investigations or proceedings.

(5) Proceedings in a magistrates' court in which the court sends an assisted person for trial in the Crown Court under section 51 of the *Crime and Disorder Act* 1998 are to be regarded as preliminary to the proceedings in the Crown Court.

[This regulation is printed as amended by the *Criminal Defence Service (General) (No. 2) (Amendment) Regulations* 2002, *Criminal Defence Service (General) (No.2) (Amendment) Regulations* 2004, the *Criminal Defence Service (General) (No. 2) (Amendment) Regulations* 2005, *Criminal Defence Service (General) (No. 2) (Amendment) Regulations* 2007, *Criminal Defence Service (General) (No. 2) (Amendment) Regulations* 2008, *Criminal Defence Service (General) (No. 2) (Amendment No. 2) Regulations* 2009, *Criminal Defence Service (General) (No.2) (Amendment No.3) Regulations* 2009, the *Football (Disorder) Act* 2000 and the *Criminal Justice Act* 2003]

General amendments have added several types of proceedings to the list of matters defined as criminal proceedings for the purposes of Legal Aid. Drink banning orders and violent offender orders have both been added in 2009.

E. REPRESENTATION

(2) The right to representation

29–23   The *Criminal Defence Service (Provisional Representation Orders) Regulations* 2009 S.I. 2009 No. 1995 came into force on August 1, 2009 but will expire on December 31, 2011. These regulations allow the Legal Services Commission to grant a provisional right to representation in cases of the investigation of serious or complex fraud where the Attorney General's Guidelines on plea discussions with the Crown Prosecution apply. As such provisional representation is still very limited in its application to such preliminary matters in these specialised prosecutions and on a temporary basis only.

(4) Selection of the representative

Criminal Defence Service (General) (No.2) Regulations 2001, reg.16A

Change of representative

16.—(1) Where a representation order has been granted an application may be made to the **29–36** court before which the proceedings are heard to select a litigator in place of a litigator previously selected, and any such application shall state the grounds on which it is made.

(2) The court may:

    (a) grant the application where:

        (i) the litigator considers himself to be under a duty to withdraw from the case in accordance with his professional rules of conduct and, in such a case, the litigator shall provide details of the nature of such duty;

        (ii) there is a breakdown in the relationship between the assisted person and the litigator such that effective representation can no longer be provided and, in such a case, the litigator shall provide details of the nature of such breakdown;

        (iii) through circumstances beyond his control, the litigator is no longer able to represent the assisted person; or

        (iv) some other substantial compelling reason exists; or

    (b) refuse the application.

(3) Paragraphs (1) and (2) apply to provisional representation orders as they apply to representation orders, but as if "the Commission" were substituted for "the court" in each place where it appears.

[This regulation is printed as amended by the *Criminal Defence Service (General) (No. 2) (Amendment) Regulations* 2009 with effect from August 4, 2009 S,I, 2009 no. 1853]

Selection of representative by two or more co-defendants etc.

16A. Where—

    (a) an individual who is granted a right to representation is one of two or more co-defendants whose cases are to be heard together, or

    (b) an individual who is provisionally granted a right to representation is one of two or more people involved in an investigation whose cases, if proceedings were to result from the investigation, would be likely to be heard together, that individual must select the same litigator as a co-defendant, unless there is or is likely to be a conflict of interest.

CHAPTER 30

COSTS

I. INTRODUCTION

The *Criminal Procedure Rules* 2005 have been amended by the *Criminal Proce-* **30–1** *dure (Amendment) Rules* 2009 S.I. No. 2087 of 2009 which came into force on October 5, 2009. The existing rules about costs have been revised and simplified and they now cover all applications for costs orders in the criminal courts. A new Pt 76 has been inserted replacing the rules in Pt 78. There are five sections which cover general information, costs out of central funds, costs paid by one party to another, other costs orders and the assessment of costs. The *Criminal Procedure Rules* 2010 are a consolidation of all recent amendments including Pt 76. The come into force on April 5, 2010. See Appendix G.

The *Costs in Criminal Cases (General) (Amendment) Regulations* 2009 S.I. No. 2720 of 2009 came into force on October 30, 2009. Procedural elements are removed from some of the existing regulations as these aspects are now covered by the new Pt 76 of the *Criminal Procedure Rules* 2010. In addition a new regulation 7 provides that the Lord Chancellor in agreement with the Treasury shall set the rates and scales at which payment for legal costs and disbursements are paid from central funds. (See below).

II. COSTS, ORDERS AND ENFORCEMENT

B. DEFENDANT'S COSTS ORDERS

In *Emohare v. Thames Magistrates' Court* (2009) 173 JP 303 a Defendants Costs **30–7** Order was refused following an acquittal for an offence of assaulting a police officer in the execution of his duty. The court said that the defendant's behaviour had been reprehensible and he had brought the prosecution on himself. It was also observed by the court that the defendant had been fortunate not to have faced a charge under the *Public Order Act* 1986. The reasoning of the court was held on appeal to be suggestive of the fact that the court regarded him as guilty despite the acquittal and this was not a proper basis for refusing the costs order. The Practice Direction had to be followed closely and the presumption of innocence should not be seen to be infringed by a refusal of costs.

In *R. (On the application of Spiteri) v. Basildon Crown Court* [2009] EWHC 665 Admin the defendant was acquitted in a drink and drive case as a result of what was described as an "unmeritorious technicality". Costs were refused because it was said that he had brought the prosecution on himself. On appeal it was held to be wrong in principle and contrary to the presumption of innocence to approach the issue of costs on the basis that the defendant was really guilty of the offence. It was also said that the bringing of the prosecution on oneself alone was not a sufficient positive reason to refuse costs as the Practice Direction went on to say that there must also have been some misleading of the prosecution into thinking that the case against the defendant was stronger than it was.

Costs in Criminal Cases (General) Regulations 1986, regs 4–8, 12

Determination of rates and scales of costs payable out of central funds

7.—(1) The appropriate authority shall consider the claim, any further particulars, informa- **30–14** tion or documents submitted by the applicant under regulation 6 and shall allow costs in respect of—

(a) such work as appears to it to have been actually and reasonably done; and

(b) such disbursements as appear to it to have been actually and reasonably incurred.

(2) Any doubts which the appropriate authority may have as to whether the costs were reasonably incurred or were reasonable in amount shall be resolved against the applicant.

(3) The costs awarded shall not exceed the costs actually incurred.

(4) The Lord Chancellor shall, with the consent of the Treasury and for the purposes of this regulation, determine the rates and scales of costs in respect of work and disbursements payable out of central funds.

[This regulation is printed as amended by the *Costs in Criminal Cases (General) (Amendment) Regulations* 2009 S.I. No. 2720 of 2009 which came into force with effect from October 30, 2009]

This Regulation has been amended to provide for official determination of rates and scales of costs.

F. Orders for Costs against Legal Representatives

Costs in Criminal Cases (General) Regulations 1986, regs 3A–3D

General

30–38   **3B.**—(1) A wasted costs order may provide for the whole or any part of the wasted costs to be disallowed or ordered to be paid and the court shall specify the amount of such costs.

(2) *Repealed.   .   ...*

(3) When making a wasted costs order the court may take into account any other order as to costs in respect of the proceedings and order into account when making any other such order.

(4) *Repealed.   .   ...*

[This regulation is printed as amended by the *Costs in Criminal Cases (General) (Amendment) Regulations* 2009 S.I. No. 2720 of 2009 which came into force with effect from October 30, 2009]

Appeals

30–39   **3C.**—(1) A legal or other representative against whom the wasted costs order is made may appeal—

(a) in the case of an order made by a magistrates' court, to the Crown Court, and

(b) in the case of an order made at first instance by the Crown Court, to the Court of Appeal.

(2) - (5) *Repealed .   .   .*

(6) The appeal court may affirm, vary or revoke the order as it thinks fit

[This regulation is printed as amended by the *Costs in Criminal Cases (General) (Amendment) Regulations* 2009 S.I. No. 2720 of 2009 which came into force with effect from October 30, 2009]

These Regulations have been amended to delete procedural requirements now found in the *Criminal Procedure Rules.*

ATTORNEY-GENERAL'S GUIDELINES

I. INTRODUCTION

The Attorney-General has issued revised guidelines on the acceptance of pleas and **C–1** the prosecutor's role in the sentencing exercise (revised November 5, 2009, and having effect as from December 1, 2009).

IV. ATTORNEY-GENERAL'S GUIDELINES ON THE ACCEPTANCE OF PLEAS AND THE PROSECUTOR'S ROLE IN THE SENTENCING EXERCISE

A. FOREWORD

A1. Prosecutors have an important role in protecting the victim's interests **C–27** in the criminal justice process, not least in the acceptance of pleas and the sentencing exercise. The basis of plea, particularly in a case that is not contested, is the vehicle through which the victim's voice is heard. Factual inaccuracies in pleas in mitigation cause distress and offence to victims, the families of victims and witnesses. This can take many forms but may be most acutely felt when the victim is dead and the family hears inaccurate assertions about the victim's character or lifestyle. Prosecution advocates are reminded that they are required to adhere to the standards set out in the Victim's Charter, which places the needs of the victim at the heart of the criminal justice process, and that they are subject to a similar obligation in respect of the Code of Practice for Victims of Crime.

A2. The principle of fairness is central to the administration of justice. The implementation of the *Human Rights Act* 1998 in October 2000 incorporated into domestic law the principle of fairness to the accused articulated in the European Convention on Human Rights. Accuracy and reasonableness of plea plays an important part in ensuring fairness both to the accused and to the victim.

A3. The Attorney General's Guidelines on the Acceptance of Pleas issued on December 7, 2000 highlighted the importance of transparency in the conduct of justice. The basis of plea agreed by the parties in a criminal trial is central to the sentencing process. An illogical or unsupported basis of plea can lead to an unduly lenient sentence being passed, and has a consequential effect where consideration arises as to whether to refer the sentence to the Court of Appeal under s.36 of the *Criminal Justice Act* 1988.

A4. These Guidelines, which replace the Guidelines issued in October 2005, give guidance on how prosecutors should meet these objectives of protection of victims' interests and of securing fairness and transparency in the process. They take into account paras IV.45.4 and following of the Consolidated Criminal Practice Direction, amended May 2009 and the guidance issued by the Court of Appeal (Criminal) Division in *R. v. Beswick*

93

[1996] 1 Cr.App.R. 343, *R v. Tolera* [1999] 1 Cr.App.R. 25 and *R. v. Underwood* [2005] 1 Cr.App.R 178. They complement the Bar Council Guidance on Written Standards for the Conduct of Professional Work issued with the 7th edition of the Code of Conduct for the Bar of England and Wales and the Law Society's Professional Conduct Rules. When considering the acceptance of a guilty plea prosecution advocates are also reminded of the need to apply "The Farquharson Guidelines on The Role and Responsibilities of the Prosecution Advocate".

A5. The Guidelines should be followed by all prosecutors and those persons designated under s.7 of the *Prosecution of Offences Act* 1985 (designated caseworkers) and apply to prosecutions conducted in England and Wales.

B. GENERAL PRINCIPLES

C–28
B1. Justice in this jurisdiction, save in the most exceptional circumstances, is conducted in public. This includes the acceptance of pleas by the prosecution and sentencing.

B2. The Code for Crown Prosecutors governs the prosecutor's decision-making prior to the commencement of the trial hearing and sets out the circumstances in which pleas to a reduced number of charges, or less serious charges, can be accepted.

B3. When a case is listed for trial and the prosecution form the view that the appropriate course is to accept a plea before the proceedings commence or continue, or to offer no evidence on the indictment or any part of it, the prosecution should whenever practicable speak to the victim or the victim's family, so that the position can be explained. The views of the victim or the family may assist in informing the prosecutor's decision as to whether it is the public interest, as defined by the Code for Crown Prosecutors, to accept or reject the plea. The victim or victim's family should then be kept informed and decisions explained once they are made at court.

B4. The appropriate disposal of a criminal case after conviction is as much a part of the criminal justice process as the trial of guilt or innocence. The prosecution advocate represents the public interest, and should be ready to assist the court to reach its decision as to the appropriate sentence. This will include drawing the court's attention to:

—any victim personal statement or other information available to the prosecution advocate as to the impact of the offence on the victim;

—where appropriate, to any evidence of the impact of the offending on a community;

—any statutory provisions relevant to the offender and the offences under consideration;

—any relevant sentencing guidelines and guideline cases; and

—the aggravating and mitigating factors of the offence under consideration.

B5. The prosecution advocate may also offer assistance to the court by making submissions, in the light of all these factors, as to the appropriate sentencing range. In all cases, it is the prosecution advocate's duty to apply for appropriate ancillary orders, such as anti-social behaviour orders and confiscation orders. When considering which ancillary orders to apply for, prosecution advocates must always have regard to the victim's needs, including the question of his or her future protection.

C. THE BASIS OF PLEA

C1. The basis of a guilty plea must not be agreed on a misleading or **C–29** untrue set of facts and must take proper account of the victim's interests. An illogical or insupportable basis of plea will inevitably result in the imposition of an inappropriate sentence and is capable of damaging public confidence in the criminal justice system. In cases involving multiple defendants the bases of plea for each defendant must be factually consistent with each other.

C2. When the defendant indicates an acceptable plea, the defence advocate should reduce the basis of the plea to writing. This must be done in all cases save for those in which the defendant has indicated that the guilty plea has been or will be tendered on the basis of the prosecution case.

C3. The written basis of plea must be considered with great care, taking account of the position of any other relevant defendant where appropriate. The prosecution should not lend itself to any agreement whereby a case is presented to the sentencing judge on a misleading or untrue set of facts or on a basis that is detrimental to the victim's interests. There will be cases where a defendant seeks to mitigate on the basis of assertions of fact which are outside the scope of the prosecution's knowledge. A typical example concerns the defendant's state of mind. If a defendant wishes to be sentenced on this basis, the prosecution advocate should invite the judge not to accept the defendant's version unless he or she gives evidence on oath to be tested in cross-examination. Paragraph IV.45.14 of the *Consolidated Criminal Practice Direction* states that in such circumstances the defence advocate should be prepared to call the defendant and, if the defendant is not willing to testify, subject to any explanation that may be given, the judge may draw such inferences as appear appropriate.

C4. The prosecution advocate should show the prosecuting authority any written record relating to the plea and agree with them the basis on which the case will be opened to the court. If, as may well be the case, the basis of plea differs in its implications for sentencing or the making of ancillary orders from the case originally outlined by the prosecution, the prosecution advocate must ensure that such differences are accurately reflected in the written record prior to showing it to the prosecuting authority.

C5. It is the responsibility of the prosecution advocate thereafter to ensure that the defence advocate is aware of the basis on which the plea is accepted by the prosecution and the way in which the prosecution case will be opened to the court.

C6. In all cases where it is likely to assist the court where the sentencing issues are complex or unfamiliar the prosecution must add to the written outline of the case which is served upon the court a summary of the key considerations. This should take the form of very brief notes on:
—any relevant statutory limitations
—the names of any relevant sentencing authorities or guidelines
—the scope for any ancillary orders (e.g. concerning anti-social behaviour, confiscation or deportation will need to be considered.
—The outline should also include the age of the defendant and information regarding any outstanding offences.

C7. It remains open to the prosecutor to provide further written information (for example to supplement and update the analysis at later stages of the case) where he or she thought that likely to assist the court, or if the judge requests it.

C8. When the prosecution advocate has agreed the written basis of plea submitted by the defence advocate, he or she should endorse the document accordingly. If the prosecution advocate takes issue with all or part of the written basis of plea, the procedure set out in the *Consolidated Criminal Practice Direction* (and in Pt 37.10(5) of the *Criminal Procedure Rules*) should be followed. The defendant's basis of plea must be set out in writing identifying what is in dispute; the court may invite the parties to make representations about whether the dispute is material to sentence; and if the court decides that it is a material dispute, the court will invite further representations or evidence as it may require and decide the dispute in accordance with the principles set out in *R. v. Newton*, 77 Cr.App.R. 13, CA. The signed original document setting out the disputed factual matters should be made available to the trial judge and thereafter lodged with the court papers, as it will form part of the record of the hearing.

C9. Where the basis of plea cannot be agreed and the discrepancy between the two accounts is such as to have a potentially significant effect on the level of sentence, it is the duty of the defence advocate so to inform the court before the sentencing process begins. There remains an overriding duty on the prosecution advocate to ensure that the sentencing judge is made aware of the discrepancy and of the consideration which must be given to holding a Newton hearing to resolve the issue. The court should be told where a derogatory reference to a victim, witness or third party is not accepted, even though there may be no effect on sentence.

C10. As emphasised in para. IV.45.10 of the *Consolidated Criminal Practice Direction*, whenever an agreement as to the basis of plea is made between the prosecution and defence, any such agreement will be subject to the approval of the trial judge, who may of his or her own motion disregard the agreement and direct that a Newton hearing should be held to determine the proper basis on which sentence should be passed.

C11. Where a defendant declines to admit an offence that he or she previously indicated should be taken into consideration, the prosecution advocate should indicate to the defence advocate and the court that, subject to further review, the offence may now form the basis of a new prosecution.

D. Sentence Indications

C–30   D1. Only in the Crown Court may sentence indications be sought. Advocates there are reminded that indications as to sentence should not be sought from the trial judge unless issues between the prosecution and defence have been addressed and resolved. Therefore, in difficult or complicated cases, no less than seven days notice in writing of an intention to seek an indication should normally be given to the prosecution and the court. When deciding whether the circumstances of a case require such notice to be given, defence advocates are reminded that prosecutors should not agree a basis of plea unless and until the necessary consultation has taken place first with the victim and/or the victim's family and second, in the case of an independent prosecution advocate, with the prosecuting authority.

D2. If there is no final agreement about the plea to the indictment, or the basis of plea, and the defence nevertheless proceeds to seek an indication of sentence, which the judge appears minded to give, the prosecution advocate should remind him or her of the guidance given in *R. v. Goodyear (Karl)* [2005] EWCA Crim. 888 that normally speaking an indication of sentence should not be given until the basis of the plea has been agreed or the judge has concluded that he or she can properly deal with the case without the need for a trial of the issue.

D3. If an indication is sought, the prosecution advocate should normally enquire whether the judge is in possession of or has access to all the evidence relied on by the prosecution, including any victim personal statement, as well as any information about relevant previous convictions recorded against the defendant.

D4. Before the judge gives the indication, the prosecution advocate should draw the judge's attention to any minimum or mandatory statutory sentencing requirements. Where the prosecution advocate would be expected to offer the judge assistance with relevant guideline cases or the views of the Sentencing Guidelines Council, he or she should invite the judge to allow them to do so. Where it applies, the prosecution advocate should remind the judge that the position of the Attorney General to refer any sentencing decision as unduly lenient is unaffected. In any event, the prosecution advocate should not say anything which may create the impression that the sentence indication has the support or approval of the Crown.

E. Pleas in Mitigation

E1. The prosecution advocate must challenge any assertion by the defence **C–31** in mitigation which is derogatory to a person's character, (for instance, because it suggests that his or her conduct is or has been criminal, immoral or improper) and which is either false or irrelevant to proper sentencing considerations. If the defence advocate persists in that assertion, the prosecution advocate should invite the court to consider holding a Newton hearing to determine the issue.

E2. The defence advocate must not submit in mitigation anything that is derogatory to a person's character without giving advance notice in writing so as to afford the prosecution advocate the opportunity to consider their position under paragraph E1. When the prosecution advocate is so notified they must take all reasonable steps to establish whether the assertions are true. Reasonable steps will include seeking the views of the victim. This will involve seeking the views of the victim's family if the victim is deceased, and the victim's parents or legal guardian where the victim is a child. Reasonable steps may also include seeking the views of the police or other law enforcement authority, as appropriate. An assertion which is derogatory to a person's character will rarely amount to mitigation unless it has a causal connection to the circumstances of the offence or is otherwise relevant to proper sentencing considerations.

E3. Where notice has not been given in accordance with paragraph E2, the prosecution advocate must not acquiesce in permitting mitigation which is derogatory to a person's character. In such circumstances, the prosecution advocate should draw the attention of the court to the failure to give advance notice and seek time, and if necessary, an adjournment to investigate the assertion in the same way as if proper notice had been given. Where, in the opinion of the prosecution advocate, there are substantial grounds for believing that such an assertion is false or irrelevant to sentence, he or she should inform the court of their opinion and invite the court to consider making an order under section 58(8) of the *Criminal Procedure and Investigations Act* 1996, preventing publication of the assertion.

E4. Where the prosecution advocate considers that the assertion is, if true, relevant to sentence, or the court has so indicated, he or she should seek time, and if necessary an adjournment, to establish whether the assertion is true. If the matter cannot be resolved to the satisfaction of the parties, the prosecution advocate should invite the court to consider holding a *Newton* hearing to determine the issue.

CODE FOR CROWN PROSECUTORS

The Director of Public Prosecution has issued a consultation document seeking views **E–1** on proposed changes to the Code for Crown Prosecutors. The consultation ended on January 11, 2010.

APPENDIX F

CONSOLIDATED CRIMINAL PRACTICE DIRECTION

History of amendment

With effect from October 5, 2009, *Amendment No. 23 to the Consolidated Criminal* **F–1** *Practice Direction (Criminal Proceedings: Forms)* [2009] 1 W.L.R. 2239 amends Annex D to the *Consolidated Criminal Practice Direction* so as to set out new forms for use in connection with new Pts 22 (disclosure), 27 (witness statements), and 62 (contempt of court) of the *Criminal Procedure Rules* 2005. Those amendments coincide with the amendments made by the *Criminal Procedure (Amendment) Rules* 2009 (S.I. 2009 No. 2087) (as to which, see Appendix G).

CRIMINAL PROCEDURE RULES

The *Criminal Procedure Rules* 2005 (S.I. 2005 No. 384) were further amended (with effect from October 5, 2009) by the *Criminal Procedure (Amendment) Rules* 2009 (S.I. 2009 No. 2087); and then revoked and replaced (with effect from April 5, 2010) by the *Criminal Procedure Rules* 2010 (S.I. 2010 No. 60). The 2010 rules represent a consolidation of the amendments made to the 2005 rules (by (S.I. 2006 No. 353, S.I. 2006 No. 2636, S.I. 2007 No. 699, S.I. 2007 No. 2317, S.I. 2007 No. 3662, S.I. 2008 No. 2076, S.I. 2008 No. 3269 and S.I. 2009 No. 2087), together with further amendments to the content of the rules.

Summary of changes to the rules

As to the amendments made by the *Criminal Procedure (Amendment) Rules* 2009, an amendment was made to r.3.8 so as to require a court to take every reasonable step to facilitate the attendance of a witness at trial. Rule 4.7 was amended so as to require personal service of an application to punish a person for contempt of court. A new Part 5 (forms and court records) was substituted, which incorporates into a single part the rules contained in the existing Parts 5 (forms) and 6 (court records); and a new Part 6 (investigation orders) was inserted. In Part 19, new rr.19.26 (grant of bail subject to electronic monitoring requirements) and 19.27 (grant of bail subject to accommodation or support requirements) were inserted. A new Part 22 (disclosure) was inserted, so as to consolidate and revise the rules previously in Parts 24 (disclosure of expert evidence), 25 (applications for public interest immunity and specific disclosure) and 26 (confidential material). Parts 23 to 26 now contain no rules. A new Part 27 (witness statements) was substituted, so as to revise and simplify the rules relating to the content and service of written witness statements. A number of amendments were made to Part 32 (international co-operation). A new Part 33 (expert evidence) was substituted, so as to incorporate and revise the part of the existing Part 24 which dealt with service of expert evidence. A new Part 62 (contempt of court) was inserted; as was a new Part 76 (costs), which replaced the rules in what used to be Part 78 (costs orders against the parties). There is now no Parts 77 and 78 to the rules.

As to the changes in the *Criminal Procedure Rules* 2010 (S.I. 2010 No. 60), new Parts 29 (measures to assist a witness or defendant to give evidence), 34 (hearsay), 35 (bad character) and 75 (request to the European Court for a preliminary ruling) have been substituted. Further, rr.3.9 (readiness for trial or appeal) and 3.10 (conduct of a trial or appeal) now apply to appeals to magistrates' courts; Part 6 (investigation orders) has been amended so as to make provision in relation to investigation anonymity orders under the Coroners and Justice Act 2009. A revised rule 10.4 (objection to committal statements being read at trial) is substituted. Rule 37.3 (procedure on plea of not guilty) is amended so as to make clear that the prosecutor may make a closing address in a summary trial where the defendant is legally represented or has introduced evidence other than his own. The rules in Part 52 (enforcement of fines) are renumbered. A minor amendment has been made to r.55.3 and a new r.55.5 (appeal to a magistrates' court against recognition of foreign driving disqualification) is inserted. Rule 63.1 (appeal to the Crown Court) is amended to include references to appeals under the*Violent Crime Reduction Act* 2006 and the *Counter-Terrorism Act* 2008. The rules in Part 64 (appeal to the High Court by way of case stated) are renumbered.

Commencement of the 2010 rules

The *Criminal Procedure Rules* 2010 (S.I. 2010 No. 60) have effect from April 5,

2010; but, unless the court otherwise directs, the new rules do not affect any right or duty existing under the 2005 rules, or the application of Part 29, 34 or 35 of the 2005 rules in a case in which an application or notice under the part concerned has been served before that date.

Criminal Procedure Rules 2010 (S.I. 2010 No. 60)

ARRANGEMENT OF RULES
General matters

PART 1 THE OVERRIDING OBJECTIVE

Contents of this Part

The overriding objective

G–1   **1.1.**—(1) The overriding objective of this new code is that criminal cases be dealt with justly.

(2) Dealing with a criminal case justly includes—

(a) acquitting the innocent and convicting the guilty;

(b) dealing with the prosecution and the defence fairly;

(c) recognising the rights of a defendant, particularly those under Article 6 of the European Convention on Human Rights;

(d) respecting the interests of witnesses, victims and jurors and keeping them informed of the progress of the case;

(e) dealing with the case efficiently and expeditiously;

(f) ensuring that appropriate information is available to the court when bail and sentence are considered; and

(g) dealing with the case in ways that take into account—

(i) the gravity of the offence alleged,

(ii) the complexity of what is in issue,

(iii) the severity of the consequences for the defendant and others affected, and

(iv) the needs of other cases.

The duty of the participants in a criminal case

G–1a   **1.2.**—(1) Each participant, in the conduct of each case, must—

(a) prepare and conduct the case in accordance with the overriding objective;

(b) comply with these Rules, practice directions and directions made by the court; and

(c) at once inform the court and all parties of any significant failure (whether or not that participant is responsible for that failure) to take any procedural step required by these Rules, any practice direction or any direction of the court. A failure is significant if it might hinder the court in furthering the overriding objective.

(2) Anyone involved in any way with a criminal case is a participant in its conduct for the purposes of this rule.

The application by the court of the overriding objective

G–1b   **1.3.** The court must further the overriding objective in particular when—

(a) exercising any power given to it by legislation (including these Rules);

(b) applying any practice direction; or

(c) interpreting any rule or practice direction.

PART 2 UNDERSTANDING AND APPLYING THE RULES

Contents of this Part

When the Rules apply

2.1.—(1) In general, the Criminal Procedure Rules apply—   **G–2**

    (a) in all criminal cases in magistrates' courts and in the Crown Court; and

    (b) in all cases in the criminal division of the Court of Appeal.

(2) If a rule applies only in one or two of those courts, the rule makes that clear.

(3) The Rules apply on and after 5th April, 2010, but unless the court otherwise directs they do not affect—

    (a) a right or duty existing under The Criminal Procedure Rules 2005; or

    (b) the application of Part 29, Part 34 or Part 35 of The Criminal Procedure Rules 2005 in a case in which an application or notice under the Part concerned has been served before that date.

Definitions

2.2—(1) In these Rules, unless the context makes it clear that something different is meant: **G–2a**

'business day' means any day except Saturday, Sunday, Christmas Day, Boxing Day, Good Friday, Easter Monday or a bank holiday;

'court' means a tribunal with jurisdiction over criminal cases. It includes a judge, recorder, District Judge (Magistrates' Court), lay justice and, when exercising their judicial powers, the Registrar of Criminal Appeals, a justices' clerk or assistant clerk;

'court officer means the appropriate member of the staff of a court;

'justices' legal adviser' means a justices' clerk or an assistant to a justices' clerk;

'live link' means an arrangement by which a person can see and hear, and be seen and heard by, the court when that person is not in court;

'Practice Direction' means the Lord Chief Justice's Consolidated Criminal Practice Direction, as amended; and

'public interest ruling' means a ruling about whether it is in the public interest to disclose prosecution material under sections 3(6), 7A(8) or 8(5) of the *Criminal Procedure and Investigations Act* 1996.

(2) Definitions of some other expressions are in the rules in which they apply.

References to Acts of Parliament and to Statutory Instruments

2.3. In these Rules, where a rule refers to an Act of Parliament or to subordinate legislation   **G–2b** by title and year, subsequent references to that Act or to that legislation in the rule are shortened: so, for example, after a reference to the *Criminal Procedure and Investigations Act* 1996 that Act is called 'the 1996 Act'; and after a reference to The *Criminal Procedure and Investigations Act 1996 (Defence Disclosure Time Limits) Regulations* 1997 those Regulations are called 'the 1997 Regulations'.

The glossary

2.4. The glossary at the end of the Rules is a guide to the meaning of certain legal expres-   **G–2c** sions used in them.

Representatives

G-2d   **2.5.**—(1) Under these Rules, unless the context makes it clear that something different is meant, anything that a party may or must do may be done—

(a) by a legal representative on that party's behalf;

(b) by a person with the corporation's written authority, where that party is a corporation;

(c) with the help of a parent, guardian or other suitable supporting adult where that party is a defendant—

(i) who is under 18, or

(ii) whose understanding of what the case involves is limited.

(2) Anyone with a prosecutor's authority to do so may, on that prosecutor's behalf—

(a) serve on the magistrates' court officer, or present to a magistrates' court, an information under section 1 of the Magistrates' Courts Act 1980; or

(b) issue a written charge and requisition under section 29 of the *Criminal Justice Act* 2003.

PART 3 CASE MANAGEMENT

Contents of this Part

The scope of this Part

G-3   **3.1.** This Part applies to the management of each case in a magistrates' court and in the Crown Court (including an appeal to the Crown Court) until the conclusion of that case.

The duty of the court

G-4   **3.2.**—(1) The court must further the overriding objective by actively managing the case.

(2) Active case management includes—

(a) the early identification of the real issues;

(b) the early identification of the needs of witnesses;

(c) achieving certainty as to what must be done, by whom, and when, in particular by the early setting of a timetable for the progress of the case;

(d) monitoring the progress of the case and compliance with directions;

(e) ensuring that evidence, whether disputed or not, is presented in the shortest and clearest way;

(f) discouraging delay, dealing with as many aspects of the case as possible on the same occasion, and avoiding unnecessary hearings;

(g) encouraging the participants to co-operate in the progression of the case; and

(h) making use of technology.

(3) The court must actively manage the case by giving any direction appropriate to the needs of that case as early as possible

The duty of the parties

G-5   **3.3.** Each party must—

(a) actively assist the court in fulfilling its duty under rule 3.2, without or if necessary with a direction; and

(b) apply for a direction if needed to further the overriding objective.

Case progression officers and their duties

3.4.—(1) At the beginning of the case each party must, unless the court otherwise directs— **G–6**

(a) nominate an individual responsible for progressing that case; and

(b) tell other parties and the court who he is and how to contact him.

(2) In fulfilling its duty under rule 3.2, the court must where appropriate—

(a) nominate a court officer responsible for progressing the case; and

(b) make sure the parties know who he is and how to contact him.

(3) In this Part a person nominated under this rule is called a case progression officer.

(4) A case progression officer must—

(a) monitor compliance with directions;

(b) make sure that the court is kept informed of events that may affect the progress of that case;

(c) make sure that he can be contacted promptly about the case during ordinary business hours;

(d) act promptly and reasonably in response to communications about the case; and

(e) if he will be unavailable, appoint a substitute to fulfil his duties and inform the other case progression officers.

The court's case management powers

3.5.—(1) In fulfilling its duty under rule 3.2 the court may give any direction and take any **G–7** step actively to manage a case unless that direction or step would be inconsistent with legislation, including these Rules.

(2) In particular, the court may—

(a) nominate a judge, magistrate or justices' legal adviser to manage the case;

(b) give a direction on its own initiative or on application by a party;

(c) ask or allow a party to propose a direction;

(d) for the purpose of giving directions, receive applications and representations by letter, by telephone or by any other means of electronic communication, and conduct a hearing by such means;

(e) give a direction without a hearing;

(f) fix, postpone, bring forward, extend or cancel a hearing;

(g) shorten or extend (even after it has expired) a time limit fixed by a direction;

(h) require that issues in the case should be determined separately, and decide in what order they will be determined; and (i) specify the consequences of failing to comply with a direction.

(3) A magistrates' court may give a direction that will apply in the Crown Court if the case is to continue there.

(4) The Crown Court may give a direction that will apply in a magistrates' court if the case is to continue there.

(5) Any power to give a direction under this Part includes a power to vary or revoke that direction.

(6) If a party fails to comply with a rule or a direction, the court may—

(a) fix, postpone, bring forward, extend, cancel or adjourn a hearing;

(b) exercise its powers to make a costs order; and

(c) impose such other sanction as may be appropriate.

Application to vary a direction

3.6.—(1) A party may apply to vary a direction if— **G–8**

(a) the court gave it without a hearing;

(b) the court gave it at a hearing in his absence; or

(c) circumstances have changed.

(2) A party who applies to vary a direction must—

(a) apply as soon as practicable after he becomes aware of the grounds for doing so; and

(b) give as much notice to the other parties as the nature and urgency of his application permits.

Agreement to vary a time limit fixed by a direction

G–9   **3.7.**—(1) The parties may agree to vary a time limit fixed by a direction, but only if—

(a) the variation will not—
     (i) affect the date of any hearing that has been fixed, or
     (ii) significantly affect the progress of the case in any other way;

(b) the court has not prohibited variation by agreement; and

(c) the court's case progression officer is promptly informed.

(2) The court's case progression officer must refer the agreement to the court if he doubts the condition in paragraph (1)(a) is satisfied.

Case preparation and progression

G–10   **3.8.**—(1) At every hearing, if a case cannot be concluded there and then the court must give directions so that it can be concluded at the next hearing or as soon as possible after that.

(2) At every hearing the court must, where relevant—

(a) if the defendant is absent, decide whether to proceed nonetheless;

(b) take the defendant's plea (unless already done) or if no plea can be taken then find out whether the defendant is likely to plead guilty or not guilty;

(c) set, follow or revise a timetable for the progress of the case, which may include a timetable for any hearing including the trial or (in the Crown Court) the appeal;

(d) in giving directions, ensure continuity in relation to the court and to the parties' representatives where that is appropriate and practicable; and

(e) where a direction has not been complied with, find out why, identify who was responsible, and take appropriate action.

(3) In order to prepare for a trial in the Crown Court, the court must conduct a plea and case management hearing unless the circumstances make that unnecessary.

(4) In order to prepare for the trial, the court must take every reasonable step to encourage and to facilitate the attendance of witnesses when they are needed.

Readiness for trial or appeal

G–11   **3.9.**—(1) This rule applies to a party's preparation for trial or appeal, and in this rule and rule 3.10 trial includes any hearing at which evidence will be introduced.

(2) In fulfilling his duty under rule 3.3, each party must—

(a) comply with directions given by the court;

(b) take every reasonable step to make sure his witnesses will attend when they are needed;

(c) make appropriate arrangements to present any written or other material; and

(d) promptly inform the court and the other parties of anything that may—
     (i) affect the date or duration of the trial or appeal, or
     (ii) significantly affect the progress of the case in any other way.

(3) The court may require a party to give a certificate of readiness.

Conduct of a trial or an appeal

G–12   **3.10.** In order to manage a trial or an appeal—

(a) the court must establish, with the active assistance of the parties, what disputed issues they intend to explore; and (b) the court may require a party to identify—
     (i) which witnesses that party wants to give oral evidence,
     (ii) the order in which that party wants those witnesses to give their evidence,
     (iii) whether that party requires an order compelling the attendance of a witness,
     (iv) what arrangements are desirable to facilitate the giving of evidence by a witness,
     (v) what arrangements are desirable to facilitate the participation of any other person, including the defendant,
     (vi) what written evidence that party intends to introduce,
     (vii) what other material, if any, that person intends to make available to the court in the presentation of the case,

(viii) whether that party intends to raise any point of law that could affect the conduct of the trial or appeal, and

(ix) what timetable that party proposes and expects to follow.

Case management forms and records

3.11.—(1) The case management forms set out in the Practice Direction must be used, and **G–13** where there is no form then no specific formality is required.

(2) The court must make available to the parties a record of directions given.

PART 4 SERVICE OF DOCUMENTS

Contents of this Part

When this Part applies

4.1. The rules in this Part apply to the service of every document in a case to which these **G–14** Rules apply, subject to any special rules in other legislation (including other Parts of these Rules) or in the Practice Direction.

Methods of service

4.2. A document may be served by any of the methods described in rules 4.3 to 4.6 (subject **G–15** to rule 4.7), or in rule 4.8.

Service by handing over a document

4.3.—(1) A document may be served on— **G–16**

(a) an individual by handing it to him or her;

(b) a corporation by handing it to a person holding a senior position in that corporation;

(c) an individual or corporation who is legally represented in the case by handing it to that representative;

(d) the prosecution by handing it to the prosecutor or to the prosecution representative;

(e) the court officer by handing it to a court officer with authority to accept it at the relevant court office; and

(f) the Registrar of Criminal Appeals by handing it to a court officer with authority to accept it at the Criminal Appeal Office.

(2) If an individual is 17 or under, a copy of a document served under paragraph (1)(a) must be handed to his or her parent, or another appropriate adult, unless no such person is readily available.

Service by leaving or posting a document

4.4—(1) A document may be served by leaving it at the appropriate address for service under **G–17** this rule or by sending it to that address by first class post or by the equivalent of first class post.

(2) The address for service under this rule on—

    (a) an individual is an address where it is reasonably believed that he or she will receive it;

    (b) a corporation is its principal office, and if there is no readily identifiable principal office then any place where it carries on its activities or business;

    (c) an individual or corporation who is legally represented in the case is that representative's office;

    (d) the prosecution is the prosecutor's office;

    (e) the court officer is the relevant court office; and

    (f) the Registrar of Criminal Appeals is the Criminal Appeal Office, Royal Courts of Justice, Strand, London, WC2A 2LL.

Service through a document exchange

G–18   **4.5.** A document may be served by document exchange (DX) where—

    (a) the writing paper of the person to be served gives a DX box number; and

    (b) that person has not refused to accept service by DX.

Service by fax, e-mail or other electronic means

G–19   **4.6.**—(1) A document may be served by fax, e-mail or other electronic means where—

    (a) the person to be served has given a fax, e-mail or other electronic address; and

    (b) that person has not refused to accept service by that means.

(2) Where a document is served under this rule the person serving it need not provide a paper copy as well.

Documents that must be served only by handing them over, leaving or posting them

G–20   **4.7.**—(1) The documents listed in paragraph (2) may be served—

    (a) on an individual, only under rule 4.3(1)(a) (handing over) or rule 4.4(1) and (2)(a) (leaving or posting); and

    (b) on a corporation, only under rule 4.3(1)(b) (handing over) or rule 4.4(1) and (2)(b) (leaving or posting).

(2) Those documents are—

    (a) a summons, requisition or witness summons;

    (b) notice of an order under section 25 of the *Road Traffic Offenders Act* 1988;

    (c) a notice of registration under section 71(6) of that Act;

    (d) a notice of discontinuance under section 23(4) of the *Prosecution of Offences Act* 1985;

    (e) notice under rule 37.3(1) of the date, time and place to which the trial of an information has been adjourned, where it was adjourned in the defendant's absence;

    (f) a notice of fine or forfeited recognizance required by rule 52.1(1);

    (g) notice under section 86 of the *Magistrates' Courts Act* 1980 of a revised date to attend a means inquiry;

    (h) notice of a hearing to review the postponement of the issue of a warrant of commitment under section 77(6) of the *Magistrates' Courts Act* 1980;

    (i) a copy of the minute of a magistrates' court order required by rule 52.7(1);

    (j) an invitation to make observations or attend a hearing under rule 53.1(2) on the review of a compensation order under section 133 of the Powers of Criminal Courts (Sentencing) Act 2000;

    (k) any notice or document served under Part 19.

(3) An application under rule 62.3 for the court to punish for contempt of court may be served—

    (a) on an individual, only under rule 4.3(1)(a) (by handing it to him or her);

    (b) on a corporation, only under rule 4.3(1)(b) (by handing it to a person holding a senior position in that corporation).

Service by person in custody

G–21   **4.8.**—(1) A person in custody may serve a document by handing it to the custodian addressed to the person to be served.

(2) The custodian must—

(a) endorse it with the time and date of receipt;

(b) record its receipt; and

(c) forward it promptly to the addressee.

Service by another method

4.9.—(1) The court may allow service of a document by a method other than those described **G–22** in rules 4.3 to 4.6 and in rule 4.8.

(2) An order allowing service by another method must specify—

(a) the method to be used; and

(b) the date on which the document will be served.

Date of service

4.10.—(1) A document served under rule 4.3 or rule 4.8 is served on the day it is handed **G–23** over.

(2) Unless something different is shown, a document served on a person by any other method is served—

(a) in the case of a document left at an address, on the next business day after the day on which it was left;

(b) in the case of a document sent by first class post or by the equivalent of first class post, on the second business day after the day on which it was posted or despatched;

(c) in the case of a document served by document exchange, on the second business day after the day on which it was left at the addressee's DX or at a correspondent DX;

(d) in the case of a document transmitted by fax, e-mail or other electronic means, on the next business day after it was transmitted; and

(e) in any case, on the day on which the addressee responds to it if that is earlier.

(3) Unless something different is shown, a document produced by a court computer system is to be taken as having been sent by first class post or by the equivalent of first class post to the addressee on the business day after the day on which it was produced.

(4) Where a document is served on or by the court officer, 'business day' does not include a day on which the court office is closed.

Proof of service

4.11. The person who serves a document may prove that by signing a certificate explaining **G–24** how and when it was served.

Court's power to give directions about service

4.12.—(1) The court may specify the time as well as the date by which a document must be— **G–25**

(a) served under rule 4.3 or rule 4.8; or

(b) transmitted by fax, e-mail or other electronic means if it is served under rule 4.6.

(2) The court may treat a document as served if the addressee responds to it even if it was not served in accordance with the rules in this Part.

PART 5 FORMS AND COURT RECORDS

Contents of this Part

Section 1: forms

SECTION 1: FORMS

Forms

G–26   **5.1.** The forms set out in the Practice Direction shall be used as appropriate in connection with the rules to which they apply.

Magistrates' courts forms in Welsh

G–27   **5.2.**—(1) Subject to the provisions of this rule, the Welsh language forms set out in the Practice Direction or forms to the like effect may be used in connection with proceedings in magistrates' courts in Wales.

(2) Both a Welsh form and an English form may be used in the same document.

(3) When only a Welsh form set out in the Practice Direction accompanying this rule, or only the corresponding English form, is used in connection with proceedings in magistrates' courts in Wales, there shall be added the following words in Welsh and English:

"Darperir y ddogfen hon yn Gymraeg / Saesneg os bydd arnoch ei heisiau. Dylech wneud cais yn ddi-oed i (Glerc Llys yr Ynadon) (rhodder yma'r cyfeiriad) .. ..

This document will be provided in Welsh / English if you require it. You should apply immediately to (the Justices' Clerk to the Magistrates' Court) (address) .. .."

(If a person other than a justices' clerk is responsible for sending or giving the document, insert that person's name instead.)

(4) The justices' clerk or other person responsible for the service of a form bearing the additional words set out in paragraph (3) above shall, if any person upon whom the form is served so requests, provide him with the corresponding English or Welsh form.

(5) In this rule any reference to serving a document shall include the sending, giving or other delivery of it.

(6) In the case of a discrepancy between an English and Welsh text the English text shall prevail.

Signature of magistrates' courts forms by justices' clerk

G–28   **5.3.**—(1) Subject to paragraph (2) below, where any form prescribed by these Rules contains provision for signature by a justice of the peace only, the form shall have effect as if it contained provision in the alternative for signature by the justices' clerk.

(2) This rule shall not apply to any form of information, complaint, statutory declaration or warrant, other than a warrant of commitment or of distress.

(3) In this rule where a signature is required on a form or warrant other than an arrest, remand or commitment warrant, an electronic signature incorporated into the document will satisfy this requirement.

SECTION 2: COURT RECORDS

Magistrates' court register

G–29   **5.4.**—(1) A magistrates' court officer shall keep a register in which there shall be entered—

     (a) a minute or memorandum of every adjudication of the court; and

     (b) a minute or memorandum of every other proceeding or thing required by these Rules or any other enactment to be so entered.

(2) The register may be stored in electronic form on the court computer system and entries in the register shall include, where relevant, the following particulars—

(a) the name of the informant, complainant or applicant;
(b) the name and date of birth (if known) of the defendant or respondent;
(c) the nature of offence, matter of complaint or details of the application;
(d) the date of offence or matter of complaint;
(e) the plea or consent to order; and
(f) the minute of adjudication.

(3) Particulars of any entry relating to a decision about bail, or the reasons for any such decision, or the particulars of any certificate granted under section 5(6A) of the Bail Act 1976, may be made in a record separate from that in which the entry recording the decision itself is made; but any such separate record shall be regarded as forming part of the register.

(4) Where, by virtue of section 128(3A) of the *Magistrates' Courts Act* 1980, an accused gives his consent to the hearing and determination in his absence of any application for his remand on an adjournment of the case under sections 5, 10(1) or 18(4)(61) of that Act, the court shall cause the consent of the accused, and the date on which it was notified to the court, to be entered in the register.

(5) Where any consent mentioned in paragraph (4) is withdrawn, the court shall cause the withdrawal of the consent and the date on which it was notified to the court to be entered in the register.

(6) On the summary trial of an information, the accused's plea shall be entered in the register.

(7) Where a court tries any person summarily in any case in which he may be tried summarily only with his consent, the court shall cause his consent to be entered in the register and, if the consent is signified by a person representing him in his absence, the court shall cause that fact also to be entered in the register.

(8) Where a person is charged before a magistrates' court with an offence triable either way, the court shall cause the entry in the register to show whether he was present when the proceedings for determining the mode of trial were conducted; and, if they were conducted in his absence, whether they were so conducted by virtue of section 18(3) of the 1980 Act (disorderly conduct on his part) or by virtue of section 23(1) of that Act (consent signified by person representing him).

(9) In any case to which section 22 of the 1980 Act (certain offences triable either way to be tried summarily if value involved is small) applies, the court shall cause its decision as to the value involved or, as the case may be, the fact that it is unable to reach such a decision to be entered in the register.

(10) Where a court has power under section 53(3) of the 1980 Act to make an order with the consent of the defendant without hearing evidence, the court shall cause any consent of the defendant to the making of the order to be entered in the register.

(11) In the case of conviction or dismissal, the register shall clearly show the nature of the offence of which the accused is convicted or, as the case may be, the nature of the offence charged in the information that is dismissed.

(12) An entry of a conviction in the register shall state the date of the offence.

(13) Where a court is required under section 130(3) of the *Powers of Criminal Courts (Sentencing) Act* 2000 to give reasons for not making a compensation order the court shall cause the reasons given to be entered in the register.

(14) Where a court passes a custodial sentence, the court shall cause a statement of whether it obtained and considered a pre-sentence report before passing sentence to be entered in the register.

(15) Every register shall be open to inspection during reasonable hours by any justice of the peace, or any person authorised in that behalf by a justice of the peace or the Lord Chancellor.

(16) A record of summary conviction or order made on complaint required for an appeal or other legal purpose may be in the form of certified extract from the court register.

(17) Such part of the register as relates to proceedings in a youth court may be recorded separately and stored in electronic form on the court computer system.

Registration of endorsement of licence under section 57 of the Road Traffic Offenders Act 1988

5.5 A magistrates' court officer or justices' clerk who, as a fixed penalty clerk within the mean- **G–30** ing of section 69(4) of the *Road Traffic Offenders Act* 1988, endorses a driving licence under section 57(3) or (4) of that Act(66) (endorsement of licences without hearing) shall register the particulars of the endorsement in a record separate from the register kept under rule 5.4; but any such record shall be regarded as forming part of the register.

Registration of certificate issued under section 70 of the Road Traffic Offenders Act 1988

G–31   **5.6.** A magistrates' court officer shall register receipt of a registration certificate issued under section 70 of the *Road Traffic Offenders Act* 1988 (sum payable in default of fixed penalty to be enforced as a fine) in a record separate from the register kept under rule 5.4; but any such record shall be regarded as forming part of the register.

Proof of proceedings in magistrates' courts

G–32   **5.7.** The register of a magistrates' court, or an extract from the register certified by the magistrates' court officer as a true extract, shall be admissible in any legal proceedings as evidence of the proceedings of the court entered in the register.

PART 6 INVESTIGATION ORDERS

Contents of this Part

SECTION 1: UNDERSTANDING AND APPLYING THIS PART

When this Part applies

G–32a   **6.1.**—(1) Sections 2 and 3 of this Part apply where, for the purposes of a terrorist investigation—

     (a) a Circuit judge can make, vary or discharge—

         (i) an order for the production of, or for giving access to, material, or for a statement of its location, under paragraphs 5 and 10 of Schedule 5 to the *Terrorism Act* 2000,

         (ii) an explanation order, under paragraphs 10 and 13 of Schedule 5 to the 2000 Act,

         (iii) a customer information order, under paragraphs 1 and 4 of Schedule 6 to the 2000 Act;

     (b) a Circuit judge can make, and the Crown Court can vary or discharge, an account monitoring order, under paragraphs 2 and 4 of Schedule 6A to the 2000 Act.

(2) Sections 2 and 4 of this Part apply where, for the purposes of a confiscation investigation or a money laundering investigation, a Crown Court judge can make, and the Crown Court can vary or discharge—

(a) a production order, under sections 345 and 351 of the *Proceeds of Crime Act* 2002;

(b) an order to grant entry, under sections 347 and 351 of the 2002 Act;

(c) a disclosure order, under sections 357 and 362 of the 2002 Act;

(d) a customer information order, under sections 363 and 369 of the 2002 Act;

(e) an account monitoring order, under sections 370 and 375 of the 2002 Act(75).

(3) Rule 6.5 and Section 5 of this Part apply where—

(a) a justice of the peace can make or discharge an investigation anonymity order, under sections 76 and 80 of the *Coroners and Justice Act* 2009;

(b) a Crown Court judge can determine an appeal against—

    (i) (i) a refusal of such an order, under section 79 of the 2009 Act,

    (ii) a decision on an application to discharge such an order, under section 80(6) of the 2009 Act.

Meaning of 'court', 'applicant' and 'respondent'

6.2. In this Part—   **G–32b**

(a) a reference to the 'court' includes a reference to any justice of the peace or judge who can exercise a power to which this Part applies;

(b) 'applicant' means any person who can apply for an order to which this Part applies; and

(c) 'respondent' means a person against whom such an order is sought or made.

SECTION 2: GENERAL RULES

Exercise of court's powers

6.3.—(1) The court must determine an application for an order—   **G–32c**

(a) at a hearing (which will be in private unless the court otherwise directs); and

(b) in the applicant's presence.

(2) The court must not determine such an application in the absence of the respondent or any other person affected, unless—

(a) the absentee has had at least 2 business days in which to make representations; or

(b) the court is satisfied that—

    (i) the applicant cannot identify or contact the absentee,

    (ii) it would prejudice the investigation if the absentee were present, or

    (iii) it would prejudice the investigation to adjourn or postpone the application so as to allow the absentee to attend.

(3) The court may determine an application to vary or discharge an order—

(a) at a hearing (which will be in private unless the court otherwise directs), or without a hearing; and

(b) in the absence of—

    (i) the applicant,

    (ii) the respondent,

    (iii) any other person affected by the order.

Court's power to vary requirements under this Part

6.4.—(1) The court may—   **G–32d**

(a) shorten or extend (even after it has expired) a time limit under this Part;

(b) dispense with a requirement for service under this Part (even after service was required); and

(c) consider an application made orally instead of in writing.

(2) A person who wants an extension of time must—

(a) apply when serving the application for which it is needed; and

(b) explain the delay.

Custody of documents

G–32e   **6.5.** Unless the court otherwise directs, the court officer may—

    (a) keep a written application; or

    (b) arrange for the whole or any part to be kept by some other appropriate person, subject to any conditions that the court may impose.

SECTION 5: ORDERS UNDER THE CORONERS AND JUSTICE ACT 2009

Exercise of court's powers

G–32f   **6.23.**—(1) The court may determine an application for an investigation anonymity order, and any appeal against the refusal of such an order—

    (a) at a hearing (which will be in private unless the court otherwise directs); or

    (b) without a hearing.

(2) The court must determine an application to discharge an investigation anonymity order, and any appeal against the decision on such an application—

    (a) at a hearing (which will be in private unless the court otherwise directs); and

    (b) in the presence of the person specified in the order, unless—

        (i) that person applied for the discharge of the order,

        (ii) that person has had an opportunity to make representations, or

        (iii) the court is satisfied that it is not reasonably practicable to communicate with that person.

(3) The court may consider an application or an appeal made orally instead of in writing.

Application for an investigation anonymity order

G–32g   **6.24.**—(1) This rule applies where an applicant wants a magistrates' court to make an investigation anonymity order.

(2) The applicant must—

    (a) apply in writing;

    (b) serve the application on the court officer;

    (c) identify the person to be specified in the order, unless—

        (i) the applicant wants the court to determine the application at a hearing, or

        (ii) · the court otherwise directs;

    (d) explain how the proposed order meets the conditions prescribed by section 78 of the *Coroners and Justice Act* 2009;

    (e) say if the applicant intends to appeal should the court refuse the order;

    (f) attach any material on which the applicant relies; and

    (g) propose the terms of the order.

(3) At any hearing of the application, the applicant must—

    (a) identify to the court the person to be specified in the order, unless—

        (i) the applicant has done so already, or

        (ii) the court otherwise directs; and

    (b) unless the applicant has done so already, inform the court if the applicant intends to appeal should the court refuse the order.

Application to discharge an investigation anonymity order

G–32h   **6.25.**—(1) This rule applies where one of the following wants a magistrates' court to discharge an investigation anonymity order—

    (a) an applicant; or

    (b) the person specified in the order.

(2) That applicant or the specified person must—

    (a) apply in writing as soon as practicable after becoming aware of the grounds for doing so;

    (b) serve the application on—

        (i) the court officer, and as applicable

     (ii) the applicant for the order, and

     (iii) the specified person;

  (c) explain—

     (i) what material circumstances have changed since the order was made, or since any previous application was made to discharge it, and

     (ii) why it is appropriate for the order to be discharged; and

  (d) attach—.

     (i) a copy of the order, and

     (ii) any material on which the applicant relies.

  (3) A party must inform the court if that party intends to appeal should the court discharge the order

Appeal

  6.26.—(1) This rule applies where one of the following ('the appellant') wants to appeal to   **G–32i** the Crown Court—

  (a) the applicant for an investigation anonymity order, where a magistrates' court has refused to make the order;

  (b) a party to an application to discharge such an order, where a magistrates' court has decided that application.

  (2) The appellant must—

  (a) serve on the Crown Court officer a copy of the application to the magistrates' court; and

  (b) where the appeal concerns a discharge decision, notify each other party, not more that 21 days after the decision against which the appellant wants to appeal.

  (3) The Crown Court must hear the appeal without justices of the peace.

PART 7 STARTING A PROSECUTION IN A MAGISTRATES' COURT

Contents of this Part

When this Part applies

  7.1.—(1) This Part applies in a magistrates' court where—   **G–33**

  (a) a prosecutor wants the court to issue a summons or warrant under section 1 of the *Magistrates' Courts Act* 1980;

  (b) a public prosecutor—

     (i) wants the court to issue a warrant under section 1 of the *Magistrates' Courts Act* 1980, or

     (ii) issues a written charge and requisition under section 29 of the *Criminal Justice Act* 2003; or

  (c) a person who is in custody is charged with an offence.

  (2) In this Part, 'public prosecutor' means one of those public prosecutors listed in section 29 of the *Criminal Justice Act* 2003.

Information and written charge

  7.2.—(1) A prosecutor who wants the court to issue a summons must—   **G–34**

  (a) serve an information in writing on the court officer; or

  (b) unless other legislation prohibits this, present an information orally to the court, with a written record of the allegation that it contains.

  (2) A prosecutor who wants the court to issue a warrant must—

    (a) serve on the court officer—

        (i) an information in writing, or

        (ii) a copy of a written charge that has been issued; or

    (b) present to the court either of those documents.

(3) A public prosecutor who issues a written charge must notify the court officer immediately.

(4) A single document may contain—

    (a) more than one information; or

    (b) more than one written charge.

(5) Where an offence can be tried only in a magistrates' court, then unless other legislation otherwise provides—

    (a) a prosecutor must serve an information on the court officer or present it to the court; or

    (b) a public prosecutor must issue a written charge, not more than 6 months after the offence alleged.

(6) Where an offence can be tried in the Crown Court then—

    (a) a prosecutor must serve an information on the court officer or present it to the court; or

    (b) a public prosecutor must issue a written charge, within any time limit that applies to that offence.

Allegation of offence in information or charge

G–35   7.3.—(1) An allegation of an offence in an information or charge must contain—

    (a) a statement of the offence that—

        (i) describes the offence in ordinary language, and

        (ii) identifies any legislation that creates it; and

    (b) such particulars of the conduct constituting the commission of the offence as to make clear what the prosecutor alleges against the defendant.

(2) More than one incident of the commission of the offence may be included in the allegation if those incidents taken together amount to a course of conduct having regard to the time, place or purpose of commission.

Summons, warrant and requisition

G–36   7.4.—(1) The court may issue or withdraw a summons or warrant—

    (a) without giving the parties an opportunity to make representations; and

    (b) without a hearing, or at a hearing in public or in private.

(2) A summons, warrant or requisition may be issued in respect of more than one offence.

(3) A summons or requisition must—

    (a) contain notice of when and where the defendant is required to attend the court;

    (b) specify each offence in respect of which it is issued; and

    (c) identify the person under whose authority it is issued.

(4) A summons may be contained in the same document as an information.

(5) A requisition may be contained in the same document as a written charge.

(6) Where the court issues a summons—

    (a) the prosecutor must—

        (i) serve it on the defendant, and

        (ii) notify the court officer; or

    (b) the court officer must—

        (i) serve it on the defendant, and

        (ii) notify the prosecutor.

(7) Where a public prosecutor issues a requisition that prosecutor must—

    (a) serve on the defendant—

        (i) the requisition, and

        (ii) the written charge; and

    (b) serve a copy of each on the court officer.

(8) Unless it would be inconsistent with other legislation, a replacement summons or requisition may be issued without a fresh information or written charge where the one replaced—

(a) was served by leaving or posting it under rule 4.7 (documents that must be served only by handing them over, leaving or posting them); but

(b) is shown not to have been received by the addressee.

(9) A summons or requisition issued to a defendant under 18 may require that defendant's parent or guardian to attend the court with the defendant, or a separate summons or requisition may be issued for that purpose.

[The next paragraph is § G-42.]

PART 8 OBJECTING TO THE DISCONTINUANCE OF PROCEEDINGS IN A MAGISTRATES' COURT

Contents of this Part

Time for objecting

8.1. The period within which an accused person may give notice under section 23(7) of the *Prosecution of Offences Act* 1985 that he wants proceedings against him to continue is 35 days from the date when the proceedings were discontinued under that section. **G–42**

Form of notice

8.2. Notice under section 23(3), (4) or (7) of the *Prosecution of Offences Act* 1985 shall be given in writing and shall contain sufficient particulars to identify the particular offence to which it relates. **G–43**

Duty of Director of Public Prosecutions

8.3. On giving notice under section 23(3) or (4) of the *Prosecution of Offences Act* 1985 the Director of Public Prosecutions shall inform any person who is detaining the accused person for the offence in relation to which the notice is given that he has given such notice and of the effect of the notice. **G–44**

Duty of magistrates' court

8.4. On being given notice under section 23(3) of the Prosecution of Offences Act 1985 in relation to an offence for which the accused person has been granted bail by a court, a magistrates' court officer shall inform— **G–45**

(a) any sureties of the accused; and

(b) (b) any persons responsible for securing the accused's compliance with any conditions of bail

that he has been given such notice and of the effect of the notice.

[The next paragraph is § G-47.]

PART 10 COMMITTAL FOR TRIAL

Contents of this Part

Restrictions on reports of committal proceedings

G–47 **10.1.**—(1) Except in a case where evidence is, with the consent of the accused, to be tendered in his absence under section 4(4)(b) of the *Magistrates' Courts Act* 1980 (absence caused by ill health), a magistrates' court acting as examining justices shall before admitting any evidence explain to the accused the restrictions on reports of committal proceedings imposed by section 8 of that Act and inform him of his right to apply to the court for an order removing those restrictions.

(2) Where a magistrates' court has made an order under section 8(2) of the 1980 Act removing restrictions on the reports of committal proceedings, such order shall be entered in the register.

(3) Where the court adjourns any such proceedings to another day, the court shall, at the beginning of any adjourned hearing, state that the order has been made.

Committal for trial without consideration of the evidence

G–48 **10.2.**—(1) This rule applies to committal proceedings where the accused has a solicitor acting for him in the case and where the court has been informed that all the evidence falls within section 5A(2) of the *Magistrates' Courts Act* 1980.

(2) A magistrates' court inquiring into an offence in committal proceedings to which this rule applies shall cause the charge to be written down, if this has not already been done, and read to the accused and shall then ascertain whether he wishes to submit that there is insufficient evidence to put him on trial by jury for the offence with which he is charged.

(3) If the court is satisfied that the accused or, as the case may be, each of the accused does not wish to make such a submission as is referred to in paragraph (2) it shall, after receiving any written evidence falling within section 5A(3) of the 1980 Act, determine whether or not to commit the accused for trial without consideration of the evidence, and where it determines not to so commit the accused it shall proceed in accordance with rule 10.3.

Consideration of evidence at committal proceedings

G–49 **10.3.**—(1) This rule does not apply to committal proceedings where under section 6(2) of the *Magistrates' Courts Act* 1980 a magistrates' court commits a person for trial without consideration of the evidence.

(2) A magistrates' court inquiring into an offence as examining justices, having ascertained—

 (a) that the accused has no legal representative acting for him in the case; or

 (b) that the accused's legal representative has requested the court to consider a submission that there is insufficient evidence to put the accused on trial by jury for the offence with which he is charged, as the case may be, shall permit the prosecutor to make an opening address to the court, if he so wishes, before any evidence is tendered.

(3) After such opening address, if any, the court shall cause evidence to be tendered in accordance with sections 5B(4), 5C(4), 5D(5) and 5E(3) of the 1980 Act, that is to say by being read out aloud, except where the court otherwise directs or to the extent that it directs that an oral account be given of any of the evidence.

(4) The court may view any exhibits produced before the court and may take possession of them.

(5) After the evidence has been tendered the court shall hear any submission which the accused may wish to make as to whether there is sufficient evidence to put him on trial by jury for any indictable offence.

(6) The court shall permit the prosecutor to make a submission—

 (a) in reply to any submission made by the accused in pursuance of paragraph (5); or

(b) where the accused has not made any such submission but the court is nevertheless minded not to commit him for trial.

(7) After hearing any submission made in pursuance of paragraph (5) or (6) the court shall, unless it decides not to commit the accused for trial, cause the charge to be written down, if this has not already been done, and, if the accused is not represented by counsel or a solicitor, shall read the charge to him and explain it in ordinary language.

Objection to committal statements being read at trial

10.4.—(1) This rule applies where— **G–50**
    (a) a written statement is admitted as evidence in committal proceedings;
    (b) under Schedule 2 to the *Criminal Procedure and Investigations Act* 1996, the statement may be introduced in evidence at trial; and
    (c) a party wants to object to that.

(2) Such a party must serve notice of objection—
    (a) on each other party and on the Crown Court officer;
    (b) not more than 14 days after the defendant is committed for trial.

(3) A prosecutor who introduces a written statement in committal proceedings must serve with it on the defendant a notice—
    (a) of the right to object, and of the time limit; and
    (b) that if the defendant does not object, the prosecutor may decide not to call the witness to give evidence in person at trial, but to rely on the written statement instead.

(4) The magistrates' court that commits the defendant for trial must remind the defendant of that right to object.

(5) The Crown Court may extend the time limit under this rule, even after it has expired.

Material to be sent to court of trial

10.5.—(1) As soon as practicable after the committal of any person for trial, and in any case **G–51** within 4 days from the date of his committal (not counting Saturdays, Sundays, Good Friday, Christmas Day or Bank Holidays), the magistrates' court officer shall, subject to the provisions of section 7 of the *Prosecution of Offences Act* 1985 (which relates to the sending of documents and things to the Director of Public Prosecutions), send to the Crown Court officer—
    (a) the information, if it is in writing;
    (b)
        (i) the evidence tendered in accordance with section 5A of the *Magistrates' Courts Act* 1980 and, where any of that evidence consists of a copy of a deposition or documentary exhibit which is in the possession of the court, any such deposition or documentary exhibit, and
        (ii) a certificate to the effect that that evidence was so tendered;
    (c) any notification by the prosecutor under section 5D(2) of the 1980 Act regarding the admissibility of a statement under section 23 or 24 of the *Criminal Justice Act* 1988 (first hand hearsay; business documents);
    (d) a copy of the record made in pursuance of section 5 of the *Bail Act* 1976 relating to the grant or withholding of bail in respect of the accused on the occasion of the committal;
    (e) any recognizance entered into by any person as surety for the accused together with a statement of any enlargement thereof under section 129(4) of the 1980 Act;
    (f) a list of the exhibits produced in evidence before the justices or treated as so produced;
    (g) such of the exhibits referred to in paragraph (1)(f) as have been retained by the justices;
    (h) the names and addresses of any interpreters engaged for the defendant for the purposes of the committal proceedings, together with any telephone numbers at which they can be readily contacted, and details of the languages or dialects in connection with which they have been so engaged;
    (i) if the committal was under section 6(2) of the 1980 Act (committal for trial without consideration of the evidence), a statement to that effect;

(j) if the magistrates' court has made an order under section 8(2) of the 1980 Act (removal of restrictions on reports of committal proceedings), a statement to that effect;

(k) the certificate of the examining justices as to the costs of the prosecution under the Costs in Criminal Cases (General) Regulations 1986;

(l) if any person under the age of 18 is concerned in the committal proceedings, a statement whether the magistrates' court has given a direction under section 39 of the *Children and Young Persons Act* 1933 (prohibition of publication of certain matter in newspapers);

(m) a copy of any representation order previously made in the case;

(n) a copy of any application for a representation order previously made in the case which has been refused; and

(o) any documents relating to an appeal by the prosecution against the granting of bail.

(2) The period of 4 days specified in paragraph (1) may be extended in relation to any committal for so long as the Crown Court officer directs, having regard to the length of any document mentioned in that paragraph or any other relevant circumstances.

PART 11 TRANSFER FOR TRIAL OF SERIOUS FRAUD CASES OR CASES INVOLVING CHILDREN

Contents of this Part

Interpretation of this Part

G–52   **11.1.**—(1) In this Part, 'notice of transfer' means a notice referred to in section 4(1) of the *Criminal Justice Act* 1987 or section 53(1) of the *Criminal Justice Act* 1991.

(2) Where this Part requires a document to be given or sent, or a notice to be communicated in writing, it may, with the consent of the addressee, be sent by electronic communication.

(3) Electronic communication means a communication transmitted (whether from one person to another, from one device to another or from a person to a device or vice versa)—

(a) by means of an electronic communications network (within the meaning of the *Communications Act* 2003); or

(b) by other means but while in an electronic form.

Transfer on bail

G–53   **11.2.**—(1) Where a person in respect of whom notice of transfer has been given—

(a) is granted bail under section 5(3) or (7A) of the *Criminal Justice Act* 1987 by the magistrates' court to which notice of transfer was given; or

(b) is granted bail under paragraph 2(1) or (7) of Schedule 6 to the *Criminal Justice Act* 1991 by the magistrates' court to which notice of transfer was given, the magistrates' court officer shall give notice thereof in writing to the governor of the prison or remand centre to which the said person would have been committed by that court if he had been committed in custody for trial.

(2) Where notice of transfer is given under section 4(1) of the 1987 Act in respect of a corporation the magistrates' court officer shall give notice thereof to the governor of the prison to which would be committed a male over 21 committed by that court in custody for trial.

Notice where person removed to hospital

G–54   **11.3.** Where a transfer direction has been given by the Secretary of State under section 47 or

48 of the *Mental Health Act* 1983 in respect of a person remanded in custody by a magistrates' court and, before the direction ceases to have effect, notice of transfer is given in respect of that person, the magistrates' court officer shall give notice thereof in writing—

(a) to the governor of the prison to which that person would have been committed by that court if he had been committed in custody for trial; and

(b) to the managers of the hospital where he is detained.

Variation of arrangements for bail

11.4.—(1) A person who intends to make an application to a magistrates' court under section **G–55** 3(8) of the *Bail Act* 1976 as that subsection has effect under section 3(8A) of that Act shall give notice thereof in writing to the magistrates' court officer, and to the designated authority or the defendant, as the case may be, and to any sureties concerned.

(2) Where, on an application referred to in paragraph (1), a magistrates' court varies or imposes any conditions of bail, the magistrates' court officer shall send to the Crown Court officer a copy of the record made in pursuance of section 5 of the 1976 Act relating to such variation or imposition of conditions.

Documents to be sent to the Crown Court

11.5. As soon as practicable after a magistrates' court to which notice of transfer has been **G–56** given has discharged the functions reserved to it under section 4(1) of the *Criminal Justice Act* 1987 or section 53(3) of the *Criminal Justice Act* 1991, the magistrates' court officer shall send to the Crown Court officer—

(a) a list of the names, addresses and occupations of the witnesses;

(b) a copy of the record made in pursuance of section 5 of the *Bail Act* 1976 relating to the grant of withholding of bail in respect of the accused;

(c) any recognizance entered into by any person as surety for the accused together with a statement of any enlargement thereof;

(d) a copy of any representation order previously made in the case; and

(e) a copy of any application for a representation order previously made in the case which has been refused.

PART 12 SENDING FOR TRIAL

Contents of this Part

Documents to be sent to the Crown Court

12.1.—(1) As soon as practicable after any person is sent for trial (pursuant to section 51 of **G–57** the *Crime and Disorder Act* 1998), and in any event within 4 days from the date on which he is sent (not counting Saturdays, Sundays, Good Friday, Christmas Day or Bank Holidays), the magistrates' court officer shall, subject to section 7 of the *Prosecution of Offences Act* 1985 (which relates to the sending of documents and things to the Director of Public Prosecutions), send to the Crown Court officer—

(a) the information, if it is in writing;

(b) the notice required by section 51(7) of the 1998 Act;

(c) a copy of the record made in pursuance of section 5 of the *Bail Act* 1976 relating to the granting or withholding of bail in respect of the accused on the occasion of the sending;

(d) any recognizance entered into by any person as surety for the accused together with any enlargement thereof under section 129(4) of the *Magistrates' Courts Act* 1980;

(e) the names and addresses of any interpreters engaged for the defendant for the purposes of the appearance in the magistrates' court, together with any telephone numbers at which they can be readily contacted, and details of the languages or dialects in connection with which they have been so engaged;

(f) if any person under the age of 18 is concerned in the proceedings, a statement whether the magistrates' court has given a direction under section 39 of the *Children and Young Persons Act* 1933 (prohibition of publication of certain matter in newspapers);

(g) a copy of any representation order previously made in the case;

(h) a copy of any application for a representation order previously made in the case which has been refused; and

(i) any documents relating to an appeal by the prosecution against the granting of bail.

(2) The period of 4 days specified in paragraph (1) may be extended in relation to any sending for trial for so long as the Crown Court officer directs, having regard to any relevant circumstances.

Time for first appearance of accused sent for trial

G–58   **12.2.** A Crown Court officer to whom notice has been given under section 51(7) of the *Crime and Disorder Act* 1998, shall list the first Crown Court appearance of the person to whom the notice relates in accordance with any directions given by the magistrates' court.

[The next paragraph is § G-73.]

PART 16 RESTRICTIONS ON REPORTING AND PUBLIC ACCESS

Contents of this Part

Application for a reporting direction under section 46(6) of the Youth Justice and Criminal Evidence Act 1999

G–73   **16.1.**—(1) An application for a reporting direction made by a party to any criminal proceedings, in relation to a witness in those proceedings, must be made in the form set out in the Practice Direction or orally under rule 16.3.

(2) If an application for a reporting direction is made in writing, the applicant shall send that application to the court officer and copies shall be sent at the same time to every other party to those proceedings.

Opposing an application for a reporting direction under section 46(6) of the Youth Justice and Criminal Evidence Act 1999

16.2.—(1) If an application for a reporting direction is made in writing, any party to the **G–74** proceedings who wishes to oppose that application must notify the applicant and the court officer in writing of his opposition and give reasons for it.

(2) A person opposing an application must state in the written notification whether he disputes that the—

- (a) witness is eligible for protection under section 46 of the *Youth Justice and Criminal Evidence Act* 1999; or
- (b) granting of protection would be likely to improve the quality of the evidence given by the witness or the level of co-operation given by the witness to any party to the proceedings in connection with that party's preparation of its case.

(3) The notification under paragraph (1) must be given within five business days of the date the application was served on him unless an extension of time is granted under rule 16.6.

Urgent action on an application under section 46(6) of the Youth Justice and Criminal Evidence Act 1999

16.3.—(1) The court may give a reporting direction under section 46 of the *Youth Justice* **G–75** *and Criminal Evidence Act* 1999 in relation to a witness in those proceedings, notwithstanding that the five business days specified in rule 16.2(3) have not expired if—

- (a) an application is made to it for the purposes of this rule; and
- (b) it is satisfied that, due to exceptional circumstances, it is appropriate to do so.

(2) Any party to the proceedings may make the application under paragraph (1) whether or not an application has already been made under rule 16.1.

(3) An application under paragraph (1) may be made orally or in writing.

(4) If an application is made orally, the court may hear and take into account representations made to it by any person who in the court's view has a legitimate interest in the application before it.

(5) The application must specify the exceptional circumstances on which the applicant relies.

Excepting direction under section 46(9) of the Youth Justice and Criminal Evidence Act 1999

16.4.—(1) An application for an excepting direction under section 46(9) of the *Youth Justice* **G–76** *and Criminal Evidence Act* 1999 (a direction dispensing with restrictions imposed by a reporting direction) may be made by—

- (a) any party to those proceedings; or
- (b) any person who, although not a party to the proceedings, is directly affected by a reporting direction given in relation to a witness in those proceedings.

(2) If an application for an excepting direction is made, the applicant must state why—

- (a) the effect of a reporting direction imposed places a substantial and unreasonable restriction on the reporting of the proceedings; and
- (b) it is in the public interest to remove or relax those restrictions.

(3) An application for an excepting direction may be made in writing, pursuant to paragraph (4), at any time after the commencement of the proceedings in the court or orally at a hearing of an application for a reporting direction.

(4) If the application for an excepting direction is made in writing it must be in the form set out in the Practice Direction and the applicant shall send that application to the court officer and copies shall be sent at the same time to every other party to those proceedings.

(5) Any person served with a copy of an application for an excepting direction who wishes to oppose it, must notify the applicant and the court officer in writing of his opposition and give reasons for it.

(6) The notification under paragraph (5) must be given within five business days of the

date the application was served on him unless an extension of time is granted under rule 16.6.

Variation or revocation of a reporting or excepting direction under section 46 of the Youth Justice and Criminal Evidence Act 1999

G–77

16.5.—(1) An application for the court to—

(a) revoke a reporting direction; or

(b) vary or revoke an excepting direction, may be made to the court at any time after the commencement of the proceedings in the court.

(2) An application under paragraph (1) may be made by a party to the proceedings in which the direction was issued, or by a person who, although not a party to those proceedings, is in the opinion of the court directly affected by the direction.

(3) An application under paragraph (1) must be made in writing and the applicant shall send that application to the officer of the court in which the proceedings commenced, and at the same time copies of the application shall be sent to every party or, as the case may be, every party to the proceedings.

(4) The applicant must set out in his application the reasons why he seeks to have the direction varied or, as the case may be, revoked.

(5) Any person served with a copy of an application who wishes to oppose it, must notify the applicant and the court officer in writing of his opposition and give reasons for it.

(6) The notification under paragraph (5) must be given within five business days of the date the application was served on him unless an extension of time is granted under rule 16.6.

Application for an extension of time in proceedings under section 46 of the Youth Justice and Criminal Evidence Act 1999

G–78

16.6.—(1) An application may be made in writing to extend the period of time for notification under rule 16.2(3), rule 16.4(6) or rule 16.5(6) before that period has expired.

(2) An application must be accompanied by a statement setting out the reasons why the applicant is unable to give notification within that period.

(3) An application must be sent to the court officer and a copy of the application must be sent at the same time to the applicant.

Decision of the court on an application under section 46 of the Youth Justice and Criminal Evidence Act 1999

G–79

16.7.—(1) The court may—

(a) determine any application made under rules 16.1 and rules 16.3 to 16.6 without a hearing; or

(b) direct a hearing of any application.

(2) The court officer shall notify all the parties of the court's decision as soon as reasonably practicable.

(3) If a hearing of an application is to take place, the court officer shall notify each party to the proceedings of the time and place of the hearing.

(4) A court may hear and take into account representations made to it by any person who in the court's view has a legitimate interest in the application before it.

Proceedings sent or transferred to the Crown Court with direction under section 46 of the Youth Justice and Criminal Evidence Act 1999 in force

G–80

16.8. Where proceedings in which reporting directions or excepting directions have been ordered are sent or transferred from a magistrates' court to the Crown Court, the magistrates' court officer shall forward copies of all relevant directions to the Crown Court officer at the place to which the proceedings are sent or transferred.

Hearings in camera and applications under section 46 of the Youth Justice and Criminal Evidence Act 1999

G–81

16.9. If in any proceedings, a prosecutor or defendant has served notice under rule 16.10 of his intention to apply for an order that all or part of a trial be held in camera, any application under this Part relating to a witness in those proceedings need not identify the witness by name and date of birth.

Application to hold a Crown Court trial in camera

16.10.—(1) Where a prosecutor or a defendant intends to apply for an order that all or part **G–82** of a trial be held in camera for reasons of national security or for the protection of the identity of a witness or any other person, he shall not less than 7 days before the date on which the trial is expected to begin serve a notice in writing to that effect on the Crown Court officer and the prosecutor or the defendant as the case may be.

(2) On receiving such notice, the court officer shall forthwith cause a copy thereof to be displayed in a prominent place within the precincts of the Court.

(3) An application by a prosecutor or a defendant who has served such a notice for an order that all or part of a trial be heard in camera shall, unless the Court orders otherwise, be made in camera, after the defendant has been arraigned but before the jury has been sworn and, if such an order is made, the trial shall be adjourned until whichever of the following shall be appropriate—

(a) 24 hours after the making of the order, where no application for leave to appeal from the order is made; or

(b) after the determination of an application for leave to appeal, where the application is dismissed; or

(c) after the determination of the appeal, where leave to appeal is granted.

Crown Court hearings in chambers

16.11.—(1) The criminal jurisdiction of the Crown Court specified in the following paragraph **G–83** may be exercised by a judge of the Crown Court sitting in chambers.

(2) The said jurisdiction is—

(a) hearing applications for bail;

(b) issuing a summons or warrant;

(c) hearing any application relating to procedural matters preliminary or incidental to criminal proceedings in the Crown Court, including applications relating to legal aid;

(d) jurisdiction under rules 12.2 (listing first appearance of accused sent for trial), 28.2 (application for witness summons), 63.9(a) (extending time for appeal against decision of magistrates' court), and 64.6 (application to state case for consideration of High Court);

(e) hearing an application under section 41(2) of the *Youth Justice and Criminal Evidence Act* 1999 (evidence of complainant's previous sexual history);

(f) hearing applications under section 22(3) of the *Prosecution of Offences Act* 1985 (extension or further extension of custody time limit imposed by regulations made under section 22(1) of that Act);

(g) hearing an appeal brought by an accused under section 22(7) of the 1985 Act against a decision of a magistrates' court to extend, or further extend, such a time limit, or brought by the prosecution under section 22(8) of the same Act against a decision of a magistrates' court to refuse to extend, or further extend, such a time limit;

(h) hearing appeals under section 1 of the *Bail (Amendment) Act* 1993 (against grant of bail by magistrates' court); and

(i) hearing appeals under section 16 of the *Criminal Justice Act* 2003 (against condition of bail imposed by magistrates' court).

PART 17 EXTRADITION

Contents of this Part

Refusal to make an order of committal

G–84

17.1.—(1) Where a magistrates' court refuses to make an order of committal in relation to a person in respect of the offence or, as the case may be, any of the offences to which the authority to proceed relates and the state, country or colony seeking the surrender of that person immediately informs the court that it intends to make an application to the court to state a case for the opinion of the High Court, if the magistrates' court makes an order in accordance with section 10(2) of the *Extradition Act* 1989 releasing that person on bail, the court officer shall forthwith send a copy of that order to the Administrative Court Office.

(2) Where a magistrates' court refuses to make an order of committal in relation to a person in respect of the offence or, as the case may be, any of the offences to which the authority to proceed relates and the state, country or colony seeking his surrender wishes to apply to the court to state a case for the opinion of the High Court under section 10(1) of the 1989 Act, such application must be made to the magistrates' court within the period of 21 days following the day on which the court refuses to make the order of committal unless the court grants a longer period within which the application is to be made.

(3) Such an application shall be made in writing and shall identify the question or questions of law on which the opinion of the High Court is sought.

(4) Within 21 days after receipt of an application to state a case under section 10(1) of the 1989 Act, the magistrates' court officer shall send a draft case to the solicitor for the state, country or colony and to the person whose surrender is sought or his solicitor and shall allow each party 21 days within which to make representations thereon; within 21 days after the latest day on which such representations may be made the court of committal shall, after considering any such representations and making such adjustments, if any, to the draft case as it thinks fit, state and sign the case which the court officer shall forthwith send to the solicitor for the state, country or colony.

Notice of waiver

G–85

17.2.—(1) A notice given under section 14 of, or paragraph 9 of Schedule 1 to, the *Extradition Act* 1989 (notice of waiver under the simplified procedure) shall be in the form set out in the Practice Direction or a form to the like effect.

(2) Such a notice shall be signed in the presence of the Senior District Judge (Chief Magistrate) or another District Judge (Magistrates' Courts) designated by him for the purposes of the Act, a justice of the peace or a justices' clerk.

(3) Any such notice given by a person in custody shall be delivered to the Governor of the prison in whose custody he is.

(4) If a person on bail gives such notice he shall deliver it to, or send it by post in a registered letter or by recorded delivery service addressed to, the Secretary of State for the Home Department, c/o the Extradition Section, Home Office, 5th Floor, Fry Building, 2 Marsham Street, London, SW1P 4DF.

Notice of consent

G–86

17.3.—(1) A person arrested in pursuance of a warrant under section 8 of or paragraph 5 of Schedule 1 to the *Extradition Act* 1989 may at any time consent to his return; and where such consent is given in accordance with the following provisions of this rule, the Senior District

Judge (Chief Magistrate) or another District Judge (Magistrates' Courts) designated by him for the purposes of the Act may order the committal for return of that person in accordance with section 14(2) of that Act or, as the case may be, paragraph 9(2) of Schedule 1 to the Act.

(2) A notice of consent for the purposes of this rule shall be given in the form set out in the Practice Direction and shall be signed in the presence of the Senior District Judge (Chief Magistrate) or another District Judge (Magistrates' Courts) designated by him for the purposes of the 1989 Act.

Notice of consent (parties to 1995 Convention)

17.4.—(1) This rule applies as between the United Kingdom and states other than the Re- **G–87** public of Ireland that are parties to the Convention drawn up on the basis of Article 31 of the Treaty on European Union on Simplified Extradition Procedures between the Member States of the European Union, in relation to which section 14A of the *Extradition Act* 1989 applies by virtue of section 34A and Schedule 1A of that Act.

(2) Notice of consent for the purposes of section 14A(3) of the 1989 Act shall be given in the form set out in the Practice Direction and shall be signed in the presence of the Senior District Judge (Chief Magistrate) or another District Judge (Magistrates' Courts) designated by him for the purposes of that Act.

(3) The Senior District Judge (Chief Magistrate) or another District Judge (Magistrates' Courts) designated by him for the purposes of the Act may order the committal for return of a person if he gives consent under section 14A of the 1989 Act in accordance with paragraph (2) above before he is committed under section 9 of that Act.

Consent to early removal to Republic of Ireland

17.5.—(1) A notice given under section 3(1)(a) of the *Backing of Warrants (Republic of* **G–88** *Ireland) Act* 1965 (consent to surrender earlier than is otherwise permitted) shall be signed in the presence of a justice of the peace or a justices' clerk.

(2) Any such notice given by a person in custody shall be delivered to the Governor of the prison in whose custody he is.

(3) If a person on bail gives such notice, he shall deliver it to, or send it by post in a registered letter or by recorded delivery service addressed to, the police officer in charge of the police station specified in his recognizance.

(4) Any such notice shall be attached to the warrant ordering the surrender of that person.

Bail pending removal to Republic of Ireland

17.6.—(1) The person taking the recognizance of a person remanded on bail under section **G–89** 2(1) or 4(3) of the *Backing of Warrants (Republic of Ireland) Act* 1965 shall furnish a copy of the recognizance to the police officer in charge of the police station specified in the recognizance.

(2) The court officer for a magistrates' court which ordered a person to be surrendered and remanded him on bail shall deliver to, or send by post in a registered letter or by re-corded delivery service addressed to, the police officer in charge of the police station speci-fied in the recognizance the warrant ordering the person to be surrendered.

(3) The court officer for a magistrates' court which refused to order a person to be delivered under section 2 of the 1965 Act but made an order in accordance with section 2A(2) of that Act releasing that person on bail, upon the chief officer of police immediately informing the court that he intended to make an application to the court to state a case for the opinion of the High Court, shall forthwith send a copy of that order to the Administra-tive Court Office.

Delivery of warrant issued in Republic of Ireland

17.7.—(1) The court officer for a magistrates' court which ordered a person to be sur- **G–90** rendered under section 2(1) of the *Backing of Warrants (Republic of Ireland) Act* 1965 shall deliver to, or send by post in a registered letter or by recorded delivery service addressed to—

    (a) if he is remanded in custody under section 5(1)(a) of the 1965 Act, the prison Governor to whose custody he is committed;

    (b) if he is remanded on bail under section 5(1)(b) of the 1965 Act, the police officer in charge of the police station specified in the recognizance; or

    (c) if he is committed to the custody of a constable pending the taking from him of a recognizance under section 5(1) of the 1965 Act, the police officer in charge of the police station specified in the warrant of commitment, the warrant of arrest issued by a judicial authority in the Republic of Ireland and endorsed in accordance with section 1 of the 1965 Act.

(2) The Governor or police officer to whom the said warrant of arrest is delivered or sent shall arrange for it to be given to the member of the police force of the Republic into whose custody the person is delivered when the person is so delivered.

Verification of warrant etc. issued in Republic of Ireland

G–91   **17.8.**—(1) A document purporting to be a warrant issued by a judicial authority in the Republic of Ireland shall, for the purposes of section 7(a) of the *Backing of Warrants (Republic of Ireland) Act* 1965, be verified by a certificate purporting to be signed by a judicial authority, a clerk of a court or a member of the police force of the Republic and certifying that the document is a warrant and is issued by a judge or justice of a court or a peace commissioner.

(2) A document purporting to be a copy of a summons issued by a judicial authority in the Republic shall, for the purposes of section 7(a) of the 1965 Act, be verified by a certificate purporting to be signed by a judicial authority, a clerk of a court or a member of the police force of the Republic and certifying that the document is a true copy of such a summons.

(3) A deposition purporting to have been made in the Republic, or affidavit or written statement purporting to have been sworn therein, shall, for the purposes of section 7(c) of the 1965 Act, be verified by a certificate purporting to be signed by the person before whom it was sworn and certifying that it was so sworn.

Application to state a case where court declines to order removal to Republic of Ireland

G–92   **17.9.**—(1) Where a magistrates' court refuses to make an order in relation to a person under section 2 of the Backing of Warrants (Republic of Ireland) Act 1965, any application to the court under section 2A(1) of that Act to state a case for the opinion of the High Court on any question of law arising in the proceedings must be made to the court by the chief officer of police within the period of 21 days following the day on which the order was refused, unless the court grants a longer period within which the application is to be made.

(2) Such an application shall be made in writing and shall identify the question or questions of law on which the opinion of the High Court is sought.

Draft case where court declines to order removal to Republic of Ireland

G–93   **17.10.** Within 21 days after receipt of an application to state a case under section 2A(1) of the *Backing of Warrants (Republic of Ireland) Act* 1965, the magistrates' court officer shall send a draft case to the applicant or his solicitor and to the person to whom the warrant relates or his solicitor and shall allow each party 21 days within which to make representations thereon; within 21 days after the latest day on which such representations may be made the court shall, after considering such representations and making such adjustments, if any, to the draft case as it thinks fit, state and sign the case which the court officer shall forthwith send to the applicant or his solicitor.

Forms for proceedings for removal to Republic of Ireland

G–94   **17.11.** Where a requirement is imposed by the *Backing of Warrants (Republic of Ireland) Act* 1965 for the use of a form, and an appropriate form is contained in the Practice Direction, that form shall be used.

PART 18 WARRANTS

Contents of this Part

Scope of this Part and interpretation

18.1.—(1) This Part applies to any warrant issued by a justice of the peace. **G–95**

(2) Where a rule applies to some of those warrants and not others, it says so.

(3) In this Part, the 'relevant person' is the person against whom the warrant is issued.

Warrants must be signed

18.2. Every warrant under the Magistrates' Courts Act 1980 must be signed by the justice is- **G–96** suing it, unless rule 5.3 permits the justices' clerk to sign it.

Warrants issued when the court office is closed

18.3.—(1) If a warrant is issued when the court office is closed, the applicant must— **G–97**

(a) serve on the court officer any information on which that warrant is issued; and

(b) do so within 72 hours of that warrant being issued.

(2) In this rule, the court office is the office for the local justice area in which the justice is acting when he issues the warrant.

Commitment to custody must be by warrant

18.4. A justice of the peace must issue a warrant of commitment when committing a person **G–98** to—

(a) a prison;

(b) a young offender institution;

(c) a remand centre;

(d) detention at a police station under section 128(7) of the Magistrates' Courts Act 1980; or

(e) customs detention under section 152 of the *Criminal Justice Act* 1988.

Terms of a warrant of arrest

18.5. A warrant of arrest must require the persons to whom it is directed to arrest the rele- **G–99** vant person.

Terms of a warrant of commitment or detention: general rules

18.6.—(1) A warrant of commitment or detention must require— **G–100**

(a) the persons to whom it is directed to—

(i) arrest the relevant person, if he is at large,

(ii) take him to the prison or place specified in the warrant, and

(iii) deliver him with the warrant to the governor or keeper of that prison or place; and

(b) the governor or keeper to keep the relevant person in custody at that prison or place—

    (i) for as long as the warrant requires, or

    (ii) until he is delivered, in accordance with the law, to the court or other proper place or person.

(2) Where the justice issuing a warrant of commitment or detention is aware that the relevant person is already detained in a prison or other place of detention, the warrant must be delivered to the governor or keeper of that prison or place.

Terms of a warrant committing a person to customs detention

G–101   **18.7.**—(1) A warrant committing a person to customs detention under section 152 of the 1988 Act must—

    (a) be directed to the officers of Her Majesty's Revenue and Customs; and

    (b) require those officers to keep the person committed in their custody, unless in the meantime he be otherwise delivered, in accordance with the law, to the court or other proper place or person, for a period (not exceeding 192 hours) specified in the warrant.

(2) Rules 18.6(1), 18.10 and 18.12 do not apply where this rule applies.

Form of warrant where male aged 15 or 16 is committed

G–102   **18.8.**—(1) This rule applies where a male aged 15 or 16 years is remanded or committed to—

    (a) local authority accommodation, with a requirement that he be placed and kept in secure accommodation;

    (b) a remand centre; or

    (c) a prison.

(2) The court must include in the warrant of commitment a statement of any declaration that is required in connection with that remand or committal.

Information to be included in a warrant

G–103   **18.9.** A warrant of arrest, commitment or detention must contain the following information—

    (a) the name or a description of the relevant person; and

    (b) either—

        (i) a statement of the offence with which the relevant person is charged,

        (ii) a statement of the offence of which the person to be committed or detained was convicted; or

        (iii) any other ground on which the warrant is issued.

Persons who may execute a warrant

G–104   **18.10.** A warrant of arrest, commitment or detention may be executed by—

    (a) the persons to whom it is directed; or

    (b) by any of the following persons, whether or not it was directed to them—

        (i) a constable for any police area in England and Wales, acting in his own police area, and

        (ii) any person authorised under section 125A (civilian enforcement officers) or section 125B (approved enforcement agencies) of the Magistrates' Courts Act 1980.

Making an arrest under a warrant

G–105   **18.11.**—(1) The person executing a warrant of arrest, commitment or detention must, when arresting the relevant person—

    (a) either—

        (i) show the warrant (if he has it with him) to the relevant person, or

        (ii) tell the relevant person where the warrant is and what arrangements can be made to let that person inspect it;

    (b) explain, in ordinary language, the charge and the reason for the arrest; and

    (c) (unless he is a constable in uniform) show documentary proof of his identity.

(2) If the person executing the warrant is one of the persons referred to in rule

18.10(b)(ii) (civilian enforcement officers or approved enforcement agencies), he must also show the relevant person a written statement under section 125A(4) or section 125B(4) of the *Magistrates' Courts Act* 1980, as appropriate.

Place of detention

18.12.—(1) This rule applies to any warrant of commitment or detention. **G–106**

(2) The person executing the warrant is required to take the relevant person to the prison or place of detention specified in the warrant.

(3) But where it is not immediately practicable to do so, or where there is some other good reason, the relevant person may be taken to any prison or place where he may be lawfully detained until such time when he can be taken to the prison or place specified in the warrant.

(4) If (and for as long as) the relevant person is detained in a place other than the one specified in the warrant, the warrant will have effect as if it specified the place where he is in fact being detained.

(5) The court must be kept informed of the prison or place where the relevant person is in fact being detained.

(6) The governor or keeper of the prison or place, to which the relevant person is delivered, must give a receipt on delivery.

Duration of detention where bail is granted subject to pre-release conditions

18.13.—(1) This rule applies where a magistrates' court— **G–107**

(a) grants bail to a person subject to conditions which must be met prior to release on bail; and

(b) commits that person to custody until those conditions are satisfied.

(2) The warrant of commitment must require the governor or keeper of the prison or place of detention to bring the relevant person to court either before or at the end of a period of 8 clear days from the date the warrant was issued, unless section 128(3A) or section 128A of the*Magistrates' Courts Act* 1980 applies to permit a longer period.

Validity of warrants that contain errors

18.14. A warrant of commitment or detention will not be invalidated on the ground that it **G–108** contains an error, provided that the warrant—

(a) is issued in relation to a valid—

(i) conviction, or

(ii) order requiring the relevant person to do, or to abstain from doing, something; and

(b) it states that it is issued in relation to that conviction or order.

Circumstances in which a warrant will cease to have effect

18.15.—(1) A warrant issued under any of the provisions listed in paragraph (2) will cease to **G–109** have effect when—

(a) the sum in respect of which the warrant is issued (together with the costs and charges of commitment, if any) is paid to the person who is executing the warrant;

(b) that sum is offered to, but refused by, the person who is executing the warrant; or (c) a receipt for that sum given by—

(i) the court officer for the court which issued the warrant, or

(ii) the charging or billing authority is produced to the person who is executing the warrant.

(2) Those provisions are—

(a) section 76 (warrant to enforce fines and other sums);

(b) section 83(1) and (2) (warrant to secure attendance of offender for purposes of section 82);

(c) section 86(4) (warrant to arrest offender following failure to appear on day fixed for means inquiry);

(d) section 136 (committal to custody overnight at police station), of the *Magistrates' Courts Act* 1980.

(3) No person may execute, or continue to execute, a warrant that ceases to have effect under this rule.

Warrant endorsed for bail (record to be kept)

G–110   **18.16.** A person executing a warrant of arrest that is endorsed for bail under section 117 of the Magistrates' Courts Act 1980 must—

    (a) make a record stating—

        (i) the name of the person arrested,

        (ii) the charge and the reason for the arrest,

        (iii) the fact that the person is to be released on bail,

        (iv) the date, time and place at which the person is required to appear before the court, and

        (v) any other details which he considers to be relevant; and

    (b) after making the record—

        (i) sign the record,

        (ii) invite the person arrested to sign the record and, if they refuse, make a note of that refusal on the record,

        (iii) make a copy of the record and give it to the person arrested, and

        (iv) send the original record to the court officer for the court which issued the warrant.

PART 19 BAIL IN MAGISTRATES' COURTS AND THE CROWN COURT

Contents of this Part

Application to a magistrates' court to vary conditions of bail

19.1.—(1) An application under section 43B(1) of the Magistrates' Courts Act 1980, or sec- **G–111** tion 47(1E) of the Police and Criminal Evidence Act 1984, to vary conditions of police bail, shall—

    (a) be made in writing;

    (b) contain a statement of the grounds upon which it is made;

    (c) where the applicant has been bailed following charge, specify the offence with which he was charged and, in any other case, specify the offence under investigation;

    (d) specify, or be accompanied by a copy of the note of, the reasons given by the custody officer for imposing or varying the conditions of bail;

    (e) specify the name and address of any surety provided by the applicant before his release on bail to secure his surrender to custody; and

    (f) specify the address at which the applicant would reside, if the court imposed a condition of residence.

(2) Any such application shall be sent to the court officer for—

    (a) the magistrates' court appointed by the custody officer as the court before which the applicant has a duty to appear; or

    (b) if no such court has been appointed, a magistrates' court acting for the local justice area in which the police station at which the applicant was granted bail or at which the conditions of his bail were varied, as the case may be, is situated,

(3) The court officer to whom an application is sent under paragraph (2) above shall serve not less than 24 hours' notice in writing of the date, time and place fixed for the hearing of the application on—

    (a) the applicant;

    (b) the prosecutor or, if the applicant has not been charged, the chief officer of police or other investigator, together with a copy of the application; and

    (c) any surety in connection with bail in criminal proceedings granted to, or the conditions of which were varied by a custody officer in relation to, the applicant.

(4) The time fixed for the hearing shall be not later than 72 hours after receipt of the application. In reckoning for the purposes of this paragraph any period of 72 hours, no

account shall be taken of Christmas Day, Boxing Day, Good Friday, any bank holiday, or any Saturday or Sunday.

(5) A party who wants a magistrates' court to vary or impose conditions of bail under section 3(8) of the Bail Act 1976, must—

    (a) serve notice, not less than 24 hours before the hearing at which that party intends to apply, on—

        (i) the court officer, and

        (ii) the other party; and

    (b) in that notice—

        (i) specify the variation or conditions proposed, and

        (ii) explain the reasons.

(6) If the magistrates' court hearing an application under section 43B(1) of the 1980 Act or section 47(1E) of the 1984 Act discharges or enlarges any recognizance entered into by any surety or increases or reduces the amount in which that person is bound, the court officer shall forthwith give notice thereof to the applicant and to any such surety.

(7) The court—

    (a) vary or waive a time limit under paragraph (3) or (5) of this rule; and

    (b) allow a notice to be—

        (i) in a different form to one set out in the Practice Direction, or

        (ii) given orally.

Application to a magistrates' court to reconsider grant of police bail

G–112   **19.2.**—(1) The appropriate court for the purposes of section 5B of the Bail Act 1976 in relation to the decision of a constable to grant bail shall be—

    (a) the magistrates' court appointed by the custody officer as the court before which the person to whom bail was granted has a duty to appear; or

    (b) if no such court has been appointed, a magistrates' court acting for the local justice area in which the police station at which bail was granted is situated.

(2) An application under section 5B(1) of the 1976 Act shall—

    (a) be made in writing;

    (b) contain a statement of the grounds on which it is made;

    (c) specify the offence which the proceedings in which bail was granted were connected with, or for;

    (d) specify the decision to be reconsidered (including any conditions of bail which have been imposed and why they have been imposed);

    (e) specify the name and address of any surety provided by the person to whom the application relates to secure his surrender to custody; and

    (f) contain notice of the powers available to the court under section 5B of the 1976 Act.

(3) The court officer to whom an application is sent under paragraph (2) above shall serve notice in writing of the date, time and place fixed for the hearing of the application on—

    (a) the prosecutor who made the application;

    (b) the person to whom bail was granted, together with a copy of the application; and

    (c) any surety specified in the application.

(4) The time fixed for the hearing shall be not later than 72 hours after receipt of the application. In reckoning for the purpose of this paragraph any period of 72 hours, no account shall be taken of Christmas Day, Good Friday, any bank holiday or any Sunday.

(5) At the hearing of an application under section 5B of the 1976 Act the court shall consider any representations made by the person affected (whether in writing or orally) before taking any decision under that section with respect to him; and, where the person affected does not appear before the court, the court shall not take such a decision unless it is proved to the satisfaction of the court, on oath or in the manner set out by rule 4.11, that the notice required to be given under paragraph (3) of this rule was served on him before the hearing.

(6) Where the court proceeds in the absence of the person affected in accordance with paragraph (6)—

    (a) if the decision of the court is to vary the conditions of bail or impose conditions in respect of bail which has been granted unconditionally, the court officer shall notify the person affected;

(b) if the decision of the court is to withhold bail, the order of the court under section 5B(5)(b) of the 1976 Act (surrender to custody) shall be signed by the justice issuing it or state his name and be authenticated by the signature of the clerk of the court.

Notice of change of time for appearance before magistrates' court

19.3. Where— **G–113**

(a) a person has been granted bail under the *Police and Criminal Evidence Act* 1984 subject to a duty to appear before a magistrates' court and the court before which he is to appear appoints a later time at which he is to appear; or

(b) a magistrates' court further remands a person on bail under section 129 of the *Magistrates' Courts Act* 1980 in his absence, it shall give him and his sureties, if any, notice thereof.

Directions by a magistrates' court as to security, etc

19.4. Where a magistrates' court, under section 3(5) or (6) of the *Bail Act* 1976, imposes any **G–114** requirement to be complied with before a person's release on bail, the court may give directions as to the manner in which and the person or persons before whom the requirement may be complied with.

Requirements to be complied with before release on bail granted by a magistrates' court

19.5.—(1) Where a magistrates' court has fixed the amount in which a person (including any **G–115** surety) is to be bound by a recognizance, the recognizance may be entered into—

(a) in the case of a surety where the accused is in a prison or other place of detention, before the governor or keeper of the prison or place as well as before the persons mentioned in section 8(4)(a) of the *Bail Act* 1976;

(b) in any other case, before a justice of the peace, a justices' clerk, a magistrates' court officer, a police officer who either is of the rank of inspector or above or is in charge of a police station or, if the person to be bound is in a prison or other place of detention, before the governor or keeper of the prison or place; or

(c) where a person other than a police officer is authorised under section 125A or 125B of the *Magistrates' Courts Act* 1980 to execute a warrant of arrest providing for a recognizance to be entered into by the person arrested (but not by any other person), before the person executing the warrant.

(2) The court officer for a magistrates' court which has fixed the amount in which a person (including any surety) is to be bound by a recognizance or, under section 3(5), (6) or (6A) of the 1976 Act imposed any requirement to be complied with before a person's release on bail or any condition of bail shall issue a certificate showing the amount and conditions, if any, of the recognizance, or as the case may be, containing a statement of the requirement or condition of bail; and a person authorised to take the recognizance or do anything in relation to the compliance with such requirement or condition of bail shall not be required to take or do it without production of such a certificate as aforesaid.

(3) If any person proposed as a surety for a person committed to custody by a magistrates' court produces to the governor or keeper of the prison or other place of detention in which the person so committed is detained a certificate to the effect that he is acceptable as a surety, signed by any of the justices composing the court or the clerk of the court and signed in the margin by the person proposed as surety, the governor or keeper shall take the recognizance of the person so proposed.

(4) Where the recognizance of any person committed to custody by a magistrates' court or of any surety of such a person is taken by any person other than the court which committed the first-mentioned person to custody, the person taking the recognizance shall send it to the court officer for that court: Provided that, in the case of a surety, if the person committed has been committed to the Crown Court for trial or under any of the enactments mentioned in rule 43.1(1), the person taking the recognizance shall send it to the Crown Court officer.

Notice to governor of prison, etc, where release from custody is ordered by a magistrates' court

19.6. Where a magistrates' court has, with a view to the release on bail of a person in custody, **G–116**

fixed the amount in which he or any surety of such a person shall be bound or, under section 3(5), (6) or (6A) of the *Bail Act* 1976, imposed any requirement to be complied with before his release or any condition of bail—

    (a) the magistrates' court officer shall give notice thereof to the governor or keeper of the prison or place where that person is detained by sending him such a certificate as is mentioned in rule 19.5(2); and

    (b) any person authorised to take the recognizance of a surety or do anything in relation to the compliance with such requirement shall, on taking or doing it, send notice thereof by post to the said governor or keeper and, in the case of a recognizance of a surety, shall give a copy of the notice to the surety.

Release when notice received by governor of prison that recognizances have been taken or requirements complied with

G–117   **19.7.** Where a magistrates' court has, with a view to the release on bail of a person in custody, fixed the amount in which he or any surety of such a person shall be bound or, under section 3(5) or (6) of the *Bail Act* 1976, imposed any requirement to be complied with before his release and given notice thereof in accordance with this Part to the governor or keeper of the prison or place where that person is detained, the governor or keeper shall, when satisfied that the recognizances of all sureties required have been taken and that all such requirements have been complied with, and unless he is in custody for some other cause, release him.

Notice from a magistrates' court of enlargement of recognizances

G–118   **19.8.**—(1) If a magistrates' court before which any person is bound by a recognizance to appear enlarges the recognizance to a later time under section 129 of the *Magistrates' Courts Act* 1980 in his absence, it shall give him and his sureties, if any, notice thereof.

    (2) If a magistrates' court, under section 129(4) of the 1980 Act, enlarges the recognizance of a surety for a person committed for trial on bail, it shall give the surety notice thereof.

Further remand by a youth court

G–119   **19.9.** Where a child or young person has been remanded, and the period of remand is extended in his absence in accordance with section 48 of the *Children and Young Persons Act* 1933, notice shall be given to him and his sureties (if any) of the date at which he will be required to appear before the court.

Notes of argument in magistrates' court bail hearings

G–120   **19.10.** . Where a magistrates' court hears full argument as to bail, the clerk of the court shall take a note of that argument.

Bail records to be entered in register of a magistrates' court

G–121   **19.11.** Any record required by section 5 of the *Bail Act* 1976 to be made by a magistrates' court (together with any note of reasons required by section 5(4) to be included and the particulars set out in any certificate granted under section 5(6A)) shall be made by way of an entry in the register.

Notification of bail decision by a magistrate after arrest while on bail

G–122   **19.12.** Where a person who has been released on bail and is under a duty to surrender into the custody of a court is brought under section 7(4)(a) of the *Bail Act* 1976 before a justice of the peace, the justice shall cause a copy of the record made in pursuance of section 5 of that Act relating to his decision under section 7(5) of that Act in respect of that person to be sent to the court officer for that court: Provided that this rule shall not apply where the court is a magistrates' court acting for the same local justice area as that for which the justice acts.

Transfer of remand hearings

G–123   **19.13.**—(1) Where a magistrates' court, under section 130(1) of the *Magistrates' Courts Act* 1980, orders that an accused who has been remanded in custody be brought up for any subsequent remands before an alternate magistrates' court, the court officer for the first-mentioned court shall, as soon as practicable after the making of the order and in any case within 2 days thereafter (not counting Sundays, Good Friday, Christmas Day or bank holidays), send to the court officer for the alternate court—

    (a) a statement indicating the offence or offences charged;

(b) a copy of the record made by the first-mentioned court in pursuance of section 5 of the *Bail Act* 1976 relating to the withholding of bail in respect of the accused when he was last remanded in custody;

(c) a copy of any representation order previously made in the same case;

(d) a copy of any application for a representation order;

(e) if the first-mentioned court has made an order under section 8(2) of the 1980 Act (removal of restrictions on reports of committal proceedings), a statement to that effect.

(f) a statement indicating whether or not the accused has a solicitor acting for him in the case and has consented to the hearing and determination in his absence of any application for his remand on an adjournment of the case under sections 5, 10(1) and 18(4) of the 1980 Act together with a statement indicating whether or not that consent has been withdrawn;

(g) a statement indicating the occasions, if any, on which the accused has been remanded under section 128(3A) of the 1980 Act without being brought before the first-mentioned court; and

(h) if the first-mentioned court remands the accused under section 128A(198) of the 1980 Act on the occasion upon which it makes the order under section 130(1) of that Act, a statement indicating the date set under section 128A(2) of that Act.

(2) Where the first-mentioned court is satisfied as mentioned in section 128(3A) of the 1980 Act, paragraph (1) shall have effect as if for the words 'an accused who has been remanded in custody be brought up for any subsequent remands before' there were substituted the words 'applications for any subsequent remands of the accused be made to'.

(3) The court officer for an alternate magistrates' court before which an accused who has been remanded in custody is brought up for any subsequent remands in pursuance of an order made as aforesaid shall, as soon as practicable after the order ceases to be in force and in any case within 2 days thereafter (not counting Sundays, Good Friday, Christmas Day or bank holidays), send to the court officer for the magistrates' court which made the order—

(a) a copy of the record made by the alternate court in pursuance of section 5 of the 1976 Act relating to the grant or withholding of bail in respect of the accused when he was last remanded in custody or on bail;

(b) a copy of any representation order made by the alternate court;

(c) a copy of any application for a representation order made to the alternate court;

(d) if the alternate court has made an order under section 8(2) of the 1980 Act removal of restrictions on reports of committal proceedings), a statement to that effect;

(e) a statement indicating whether or not the accused has a solicitor acting for him in the case and has consented to the hearing and determination in his absence of any application for his remand on an adjournment of the case under sections 5, 10(1) and 18(4) of the 1980 Act together with a statement indicating whether or not that consent has been withdrawn; and

(f) a statement indicating the occasions, if any, on which the accused has been remanded by the alternate court under section 128(3A) of the 1980 Act without being brought before that court.

(4) Where the alternate court is satisfied as mentioned in section 128(3A) of the 1980 Act paragraph (2) above shall have effect as if for the words 'an accused who has been remanded in custody is brought up for any subsequent remands' there shall be substituted the words 'applications for the further remand of the accused are to be made'

Notice of further remand in certain cases

19.14. Where a transfer direction has been given by the Secretary of State under section 47 **G–124** of the *Mental Health Act* 1983 in respect of a person remanded in custody by a magistrates' court and the direction has not ceased to have effect, the court officer shall give notice in writing to the managers of the hospital where he is detained of any further remand under section 128 of the Magistrates' Courts Act 1980.

Cessation of transfer direction

19.15 Where a magistrates' court directs, under section 52(5) of the *Mental Health Act* **G–125** 1983, that a transfer direction given by the Secretary of State under section 48 of that Act in respect of a person remanded in custody by a magistrates' court shall cease to have effect, the court officer shall give notice in writing of the court's direction to the managers of the hospital specified in the Secretary of State's direction and, where the period of remand has not expired or the person has been committed to the Crown Court for trial or to be otherwise dealt with, to the Governor of the prison to which persons of the sex of that person are committed by the court if remanded in custody or committed in custody for trial.

Lodging an appeal against a grant of bail by a magistrates' court

G–126　　**19.16.**—(1) Where the prosecution wishes to exercise the right of appeal, under section 1 of the *Bail (Amendment) Act* 1993, to a judge of the Crown Court against a decision to grant bail, the oral notice of appeal must be given to the justices' clerk and to the person concerned, at the conclusion of the proceedings in which such bail was granted and before the release of the person concerned.

(2) When oral notice of appeal is given, the justices' clerk shall announce in open court the time at which such notice was given.

(3) A record of the prosecution's decision to appeal and the time the oral notice of appeal was given shall be made in the register and shall contain the particulars set out.

(4) Where an oral notice of appeal has been given the court shall remand the person concerned in custody by a warrant of commitment.

(5) On receipt of the written notice of appeal required by section 1(5) of the 1993 Act, the court shall remand the person concerned in custody by a warrant of commitment, until the appeal is determined or otherwise disposed of.

(6) A record of the receipt of the written notice of appeal shall be made in the same manner as that of the oral notice of appeal under paragraph (3).

(7) If, having given oral notice of appeal, the prosecution fails to serve a written notice of appeal within the two hour period referred to in section 1(5) of the 1993 Act the justices' clerk shall, as soon as practicable, by way of written notice (served by a court officer) to the persons in whose custody the person concerned is, direct the release of the person concerned on bail as granted by the magistrates' court and subject to any conditions which it imposed.

(8) If the prosecution serves notice of abandonment of appeal on a court officer, the justices' clerk shall, forthwith, by way of written notice (served by the court officer) to the governor of the prison where the person concerned is being held, or the person responsible for any other establishment where such a person is being held, direct his release on bail as granted by the magistrates' court and subject to any conditions which it imposed.

(9) A court officer shall record the prosecution's failure to serve a written notice of appeal, or its service of a notice of abandonment.

(10) Where a written notice of appeal has been served on a magistrates' court officer, he shall provide as soon as practicable to a Crown Court officer a copy of that written notice, together with—

    (a) the notes of argument made by the court officer for the court under rule 19.10; and

    (b) a note of the date, or dates, when the person concerned is next due to appear in the magistrates' court, whether he is released on bail or remanded in custody by the Crown Court.

(11) References in this rule to 'the person concerned' are references to such a person within the meaning of section 1 of the 1993 Act.

Crown Court procedure on appeal against grant of bail by a magistrates' court

G–126a　　**19.17.**—(1) This rule shall apply where the prosecution appeals under section 1 of the *Bail (Amendment) Act* 1993 against a decision of a magistrates' court granting bail and in this rule, 'the person concerned' has the same meaning as in that Act.

(2) The written notice of appeal required by section 1(5) of the 1993 Act shall be in the form set out in the Practice Direction and shall be served on—

    (a) the magistrates' court officer; and

    (b) the person concerned.

(3) The Crown Court officer shall enter the appeal and give notice of the time and place of the hearing to—

    (a) the prosecution;

    (b) the person concerned or his legal representative; and

(c) the magistrates' court officer.

(4) The person concerned shall not be entitled to be present at the hearing of the appeal unless he is acting in person or, in any other case of an exceptional nature, a judge of the Crown Court is of the opinion that the interests of justice require him to be present and gives him leave to be so.

(5) Where a person concerned has not been able to instruct a solicitor to represent him at the appeal, he may give notice to the Crown Court requesting that the Official Solicitor shall represent him at the appeal, and the court may, if it thinks fit, assign the Official Solicitor to act for the person concerned accordingly.

(6) At any time after the service of written notice of appeal under paragraph (2), the prosecution may abandon the appeal by giving notice in writing in the form set out in the Practice Direction.

(7) The notice of abandonment required by the preceding paragraph shall be served on—

(a) the person concerned or his legal representative;

(b) the magistrates' court officer; and

(c) the Crown Court officer.

(8) Any record required by section 5 of the *Bail Act* 1976 (together with any note of reasons required by subsection (4) of that section to be included) shall be made by way of an entry in the file relating to the case in question and the record shall include the following particulars, namely—

(a) the effect of the decision;

(b) a statement of any condition imposed in respect of bail, indicating whether it is to be complied with before or after release on bail; and

(c) where bail is withheld, a statement of the relevant exception to the right to bail (as provided in Schedule 1 to the 1976 Act) on which the decision is based.

(9) The Crown Court officer shall, as soon as practicable after the hearing of the appeal, give notice of the decision and of the matters required by the preceding paragraph to be recorded to—

(a) the person concerned or his legal representative;

(b) the prosecution;

(c) the police;

(d) the magistrates' court officer; and

(e) the governor of the prison or person responsible for the establishment where the person concerned is being held.

(10) Where the judge hearing the appeal grants bail to the person concerned, the provisions of rule 19.18(9) (informing the Court of any earlier application for bail) and rule 19.22 (conditions attached to bail granted by the Crown Court) shall apply as if that person had applied to the Crown Court for bail.

(11) The notices required by paragraphs (3), (5), (7) and (9) of this rule may be served under rule 4.6 (service by fax, e-mail or other electronic means) and the notice required by paragraph (3) may be given by telephone.

Application to the Crown Court relating to bail

19.18.—(1) This rule applies where an application to the Crown Court relating to bail is **G–126b** made otherwise than during the hearing of proceedings in the Crown Court.

(2) Subject to paragraph (7) below, notice in writing of intention to make such an application to the Crown Court shall, at least 24 hours before it is made, be given to the prosecutor and if the prosecution is being carried on by the Crown Prosecution Service, to the appropriate Crown Prosecutor or, if the application is to be made by the prosecutor or a constable under section 3(8) of the *Bail Act* 1976, to the person to whom bail was granted.

(3) On receiving notice under paragraph (2), the prosecutor or appropriate Crown Public Prosecutor or, as the case may be, the person to whom bail was granted shall—

(a) notify the Crown Court officer and the applicant that he wishes to be represented at the hearing of the application;

(b) notify the Crown Court officer and the applicant that he does not oppose the application; or

(c) give to the Crown Court officer, for the consideration of the Crown Court, a written statement of his reasons for opposing the application, at the same time sending a copy of the statement to the applicant.

(4) A notice under paragraph (2) shall be in the form set out in the Practice Direction or a form to the like effect, and the applicant shall give a copy of the notice to the Crown Court officer.

(5) Except in the case of an application made by the prosecutor or a constable under section 3(8) of the 1976 Act, the applicant shall not be entitled to be present on the hearing of his application unless the Crown Court gives him leave to be present.

(6) Where a person who is in custody or has been released on bail desires to make an application relating to bail and has not been able to instruct a solicitor to apply on his behalf under the preceding paragraphs of this rule, he may give notice in writing to the Crown Court of his desire to make an application relating to bail, requesting that the Official Solicitor shall act for him in the application, and the Court may, if it thinks fit, assign the Official Solicitor to act for the applicant accordingly.

(7) Where the Official Solicitor has been so assigned the Crown Court may, if it thinks fit, dispense with the requirements of paragraph (2) and deal with the application in a summary manner.

(8) Any record required by section 5 of the 1976 Act (together with any note of reasons required by section 5(4) to be included) shall be made by way of an entry in the file relating to the case in question and the record shall include the following particulars, namely—

    (a) the effect of the decision;

    (b) a statement of any condition imposed in respect of bail, indicating whether it is to be complied with before or after release on bail;

    (c) where conditions of bail are varied, a statement of the conditions as varied; and

    (d) where bail is withheld, a statement of the relevant exception to the right to bail (as provided in Schedule 1 to the 1976 Act) on which the decision is based.

(9) Every person who makes an application to the Crown Court relating to bail shall inform the Court of any earlier application to the High Court or the Crown Court relating to bail in the course of the same proceedings.

Notice to governor of prison of committal on bail

G–127   **19.19.**—(1) Where the accused is committed or sent for trial on bail, a magistrates' court officer shall give notice thereof in writing to the governor of the prison to which persons of the sex of the person committed or sent are committed or sent by that court if committed or sent in custody for trial and also, if the person committed or sent is under 21, to the governor of the remand centre to which he would have been committed or sent if the court had refused him bail.

(2) Where a corporation is committed or sent for trial, a magistrates' court officer shall give notice thereof to the governor of the prison to which would be committed or sent a man committed or sent by that court in custody for trial.

Notices on committal of person subject to transfer direction

G–128   **19.20.** Where a transfer direction has been given by the Secretary of State under section 48 of the *Mental Health Act* 1983 in respect of a person remanded in custody by a magistrates' court and, before the direction ceases to have effect, that person is committed or sent for trial, a magistrates' court officer shall give notice—

    (a) to the governor of the prison to which persons of the sex of that person are committed or sent by that court if committed or sent in custody for trial; and

    (b) to the managers of the hospital where he is detained.

Variation of arrangements for bail on committal to the Crown Court

G–129   **19.21.** Where a magistrates' court has committed or sent a person on bail to the Crown Court for trial or under any of the enactments mentioned in rule 43.1(1) and subsequently varies any conditions of the bail or imposes any conditions in respect of the bail, the magistrates' court officer shall send to the Crown Court officer a copy of the record made in pursuance of section 5 of the *Bail Act* 1976 relating to such variation or imposition of conditions.

Conditions attached to bail granted by the Crown Court

G–130   **19.22.**—(1) Where the Crown Court grants bail, the recognizance of any surety required as a condition of bail may be entered into before an officer of the Crown Court or, where the person who has been granted bail is in a prison or other place of detention, before the governor or keeper of the prison or place as well as before the persons specified in section 8(4) of the *Bail Act* 1976.

(2) Where the Crown Court under section 3(5) or (6) of the 1976 Act imposes a requirement to be complied with before a person's release on bail, the Court may give directions as to the manner in which and the person or persons before whom the requirement may be complied with.

(3) A person who, in pursuance of an order made by the Crown Court for the grant of bail, proposes to enter into a recognizance or give security must, unless the Crown Court otherwise directs, give notice to the prosecutor at least 24 hours before he enters into the recognizance or gives security as aforesaid.

(4) Where, in pursuance of an order of the Crown Court, a recognizance is entered into or any requirement imposed under section 3(5) or (6) of the 1976 Act is complied with (being a requirement to be complied with before a person's release on bail) before any person, it shall be his duty to cause the recognizance or, as the case may be, a statement of the requirement to be transmitted forthwith to the court officer; and a copy of the recognizance or statement shall at the same time be sent to the governor or keeper of the prison or other place of detention in which the person named in the order is detained, unless the recognizance was entered into or the requirement was complied with before such governor or keeper.

(5) (5) Where, in pursuance of section 3(5) of the 1976 Act, security has been given in respect of a person granted bail with a duty to surrender to the custody of the Crown Court and either—

    (a) that person surrenders to the custody of the Court; or

    (b) that person having failed to surrender to the custody of the Court, the Court decides not to order the forfeiture of the security, the court officer shall as soon as practicable give notice of the surrender to custody or, as the case may be, of the decision not to forfeit the security to the person before whom the security was given.

Estreat of recognizances in respect of person bailed to appear before the Crown Court

19.23.—(1) Where a recognizance has been entered into in respect of a person granted bail **G–131** to appear before the Crown Court and it appears to the Court that a default has been made in performing the conditions of the recognizance, other than by failing to appear before the Court in accordance with any such condition, the Court may order the recognizance to be estreated.

(2) Where the Crown Court is to consider making an order under paragraph (1) for a recognizance to be estreated, the court officer shall give notice to that effect to the person by whom the recognizance was entered into indicating the time and place at which the matter will be considered; and no such order shall be made before the expiry of 7 days after the notice required by this paragraph has been given.

Forfeiture of recognizances in respect of person bailed to appear before the Crown Court

19.24.—(1) Where a recognizance is conditioned for the appearance of an accused before **G–132** the Crown Court and the accused fails to appear in accordance with the condition, the Court shall declare the recognizance to be forfeited.

(2) Where the Crown Court declares a recognizance to be forfeited under paragraph (1), the court officer shall issue a summons to the person by whom the recognizance was entered into requiring him to appear before the Court at a time and place specified in the summons to show cause why the Court should not order the recognizance to be estreated.

(3) At the time specified in the summons the Court may proceed in the absence of the person by whom the recognizance was entered into if it is satisfied that he has been served with the summons.

Grant of bail subject to a condition of residence

19.25.—(1) The defendant must notify the prosecutor of the address at which the defendant **G–132a** would reside if released on bail with a condition of residence—

    (a) as soon as practicable after the institution of proceedings, unless already done; and

    (b) as soon as practicable after any change of that address.

(2) The prosecutor must help the court to assess the suitability of an address proposed as a condition of residence.

Grant of bail subject to electronic monitoring requirements

19.26.—(1) This rule applies where the court imposes electronic monitoring requirements **G–132b** (where available) as a condition of bail.

(2) The court officer must—
    (a) inform the person responsible for the monitoring ('the monitor') of—
      (i) the defendant's name, and telephone number (if available),
      (ii) the offence or offences with which the defendant is charged,
      (iii) details of the place at which the defendant's presence must be monitored,
      (iv) the period or periods during which the defendant's presence at that place must be monitored, and
      (v) if fixed, the date on which the defendant must surrender to custody;
    (b) inform the defendant and, where the defendant is under 16, an appropriate adult, of the monitor's name, and the means by which the monitor may be contacted; and
    (c) notify the monitor of any subsequent—
      (i) variation or termination of the electronic monitoring requirements, or
      (ii) fixing or variation of the date on which the defendant must surrender to custody.

Grant of bail subject to accommodation or support requirements
G–132c **19.27.**—(1) This rule applies where the court imposes as a condition of bail a requirement (where available) that the defendant must—
    (a) reside in accommodation provided for that purpose by, or on behalf of, a public authority;
    (b) receive bail support provided by, or on behalf of, a public authority.
(2) The court officer must—
    (a) inform the person responsible for the provision of any such accommodation or support ('the service provider') of—
      (i) the defendant's name, and telephone number (if available),
      (ii) the offence or offences with which the defendant is charged,
      (iii) details of the requirement,
      (iv) any other bail condition, and
      (v) if fixed, the date on which the defendant must surrender to custody;
    (b) inform the defendant and, where the defendant is under 16, an appropriate adult, of—
      (i) the service provider's name, and the means by which the service provider may be contacted, and
      (ii) the address of any accommodation in which the defendant must reside; and
    (c) notify the service provider of any subsequent—
      (i) variation or termination of the requirement
      (ii) variation or termination of any other bail condition, and
      (iii) fixing or variation of the date on which the defendant must surrender to custody.

PART 20 CUSTODY TIME LIMITS

Contents of this Part

Appeal to the Crown Court against decision in respect of a custody time limit
G–133 **20.1.**—(1) This rule applies—
    (a) to any appeal brought by an accused, under section 22(7) of the *Prosecution of Offences Act* 1985, against a decision of a magistrates' court to extend, or further extend, a custody time limit imposed by regulations made under section 22(1) of the 1985 Act; and
    (b) to any appeal brought by the prosecution, under section 22(8) of the 1985 Act, against a decision of a magistrates' court to refuse to extend, or further extend, such a time limit.

(2) An appeal to which this rule applies shall be commenced by the appellant's giving notice in writing of appeal—

(a) to the court officer for the magistrates' court which took the decision;

(b) if the appeal is brought by the accused, to the prosecutor and, if the prosecution is to be carried on by the Crown Prosecution Service, to the appropriate Crown Prosecutor;

(c) if the appeal is brought by the prosecution, to the accused; and

(d) to the Crown Court officer.

(3) The notice of an appeal to which this rule applies shall state the date on which the custody time limit applicable to the case is due to expire and, if the appeal is brought by the accused under section 22(7) of the 1985 Act, the date on which the custody time limit would have expired had the court decided not to extend or further extend that time limit.

(4) On receiving notice of an appeal to which this rule applies, the Crown Court officer shall enter the appeal and give notice of the time and place of the hearing to—

(a) the appellant;

(b) the other party to the appeal; and

(c) the court officer for the magistrates' court which took the decision.

(5) Without prejudice to the power of the Crown Court to give leave for an appeal to be abandoned, an appellant may abandon an appeal to which this rule applies by giving notice in writing to any person to whom notice of the appeal was required to be given by paragraph (2) of this rule not later than the third day preceding the day fixed for the hearing of the appeal:

Provided that, for the purpose of determining whether notice was properly given in accordance with this paragraph, there shall be disregarded any Saturday and Sunday and any day which is specified to be a bank holiday in England and Wales under section 1(1) of the *Banking and Financial Dealings Act* 1971.

PART 21 INITIAL DETAILS OF THE PROSECUTION CASE

Contents of this Part

When this Part applies

21.1.—(1) This Part applies in a magistrates' court, where the offence is one that can be tried in a magistrates' court.   **G–134**

(2) The court may direct that, for a specified period, this Part will not apply—

(a) to any case in that court; or

(b) to any specified category of case.

Providing initial details of the prosecution case

21.2. The prosecutor must provide initial details of the prosecution case by—   **G–135**

(a) serving those details on the court officer; and

(b) making those details available to the defendant, at, or before, the beginning of the day of the first hearing.

Content of initial details

21.3. Initial details of the prosecution case must include—   **G–136**

(a) a summary of the evidence on which that case will be based; or

(b) any statement, document or extract setting out facts or other matters on which that case will be based; or

(c) any combination of such a summary, statement, document or extract; and

(d) the defendant's previous convictions.

[The next paragraph is § G-140.]

PART 22 DISCLOSURE

Contents of this Part

When this Part applies

G–140   **22.1.** This Part applies—
    (a) in a magistrates' court and in the Crown Court;
    (b) where Parts I and II of the *Criminal Procedure and Investigations Act* 1996 apply.

Prosecution disclosure

G–140a   **22.2.**—(1) This rule applies in the Crown Court where, under section 3 of the *Criminal Procedure and Investigations Act* 1996, the prosecutor—
    (a) discloses prosecution material to the defendant; or
    (b) serves on the defendant a written statement that there is no such material to disclose.
    (2) The prosecutor must at the same time so inform the court officer.

Prosecutor's application for public interest ruling

G–140b   **22.3.**—(1) This rule applies where—
    (a) without a court order, the prosecutor would have to disclose material; and
    (b) the prosecutor wants the court to decide whether it would be in the public interest to disclose it.
    (2) The prosecutor must—
    (a) apply in writing for such a decision; and
    (b) serve the application on—
      (i) the court officer,
      (ii) any person who the prosecutor thinks would be directly affected by disclosure of the material, and
      (iii) the defendant, but only to the extent that serving it on the defendant would not disclose what the prosecutor thinks ought not be disclosed.
    (3) The application must—
    (a) describe the material, and explain why the prosecutor thinks that—
      (i) it is material that the prosecutor would have to disclose,
      (ii) it would not be in the public interest to disclose that material, and
      (iii) no measure such as the prosecutor's admission of any fact, or disclosure by summary, extract or edited copy, adequately would protect both the public interest and the defendant's right to a fair trial;
    (b) omit from any part of the application that is served on the defendant anything that would disclose what the prosecutor thinks ought not be disclosed (in which case, paragraph (4) of this rule applies); and
    (c) explain why, if no part of the application is served on the defendant.
    (4) Where the prosecutor serves only part of the application on the defendant, the prosecutor must—
    (a) mark the other part, to show that it is only for the court; and

(b) in that other part, explain why the prosecutor has withheld it from the defendant.

(5) Unless already done, the court may direct the prosecutor to serve an application on—

   (a) the defendant;

   (b) any other person who the court considers would be directly affected by the disclosure of the material.

(6) The court must determine the application at a hearing which—

   (a) will be in private, unless the court otherwise directs; and

   (b) if the court so directs, may take place, wholly or in part, in the defendant's absence.

(7) At a hearing at which the defendant is present—

   (a) the general rule is that the court will receive, in the following sequence—

      (i) representations first by the prosecutor and any other person served with the application, and then by the defendant, in the presence of them all, and then

      (ii) further representations by the prosecutor and any such other person in the defendant's absence; but

   (b) the court may direct other arrangements for the hearing.

(8) The court may only determine the application if satisfied that it has been able to take adequate account of—

   (a) such rights of confidentiality as apply to the material; and

   (b) the defendant's right to a fair trial.

(9) Unless the court otherwise directs, the court officer—

   (a) must not give notice to anyone other than the prosecutor—

      (i) of the hearing of an application under this rule, unless the prosecutor served the application on that person, or

      (ii) of the court's decision on the application;

   (b) may—

      (i) keep a written application or representations, or

      (ii) arrange for the whole or any part to be kept by some other appropriate person, subject to any conditions that the court may impose.

Defence disclosure

22.4. The defendant must serve any defence statement given under the *Criminal Procedure*   **G–140c**
and Investigations Act 1996 on—

   (a) the court officer; and

   (b) the prosecutor.

Defendant's application for prosecution disclosure

22.5.—(1) This rule applies where the defendant—   **G–140d**

   (a) has served a defence statement given under the *Criminal Procedure and Investigations Act* 1996; and

   (b) wants the court to require the prosecutor to disclose material.

(2) The defendant must serve an application on—

   (a) the court officer; and

   (b) the prosecutor.

(3) The application must—

   (a) describe the material that the defendant wants the prosecutor to disclose;

   (b) explain why the defendant thinks there is reasonable cause to believe that—

      (i) the prosecutor has that material, and

      (ii) it is material that the *Criminal Procedure and Investigations Act* 1996 requires the prosecutor to disclose; and

   (c) ask for a hearing, if the defendant wants one, and explain why it is needed.

(4) The court may determine an application under this rule—

   (a) at a hearing, in public or in private; or

   (b) without a hearing.

(5) The court must not require the prosecutor to disclose material unless the prosecutor—

(a) is present; or

(b) has had at least 14 days in which to make representations.

Review of public interest ruling

G–140e **22.6.**—(1) This rule applies where the court has ordered that it is not in the public interest to disclose material that the prosecutor otherwise would have to disclose, and

(a) the defendant wants the court to review that decision; or

(b) the Crown Court reviews that decision on its own initiative.

(2) Where the defendant wants the court to review that decision, the defendant must—

(a) serve an application on—

(i) the court officer, and

(ii) the prosecutor; and

(b) in the application—

(i) describe the material that the defendant wants the prosecutor to disclose, and

(ii) explain why the defendant thinks it is no longer in the public interest for the prosecutor not to disclose it.

(3) The prosecutor must serve any such application on any person who the prosecutor thinks would be directly affected if that material were disclosed.

(4) The prosecutor, and any such person, must serve any representations on—

(a) the court officer; and

(b) the defendant, unless to do so would in effect reveal something that either thinks ought not be disclosed.

(5) The court may direct—

(a) the prosecutor to serve any such application on any person who the court considers would be directly affected if that material were disclosed;

(b) the prosecutor and any such person to serve any representations on the defendant.

(6) The court must review a decision to which this rule applies at a hearing which—

(a) will be in private, unless the court otherwise directs; and

(b) if the court so directs, may take place, wholly or in part, in the defendant's absence.

(7) At a hearing at which the defendant is present—

(a) the general rule is that the court will receive, in the following sequence—

(i) representations first by the defendant, and then by the prosecutor and any other person served with the application, in the presence of them all, and then

(ii) further representations by the prosecutor and any such other person in the defendant's absence; but

(b) the court may direct other arrangements for the hearing.

(8) The court may only conclude a review if satisfied that it has been able to take adequate account of—

(a) such rights of confidentiality as apply to the material; and

(b) the defendant's right to a fair trial.

Defendant's application to use disclosed material

G–140f **22.7.**—(1) This rule applies where a defendant wants the court's permission to use disclosed prosecution material—

(a) otherwise than in connection with the case in which it was disclosed; or

(b) beyond the extent to which it was displayed or communicated publicly at a hearing.

(2) The defendant must serve an application on—

(a) the court officer; and

(b) the prosecutor.

(3) The application must—

(a) specify what the defendant wants to use or disclose; and

(b) explain why.

(4) The court may determine an application under this rule—

(a) at a hearing, in public or in private; or

(b) without a hearing.

(5) The court must not permit the use of such material unless—

(a) the prosecutor has had at least 28 days in which to make representations; and

(b) the court is satisfied that it has been able to take adequate account of any rights of confidentiality that may apply to the material.

Unauthorised use of disclosed material

22.8.—(1) This rule applies where a person uses disclosed prosecution material in contraven- **G–140g** tion of section 17 of the *Criminal Procedure and Investigations Act* 1996.

(2) The court may exercise its power to punish such a person for contempt of court—

(a) on an application by—

(i) the prosecutor, or

(ii) any person directly affected by the disclosure of the material; or

(b) on its own initiative.

(3) An applicant who wants the court to exercise that power must comply with the rules in Part 62 (Contempt of court).

(4) The court must not exercise its power to forfeit material used in contempt of court unless—

(a) the prosecutor; and

(b) any other person directly affected by the disclosure of the material, is present, or has had at least 14 days in which to make representations.

(5) The provisions of Schedule 3 to the*Contempt of Court Act* 1981 apply to a magistrates' court's exercise of the power to which this rule applies.

Court's power to vary requirements under this Part

22.9. The court may— **G–140h**

(a) shorten or extend (even after it has expired) a time limit under this Part;

(b) allow a defence statement to be in a different written form to one set out in the Practice Direction, as long as it contains what the*Criminal Procedure and Investigations Act* 1996 requires;

(c) allow an application under this Part to be in a different form to one set out in the Practice Direction, or to be presented orally; and

(d) specify the period within which—

(i) any application under this Part must be made, or

(ii) any material must be disclosed, on an application to which rule 22.5 applies (defendant's application for prosecution disclosure).

[The next paragraph is § G-158.]

PART 27 WITNESS STATEMENTS

Contents of this Part

When this Part applies

27.1. . This Part applies where a party wants to introduce a written statement in evidence **G–158** under section 9 of the *Criminal Justice Act* 1967.

Content of written statement

27.2. The statement must contain— **G–159**

    (a) at the beginning—
       (i) the witness' name, and
       (ii) the witness' age, if under 18;
    (b) a declaration by the witness that—
       (i) it is true to the best of the witness' knowledge and belief, and
       (ii) the witness knows that if it is introduced in evidence, then it would be an offence wilfully to have stated in it anything that the witness knew to be false or did not believe to be true;
    (c) if the witness cannot read the statement, a signed declaration by someone else that that person read it to the witness; and
    (d) the witness' signature.

Reference to exhibit

G–159a   **27.3.** Where the statement refers to a document or object as an exhibit—
    (a) the statement must contain such a description of that exhibit as to identify it clearly; and
    (b) the exhibit must be labelled or marked correspondingly, and the label or mark signed by the maker of the statement.

Written statement in evidence

G–159b   **27.4.**—(1) A party who wants to introduce in evidence a written statement must—
    (a) before the hearing at which that party wants to do so, serve a copy of the statement on—
       (i) the court officer, and
       (ii) each other party; and
    (b) at or before that hearing, serve the statement itself on the court officer.
   (2) If that party relies on only part of the statement, that party must mark the copy in such a way as to make that clear.
   (3) A prosecutor must serve on a defendant, with the copy of the statement, a notice—
    (a) of the right within 7 days of service to object to the introduction of the statement in evidence instead of the witness giving evidence in person; and
    (b) that if the defendant does not object in time, the court—
       (i) can nonetheless require the witness to give evidence in person, but
       (ii) may decide not to do so.
   (4) The court may exercise its power to require the witness to give evidence in person—
    (a) on application by any party; or
    (b) on its own initiative.
   (5) A party entitled to receive a copy of a statement may waive that entitlement by so informing—
    (a) the party who would have served it; and
    (b) the court.

PART 28 WITNESS SUMMONSES, WARRANTS AND ORDERS

Contents of this Part

Application for summons to produce a document, etc.: court's assessment of relevance and confidentiality	r.28.6 (*post*, G-165)
Application to withdraw a summons, warrant or order	r.28.7 (*post*, G-166)
Court's power to vary requirements under this Part	r.28.8 (*post*, G-167)

When this Part applies

28.1.—(1) This Part applies in magistrates' courts and in the Crown Court where—   **G–160**
    (a) a party wants the court to issue a witness summons, warrant or order under—
        (i) section 97 of the *Magistrates' Courts Act* 1980,
        (ii) section 2 of the *Criminal Procedure (Attendance of Witnesses) Act* 1965, or
        (iii) section 7 of the *Bankers' Books Evidence Act* 1879;
    (b) the court considers the issue of such a summons, warrant or order on its own initiative as if a party had applied; or
    (c) one of those listed in rule 28.7 wants the court to withdraw such a summons, warrant or order.

(2) A reference to a 'witness' in this Part is a reference to a person to whom such a summons, warrant or order is directed.

Issue etc. of summons, warrant or order with or without a hearing

28.2.—(1) The court may issue or withdraw a witness summons, warrant or order with or **G–161**
without a hearing.

(2) A hearing under this Part must be in private unless the court otherwise directs.

Application for summons, warrant or order: general rules

28.3.—(1) A party who wants the court to issue a witness summons, warrant or order must **G–162**
apply as soon as practicable after becoming aware of the grounds for doing so.

(2) The party applying must—
    (a) identify the proposed witness;
    (b) explain—
        (i) what evidence the proposed witness can give or produce,
        (ii) why it is likely to be material evidence, and
        (iii) why it would be in the interests of justice to issue a summons, order or warrant as appropriate.

(3) The application may be made orally unless—
    (a) rule 28.5 applies; or
    (b) the court otherwise directs.

Written application: form and service

28.4.—(1) An application in writing under rule 28.3 must be in the form set out in the **G–163**
Practice Direction, containing the same declaration of truth as a witness statement.

(2) The party applying must serve the application—
    (a) in every case, on the court officer and as directed by the court; and
    (b) as required by rule 28.5, if that rule applies.

Application for summons to produce a document, etc.: special rules

28.5.—(1) This rule applies to an application under rule 28.3 for a witness summons requir- **G–164**
ing the proposed witness—
    (a) to produce in evidence a document or thing; or
    (b) to give evidence about information apparently held in confidence, that relates to another person.

(2) The application must be in writing in the form required by rule 28.4.

(3) The party applying must serve the application—
    (a) on the proposed witness, unless the court otherwise directs; and
    (b) on one or more of the following, if the court so directs—
        (i) a person to whom the proposed evidence relates,
        (ii) another party.

(4) The court must not issue a witness summons where this rule applies unless—

    (a) everyone served with the application has had at least 14 days in which to make representations, including representations about whether there should be a hearing of the application before the summons is issued; and

    (b) the court is satisfied that it has been able to take adequate account of the duties and rights, including rights of confidentiality, of the proposed witness and of any person to whom the proposed evidence relates.

(5) This rule does not apply to an application for an order to produce in evidence a copy of an entry in a banker's book.

Application for summons to produce a document, etc.: court's assessment of relevance and confidentiality

G–165
    28.6.—(1) This rule applies where a person served with an application for a witness summons requiring the proposed witness to produce in evidence a document or thing objects to its production on the ground that—

    (a) it is not likely to be material evidence; or

    (b) even if it is likely to be material evidence, the duties or rights, including rights of confidentiality, of the proposed witness or of any person to whom the document or thing relates, outweigh the reasons for issuing a summons.

(2) The court may require the proposed witness to make the document or thing available for the objection to be assessed.

(3) The court may invite—

    (a) the proposed witness or any representative of the proposed witness; or

    (b) a person to whom the document or thing relates or any representative of such a person, to help the court assess the objection.

Application to withdraw a summons, warrant or order

G–166
    28.7.—(1) The court may withdraw a witness summons, warrant or order if one of the following applies for it to be withdrawn—

    (a) the party who applied for it, on the ground that it no longer is needed;

    (b) the witness, on the grounds that—

        (i) he was not aware of any application for it, and

        (ii) he cannot give or produce evidence likely to be material evidence, or

        (iii) even if he can, his duties or rights, including rights of confidentiality, or those of any person to whom the evidence relates, outweigh the reasons for the issue of the summons, warrant or order; or

    (c) any person to whom the proposed evidence relates, on the grounds that—

        (i) he was not aware of any application for it, and

        (ii) that evidence is not likely to be material evidence, or

        (iii) even if it is, his duties or rights, including rights of confidentiality, or those of the witness, outweigh the reasons for the issue of the summons, warrant or order.

(2) A person applying under the rule must—

    (a) apply in writing as soon as practicable after becoming aware of the grounds for doing so, explaining why he wants the summons, warrant or order to be withdrawn; and

    (b) serve the application on the court officer and as appropriate on—

        (i) the witness,

        (ii) the party who applied for the summons, warrant or order, and

        (iii) any other person who he knows was served with the application for the summons, warrant or order.

(3) Rule 28.6 applies to an application under this rule that concerns a document or thing to be produced in evidence.

Court's power to vary requirements under this Part

G–167
    28.8.—(1) The court may—

    (a) shorten or extend (even after it has expired) a time limit under this Part; and

    (b) where a rule or direction requires an application under this Part to be in writing, allow that application to be made orally instead.

(2) Someone who wants the court to allow an application to be made orally bunder paragraph (1)(b) of this rule must—

    (a) give as much notice as the urgency of his application permits to those on whom he would otherwise have served an application in writing; and

    (b) in doing so explain the reasons for the application and for wanting the court to consider it orally.

PART 29 MEASURES TO ASSIST A WITNESS OR DEFENDANT TO GIVE EVIDENCE

Contents of this Part

SECTION 1: UNDERSTANDING AND APPLYING THIS PART

When this Part applies

G–168   **29.1.**—(1) This Part applies—

(a) where the court can give a direction (a 'special measures direction'), under section 19 of the *Youth Justice and Criminal Evidence Act* 1999, on an application or on its own initiative, for any of the following measures—

  (i) preventing a witness from seeing the defendant (section 23 of the 1999 Act),

  (ii) allowing a witness to give evidence by live link (section 24 of the 1999 Act),

  (iii) hearing a witness' evidence in private (section 25 of the 1999 Act),

  (iv) dispensing with the wearing of wigs and gowns (section 26 of the 1999 Act),

  (v) admitting video recorded evidence (sections 27 and 28 of the 1999 Act),

  (vi) questioning a witness through an intermediary (section 29 of the 1999 Act),

  (vii) using a device to help a witness communicate (section 30 of the 1999 Act);

(b) where the court can vary or discharge such a direction, under section 20 of the 1999 Act;

(c) where the court can give, vary or discharge a direction (a 'defendant's evidence direction') for a defendant to give evidence—

  (i) by live link, under section 33A of the 1999 Act, or

  (ii) through an intermediary, under sections 33BA and 33BB of the 1999 Act;

(d) where the court can—

  (i) make a witness anonymity order, under section 86 of the *Coroners and Justice Act* 2009, or

  (ii) vary or discharge such an order, under section 91, 92 or 93 of the 2009 Act;

(e) where the court can exercise any other power it has to give, vary or discharge a direction for a measure to help a witness give evidence

Meaning of 'witness'

G–169   **29.2.** In this Part, 'witness' means anyone (other than a defendant) for whose benefit an application, direction or order is made.

SECTION 2: GENERAL RULES

Making an application for a direction or order

G–170   **29.3.** A party who wants the court to exercise its power to give or make a direction or order must—

(a) apply in writing—

  (i) as soon as reasonably practicable, and in any event

  (ii) not more than 14 days after the defendant pleads not guilty; and

(b) serve the application on—

  (i) the court officer, and

  (ii) each other party.

Decisions and reasons

G–171   **29.4.**—(1) A party who wants to introduce the evidence of a witness who is the subject of an application, direction or order must—

(a) inform the witness of the court's decision as soon as reasonably practicable; and

(b) explain to the witness the arrangements that as a result will be made for him or her to give evidence.

(2) The court must announce, at a hearing in public before the witness gives evidence, the reasons for a decision—

(a) to give, make, vary or discharge a direction or order; or

(b) to refuse to do so.

Court's power to vary requirements under this Part

29.5.—(1) The court may—

    (a) shorten or extend (even after it has expired) a time limit under this Part; and

    (b) allow an application or representations to be made in a different form to one set out in the Practice Direction, or to be made orally.

(2) A person who wants an extension of time must—

    (a) apply when serving the application or representations for which it is needed; and

    (b) explain the delay.

G–172

Custody of documents

29.6. Unless the court otherwise directs, the court officer may—

    (a) keep a written application or representations; or

    (b) arrange for the whole or any part to be kept by some other appropriate person, subject to any conditions that the court may impose.

G–173

Declaration by intermediary

29.7.—(1) This rule applies where—

    (a) a video recorded interview with a witness is conducted through an intermediary;

    (b) the court directs the examination of a witness or defendant through an intermediary.

(2) An intermediary must make a declaration—

    (a) before such an interview begins;

    (b) before the examination begins (even if such an interview with the witness was conducted through the same intermediary).

(3) The declaration must be in these terms—

"I solemnly, sincerely and truly declare [or I swear by Almighty God] that I will well and faithfully communicate questions and answers and make true explanation of all matters and things as shall be required of me according to the best of my skill and understanding."

G–174

SECTION 3: SPECIAL MEASURES DIRECTIONS

Exercise of court's powers

29.8. The court may decide whether to give, vary or discharge a special measures direction— **G–175**

    (a) at a hearing, in public or in private, or without a hearing;

    (b) in a party's absence, if that party—

        (i) applied for the direction, variation or discharge, or

        (ii) has had at least 14 days in which to make representations.

Special measures direction for a young witness

29.9.—(1) This rule applies where, under section 21 or section 22 of the Youth Justice and **G–176** Criminal Evidence Act 1999, the primary rule requires the court to give a direction for a special measure to assist a child witness or a qualifying witness—

    (a) on an application, if one is made; or

    (b) on the court's own initiative, in any other case.

(2) A party who wants to introduce the evidence of such a witness must as soon as reasonably practicable—

    (a) notify the court that the witness is eligible for assistance;

    (b) provide the court with any information that the court may need to assess the witness' views, if the witness does not want the primary rule to apply; and

    (c) serve any video recorded evidence on—

        (i) the court officer, and

        (ii) each other party.

Content of application for a special measures direction

29.10. An applicant for a special measures direction must— **G–176a**

(a) explain how the witness is eligible for assistance;

(b) explain why special measures would be likely to improve the quality of the witness' evidence;

(c) propose the measure or measures that in the applicant's opinion would be likely to maximise so far as practicable the quality of that evidence;

(d) report any views that the witness has expressed about—

 (i) his or her eligibility for assistance,

 (ii) the likelihood that special measures would improve the quality of his or her evidence, and

 (iii) the measure or measures proposed by the applicant;

(e) in a case in which a child witness or a qualifying witness does not want the primary rule to apply, provide any information that the court may need to assess the witness' views;

(f) in a case in which the applicant proposes that the witness should give evidence by live link—

 (i) identify someone to accompany the witness while the witness gives evidence,

 (ii) name that person, if possible, and

 (iii) explain why that person would be an appropriate companion for the witness, including the witness' own views;

(g) in a case in which the applicant proposes the admission of video recorded evidence, identify—

 (i) the date and duration of the recording,

 (ii) which part the applicant wants the court to admit as evidence, if the applicant does not want the court to admit all of it;

(h) attach any other material on which the applicant relies; and

(i) if the applicant wants a hearing, ask for one, and explain why it is needed.

Application to vary or discharge a special measures direction

G–176b   **29.11.**—(1) A party who wants the court to vary or discharge a special measures direction must—

(a) apply in writing, as soon as reasonably practicable after becoming aware of the grounds for doing so; and

(b) serve the application on—

 (i) the court officer, and

 (ii) each other party.

(2) The applicant must—

(a) explain what material circumstances have changed since the direction was given (or last varied, if applicable);

(b) explain why the direction should be varied or discharged; and

(c) ask for a hearing, if the applicant wants one, and explain why it is needed.

Application containing information withheld from another party

G–176c   **29.12.**—(1) This rule applies where—

(a) an applicant serves an application for a special measures direction, or for its variation or discharge; and

(b) the application includes information that the applicant thinks ought not be revealed to another party.

(2) The applicant must—

(a) omit that information from the part of the application that is served on that other party;

(b) mark the other part to show that, unless the court otherwise directs, it is only for the court; and

(c) in that other part, explain why the applicant has withheld that information from that other party.

(3) Any hearing of an application to which this rule applies—

(a) must be in private, unless the court otherwise directs; and

(b) if the court so directs, may be, wholly or in part, in the absence of a party from whom information has been withheld.

(4) At any hearing of an application to which this rule applies—

    (a) the general rule is that the court will receive, in the following sequence—

        (i) representations first by the applicant and then by each other party, in all the parties' presence, and then

        (ii) further representations by the applicant, in the absence of a party from whom information has been withheld; but

    (b) the court may direct other arrangements for the hearing.

Representations in response

29.13.—(1) This rule applies where a party wants to make representations about—   **G–176d**

    (a) an application for a special measures direction;

    (b) an application for the variation or discharge of such a direction; or

    (c) a direction, variation or discharge that the court proposes on its own initiative.

(2) Such a party must—

    (a) serve the representations on—

        (i) the court officer, and

        (ii) each other party;

    (b) do so not more than 14 days after, as applicable—

        (i) service of the application, or

        (ii) notice of the direction, variation or discharge that the court proposes; and

    (c) ask for a hearing, if that party wants one, and explain why it is needed.

(3) Where representations include information that the person making them thinks ought not be revealed to another party, that person must—

    (a) omit that information from the representations served on that other party;

    (b) mark the information to show that, unless the court otherwise directs, it is only for the court; and

    (c) with that information include an explanation of why it has been withheld from that other party.

(4) Representations against a special measures direction must explain—

    (a) why the witness is not eligible for assistance; or

    (b) if the witness is eligible for assistance, why—

        (i) no special measure would be likely to improve the quality of the witness' evidence,

        (ii) the proposed measure or measures would not be likely to maximise so far as practicable the quality of the witness' evidence, or

        (iii) the proposed measure or measures might tend to inhibit the effective testing of that evidence.

(5) Representations against the variation or discharge of a special measures direction must explain why it should not be varied or discharged.

SECTION 4: DEFENDANT'S EVIDENCE DIRECTIONS

Exercise of court's powers

29.14. The court may decide whether to give, vary or discharge a defendant's evidence   **G–176e** direction—

    (a) at a hearing, in public or in private, or without a hearing;

    (b) in a party's absence, if that party—

        (i) applied for the direction, variation or discharge, or

        (ii) has had at least 14 days in which to make representations.

Content of application for a defendant's evidence direction

29.15. An applicant for a defendant's evidence direction must—   **G–176f**

    (a) explain how the proposed direction meets the conditions prescribed by the *Youth Justice and Criminal Evidence Act* 1999;

    (b) in a case in which the applicant proposes that the defendant give evidence by live link—

        (i) identify a person to accompany the defendant while the defendant gives evidence, and

(ii) explain why that person is appropriate;

(c) ask for a hearing, if the applicant wants one, and explain why it is needed.

Application to vary or discharge a defendant's evidence direction

G–176g   **29.16.**—(1) A party who wants the court to vary or discharge a defendant's evidence direction must—

(a) apply in writing, as soon as reasonably practicable after becoming aware of the grounds for doing so; and

(b) serve the application on—

    (i) the court officer, and

    (ii) each other party.

(2) The applicant must—

(a) on an application to discharge a live link direction, explain why it is in the interests of justice to do so;

(b) on an application to discharge a direction for an intermediary, explain why it is no longer necessary in order to ensure that the defendant receives a fair trial;

(c) on an application to vary a direction for an intermediary, explain why it is necessary for the direction to be varied in order to ensure that the defendant receives a fair trial; and

(d) ask for a hearing, if the applicant wants one, and explain why it is needed.

Representations in response

G–176h   **29.17.**—(1) This rule applies where a party wants to make representations about—

(a) an application for a defendant's evidence direction;

(b) an application for the variation or discharge of such a direction; or

(c) a direction, variation or discharge that the court proposes on its own initiative.

(2) Such a party must—

(a) serve the representations on—

    (i) the court officer, and

    (ii) each other party;

(b) do so not more than 14 days after, as applicable—

    (i) service of the application, or

    (ii) notice of the direction, variation or discharge that the court proposes; and

(c) ask for a hearing, if that party wants one, and explain why it is needed.

(3) Representations against a direction, variation or discharge must explain why the conditions prescribed by the *Youth Justice and Criminal Evidence Act* 1999 are not met.

SECTION 5: WITNESS ANONYMITY ORDERS

Exercise of court's powers

G–176i   **29.18.**—(1) The court may decide whether to make, vary or discharge a witness anonymity order—

(a) at a hearing (which will be in private, unless the court otherwise directs), or without a hearing (unless any party asks for one);

(b) in the absence of a defendant.

(2) The court must not exercise its power to make, vary or discharge a witness anonymity order, or to refuse to do so—

(a) before or during the trial, unless each party has had an opportunity to make representations;

(b) on an appeal by the defendant to which applies Part 63 (appeal to the Crown Court) or Part 68 (appeal to the Court of Appeal about conviction or sentence), unless in each party's case—

    (i) that party has had an opportunity to make representations, or

    (ii) the appeal court is satisfied that it is not reasonably practicable to communicate with that party;

(c) after the trial and any such appeal are over, unless in the case of each party and the witness—

    (i)   each has had an opportunity to make representations, or

    (ii)   the court is satisfied that it is not reasonably practicable to communicate with that party or witness.

Content and conduct of application for a witness anonymity order

29.19.—(1) An applicant for a witness anonymity order must—   **G–176j**

  (a) include in the application nothing that might reveal the witness' identity;

  (b) describe the measures proposed by the applicant;

  (c) explain how the proposed order meets the conditions prescribed by section 88 of the *Coroners and Justice Act* 2009;

  (d) explain why no measures other than those proposed will suffice, such as—

    (i)   an admission of the facts that would be proved by the witness,

    (ii)   an order restricting public access to the trial,

    (iii)   reporting restrictions, in particular under section 46 of the *Youth Justice and Criminal Evidence Act* 1999 or under section 39 of the *Children and Young Persons Act* 1933,

    (iv)   a direction for a special measure under section 19 of the *Youth Justice and Criminal Evidence Act* 1999,

    (v)   introduction of the witness' written statement as hearsay evidence, under section 116 of the *Criminal Justice Act* 2003, or

    (vi)   arrangements for the protection of the witness;

  (e) attach to the application—

    (i)   a witness statement setting out the proposed evidence, edited in such a way as not to reveal the witness' identity,

    (ii)   where the prosecutor is the applicant, any further prosecution evidence to be served, and any further prosecution material to be disclosed under the Criminal Procedure and Investigations Act 1996, similarly edited, and

    (iii)   any defence statement that has been served, or as much information as may be available to the applicant that gives particulars of the defence; and

  (f) ask for a hearing, if the applicant wants one.

(2) At any hearing of the application, the applicant must—

  (a) identify the witness to the court, unless at the prosecutor's request the court otherwise directs; and

  (b) present to the court, unless it otherwise directs—

    (i)   the unedited witness statement from which the edited version has been prepared,

    (ii)   where the prosecutor is the applicant, the unedited version of any further prosecution evidence or material from which an edited version has been prepared, and

    (iii)   such further material as the applicant relies on to establish that the proposed order meets the conditions prescribed by section 88 of the 2009 Act.

(3) At any such hearing—

  (a) the general rule is that the court will receive, in the following sequence—

    (i)   representations first by the applicant and then by each other party, in all the parties' presence, and then

    (ii)   information withheld from a defendant, and further representations by the applicant, in the absence of any (or any other) defendant; but

  (b) the court may direct other arrangements for the hearing.

(4) Before the witness gives evidence, the applicant must identify the witness to the court—

  (a) if not already done;

  (b) without revealing the witness' identity to any other party or person; and

  (c) unless at the prosecutor's request the court otherwise directs.

Duty of court officer to notify the Director of Public Prosecutions

29.20. The court officer must notify the Director of Public Prosecutions of an application, un- **G–176k**
less the prosecutor is, or acts on behalf of, a public authority.

Application to vary or discharge a witness anonymity order

G–176l   **29.21.**—(1) A party who wants the court to vary or discharge a witness anonymity order, or a witness who wants the court to do so when the case is over, must—

    (a) apply in writing, as soon as reasonably practicable after becoming aware of the grounds for doing so; and

    (b) serve the application on—

        (i)   the court officer, and

        (ii)   each other party.

  (2) The applicant must—

    (a) explain what material circumstances have changed since the order was made (or last varied, if applicable);

    (b) explain why the order should be varied or discharged, taking account of the conditions for making an order; and

    (c) ask for a hearing, if the applicant wants one.

  (3) Where an application includes information that the applicant thinks might reveal the witness' identity, the applicant must—

    (a) omit that information from the application that is served on a defendant;

    (b) mark the information to show that it is only for the court and the prosecutor (if the prosecutor is not the applicant); and

    (c) with that information include an explanation of why it has been withheld.

  (4) Where a party applies to vary or discharge a witness anonymity order after the trial and any appeal are over, the party who introduced the witness' evidence must serve the application on the witness.

Representations in response

G–176m   **29.22.**—(1) This rule applies where a party or, where the case is over, a witness, wants to make representations about—

    (a) an application for a witness anonymity order;

    (b) an application for the variation or discharge of such an order; or

    (c) a variation or discharge that the court proposes on its own initiative.

  (2) Such a party or witness must—

    (a) serve the representations on—

        (i)   the court officer, and

        (ii)   each other party;

    (b) do so not more than 14 days after, as applicable—

        (i)   service of the application, or

        (ii)   notice of the variation or discharge that the court proposes; and

    (c) ask for a hearing, if that party or witness wants one.

  (3) Where representations include information that the person making them thinks might reveal the witness' identity, that person must—

    (a) omit that information from the representations served on a defendant;

    (b) mark the information to show that it is only for the court (and for the prosecutor, if relevant); and

    (c) with that information include an explanation of why it has been withheld.

  (4) Representations against a witness anonymity order must explain why the conditions for making the order are not met.

  (5) Representations against the variation or discharge of such an order must explain why it would not be appropriate to vary or discharge it, taking account of the conditions for making an order.

  (6) A prosecutor's representations in response to an application by a defendant must include all information available to the prosecutor that is relevant to the conditions and considerations specified by sections 88 and 89 of the *Coroners and Justice Act* 2009.

[The next paragraph is § G–178.]

PART 31 RESTRICTION ON CROSS-EXAMINATION BY A DEFENDANT ACTING IN PERSON

Contents of this Part

Restrictions on cross-examination of witness

31.1.—(1) This rule and rules 31.2 and 31.3 apply where an accused is prevented from **G–178** cross-examining a witness in person by virtue of section 34, 35 or 36 of the *Youth Justice and Criminal Evidence Act* 1999.

(2) The court shall explain to the accused as early in the proceedings as is reasonably practicable that he—

(a) is prevented from cross-examining a witness in person; and

(b) should arrange for a legal representative to act for him for the purpose of cross-examining the witness.

(3) The accused shall notify the court officer within 7 days of the court giving its explanation, or within such other period as the court may in any particular case allow, of the action, if any, he has taken.

(4) Where he has arranged for a legal representative to act for him, the notification shall include details of the name and address of the representative.

(5) The notification shall be in writing.

(6) The court officer shall notify all other parties to the proceedings of the name and address of the person, if any, appointed to act for the accused.

(7) Where the court gives its explanation under paragraph (2) to the accused either within 7 days of the day set for the commencement of any hearing at which a witness in respect of whom a prohibition under section 34, 35 or 36 of the 1999 Act applies may be cross-examined or after such a hearing has commenced, the period of 7 days shall be reduced in accordance with any directions issued by the court.

(8) Where at the end of the period of 7 days or such other period as the court has allowed, the court has received no notification from the accused it may grant the accused an extension of time, whether on its own motion or on the application of the accused.

(9) Before granting an extension of time, the court may hold a hearing at which all parties to the proceedings may attend and be heard.

(10) Any extension of time shall be of such period as the court considers appropriate in the circumstances of the case.

(11) The decision of the court as to whether to grant the accused an extension of time shall be notified to all parties to the proceedings by the court officer.

Appointment of legal representative by the court

31.2.—(1) Where the court decides, in accordance with section 38(4) of the *Youth Justice* **G–179** *and Criminal Evidence Act* 1999, to appoint a qualified legal representative, the court officer shall notify all parties to the proceedings of the name and address of the representative.

(2) An appointment made by the court under section 38(4) of the 1999 Act shall, except to such extent as the court may in any particular case determine, terminate at the conclusion of the cross-examination of the witness or witnesses in respect of whom a prohibition under section 34, 35 or 36 of the 1999 Act applies.

Appointment arranged by the accused

31.3.—(1) The accused may arrange for the qualified legal representative, appointed by the **G–180** court under section 38(4) of the *Youth Justice and Criminal Evidence Act* 1999, to be appointed to act for him for the purpose of cross-examining any witness in respect of whom a prohibition under section 34, 35 or 36 of the 1999 Act applies.

(2) Where such an appointment is made—

(a) both the accused and the qualified legal representative appointed shall notify the court of the appointment; and

(b) the qualified legal representative shall, from the time of his appointment, act for the accused as though the arrangement had been made under section 38(2)(a) of the 1999 Act and shall cease to be the representative of the court under section 38(4).

(3) Where the court receives notification of the appointment either from the qualified legal representative or from the accused but not from both, the court shall investigate whether the appointment has been made, and if it concludes that the appointment has not been made, paragraph (2)(b) shall not apply.

(4) An accused may, notwithstanding an appointment by the court under section 38(4) of the 1999 Act, arrange for a legal representative to act for him for the purpose of cross-examining any witness in respect of whom a prohibition under section 34, 35 or 36 of the 1999 Act applies.

(5) Where the accused arranges for, or informs the court of his intention to arrange for, a legal representative to act for him, he shall notify the court, within such period as the court may allow, of the name and address of any person appointed to act for him.

(6) Where the court is notified within the time allowed that such an appointment has been made, any qualified legal representative appointed by the court in accordance with section 38(4) of the 1999 Act shall be discharged.

(7) The court officer shall, as soon as reasonably practicable after the court receives notification of an appointment under this rule or, where paragraph (3) applies, after the court is satisfied that the appointment has been made, notify all the parties to the proceedings—

(a) that the appointment has been made;

(b) where paragraph (4) applies, of the name and address of the person appointed; and

(c) that the person appointed by the court under section 38(4) of the 1999 Act has been discharged or has ceased to act for the court.

Prohibition on cross-examination of witness

G–181   **31.4.**—(1) An application by the prosecutor for the court to give a direction under section 36 of the Youth Justice and Criminal Evidence Act 1999 in relation to any witness must be sent to the court officer and at the same time a copy thereof must be sent by the applicant to every other party to the proceedings.

(2) In his application the prosecutor must state why, in his opinion—

(a) the evidence given by the witness is likely to be diminished if cross-examination is undertaken by the accused in person;

(b) the evidence would be improved if a direction were given under section 36(2) of the 1999 Act; and

(c) it would not be contrary to the interests of justice to give such a direction.

(3) On receipt of the application the court officer must refer it—

(a) if the trial has started, to the court of trial; or

(b) if the trial has not started when the application is received—

(i) to the judge or court designated to conduct the trial, or

(ii) if no judge or court has been designated for that purpose, to such judge or court designated for the purposes of hearing that application.

(4) Where a copy of the application is received by a party to the proceedings more than 14 days before the date set for the trial to begin, that party may make observations in writing on the application to the court officer, but any such observations must be made within 14 days of the receipt of the application and be copied to the other parties to the proceedings.

(5) A party to whom an application is sent in accordance with paragraph (1) who wishes to oppose the application must give his reasons for doing so to the court officer and the other parties to the proceedings.

(6) Those reasons must be notified—

(a) within 14 days of the date the application was served on him, if that date is more than 14 days before the date set for the trial to begin;

(b) if the trial has begun, in accordance with any directions issued by the court; or

(c) if neither paragraph (6)(a) nor (b) applies, before the date set for the trial to begin.

(7) Where the application made in accordance with paragraph (1) is made before the date set for the trial to begin and—

(a) is not contested by any party to the proceedings, the court may determine the application without a hearing;

(b) is contested by a party to the proceedings, the court must direct a hearing of the application.

(8) Where the application is made after the trial has begun—

(a) the application may be made orally; and

(b) the court may give such directions as it considers appropriate to deal with the application.

(9) Where a hearing of the application is to take place, the court officer shall notify each party to the proceedings of the time and place of the hearing.

(10) A party notified in accordance with paragraph (9) may be present at the hearing and be heard.

(11) The court officer must, as soon as possible after the determination of an application made in accordance with paragraph (1), give notice of the decision and the reasons for it to all the parties to the proceedings. (12) A person making an oral application under paragraph (8)(a) must—

(a) give reasons why the application was not made before the trial commenced; and

(b) provide the court with the information set out in paragraph (2).

PART 32 INTERNATIONAL CO-OPERATION

Contents of this Part

Notice required to accompany process served outside the United Kingdom and translations

32.1.—(1) The notice which by virtue of section 3(4)(b) of the *Crime (International Co-* **G–182** *operation) Act* 2003 (general requirements for service of process) must accompany any process served outside the United Kingdom must give the information specified in paragraphs (2) and (4) below.

(2) The notice must—

(a) state that the person required by the process to appear as a party or attend as a witness can obtain information about his rights in connection therewith from the relevant authority; and

    (b) give the particulars specified in paragraph (4) about that authority.

(3) The relevant authority where the process is served—

    (a) at the request of the prosecuting authority, is that authority; or

    (b) at the request of the defendant or the prosecutor in the case of a private prosecution, is the court by which the process is served.

(4) The particulars referred to in paragraph (2) are—

    (a) the name and address of the relevant authority, together with its telephone and fax numbers and e-mail address; and

    (b) the name of a person at the relevant authority who can provide the information referred to in paragraph (2)(a), together with his telephone and fax numbers and e-mail address.

(5) The justices' clerk or Crown Court officer must send, together with any process served outside the United Kingdom—

    (a) any translation which is provided under section 3(3)(b) of the 2003 Act; and

    (b) any translation of the information required to be given by this rule which is provided to him.

(6) In this rule, 'process' has the same meaning as in section 51(3) of the 2003 Act.

Proof of service outside the United Kingdom

G–183   **32.2.**—(1) A statement in a certificate given by or on behalf of the Secretary of State—

    (a) that process has been served on any person under section 4(1) of the *Crime (International Co-operation) Act* 2003 (service of process otherwise than by post);

    (b) of the manner in which service was effected; and

    (c) of the date on which process was served; shall be admissible as evidence of any facts so stated.

(2) In this rule, 'process' has the same meaning as in section 51(3) of the 2003 Act.

Supply of copy of notice of request for assistance abroad

G–184   **32.3.** Where a request for assistance under section 7 of the *Crime (International Co-operation) Act* 2003 is made by a justice of the peace or a judge exercising the jurisdiction of the Crown Court and is sent in accordance with section 8(1) of the 2003 Act, the justices' clerk or the Crown Court officer shall send a copy of the letter of request to the Secretary of State as soon as practicable after the request has been made.

Persons entitled to appear and take part in proceedings before a nominated court, and exclusion of the public

G–185   **32.4.** A court nominated under section 15(1) of the *Crime (International Co-operation) Act* 2003 (nominating a court to receive evidence) may—

    (a) determine who may appear or take part in the proceedings under Schedule 1 to the 2003 Act before the court and whether a party to the proceedings is entitled to be legally represented; and

    (b) direct that the public be excluded from those proceedings if it thinks it necessary to do so in the interests of justice.

Record of proceedings to receive evidence before a nominated court

G–186   **32.5.**—(1) Where a court is nominated under section 15(1) of the *Crime (International Co-operation) Act* 2003 the justices' clerk or Crown Court officer shall enter in an overseas record—

    (a) details of the request in respect of which the notice under section 15(1) of the 2003 Act was given;

    (b) the date on which, and place at which, the proceedings under Schedule 1 to the 2003 Act in respect of that request took place;

    (c) the name of any witness who gave evidence at the proceedings in question;

    (d) the name of any person who took part in the proceedings as a legal representative or an interpreter;

    (e) whether a witness was required to give evidence on oath or (by virtue of section 5 of the Oaths Act 1978) after making a solemn affirmation; and

(f) whether the opportunity to cross-examine any witness was refused.

(2) When the court gives the evidence received by it under paragraph 6(1) of Schedule 1 to the 2003 Act to the court or authority that made the request or to the territorial authority for forwarding to the court or authority that made the request, the justices' clerk or Crown Court officer shall send to the court, authority or territorial authority (as the case may be) a copy of an extract of so much of the overseas record as relates to the proceedings in respect of that request.

Interpreter for the purposes of proceedings involving a television or telephone link

32.6.—(1) This rule applies where a court is nominated under section 30(3) (hearing wit- **G–187** nesses in the UK through television links) or section 31(4) (hearing witnesses in the UK by telephone) of the *Crime (International Co-operation) Act* 2003.

(2) Where it appears to the justices' clerk or the Crown Court officer that the witness to be heard in the proceedings under Part 1 or 2 of Schedule 2 to the 2003 Act ('the relevant proceedings') is likely to give evidence in a language other than English, he shall make arrangements for an interpreter to be present at the proceedings to translate what is said into English.

(3) Where it appears to the justices' clerk or the Crown Court officer that the witness to be heard in the relevant proceedings is likely to give evidence in a language other than that in which the proceedings of the court referred to in section 30(1) or, as the case may be, 31(1) of the 2003 Act ('the external court') will be conducted, he shall make arrangements for an interpreter to be present at the relevant proceedings to translate what is said into the language in which the proceedings of the external court will be conducted.

(4) Where the evidence in the relevant proceedings is either given in a language other than English or is not translated into English by an interpreter, the court shall adjourn the proceedings until such time as an interpreter can be present to provide a translation into English.

(5) Where a court in Wales understands Welsh—

    (a) paragraph (2) does not apply where it appears to the justices' clerk or Crown Court officer that the witness in question is likely to give evidence in Welsh;

    (b) paragraph (4) does not apply where the evidence is given in Welsh; and

    (c) any translation which is provided pursuant to paragraph (2) or (4) may be into Welsh instead of English.

Record of television link hearing before a nominated court

32.7.—(1) This rule applies where a court is nominated under section 30(3) of the *Crime* **G–188** *(International Co-operation) Act* 2003.

(2) The justices' clerk or Crown Court officer shall enter in an overseas record—

    (a) details of the request in respect of which the notice under section 30(3) of the 2003 Act was given;

    (b) the date on which, and place at which, the proceedings under Part 1 of Schedule 2 to that Act in respect of that request took place;

    (c) the technical conditions, such as the type of equipment used, under which the proceedings took place;

    (d) the name of the witness who gave evidence;

    (e) the name of any person who took part in the proceedings as a legal representative or an interpreter; and

    (f) the language in which the evidence was given.

(3) As soon as practicable after the proceedings under Part 1 of Schedule 2 to the 2003 Act took place, the justices' clerk or Crown Court officer shall send to the external authority that made the request a copy of an extract of so much of the overseas record as relates to the proceedings in respect of that request.

Record of telephone link hearing before a nominated court

32.8.—(1) This rule applies where a court is nominated under section 31(4) of the *Crime* **G–189** *(International Co-operation) Act* 2003.

(2) The justices' clerk or Crown Court officer shall enter in an overseas record—

    (a) details of the request in respect of which the notice under section 31(4) of the 2003 Act was given;

    (b) the date, time and place at which the proceedings under Part 2 of Schedule 2 to the 2003 Act took place;

(c) the name of the witness who gave evidence;

(d) the name of any interpreter who acted at the proceedings; and

(e) the language in which the evidence was given.

Overseas record

G–190　　　**32.9.**—(1) The overseas records of a magistrates' court shall be part of the register (within the meaning of section 150(1) of the*Magistrates' Courts Act* 1980).

(2)　The overseas records of any court shall not be open to inspection by any person except—

(a) as authorised by the Secretary of State; or

(b) with the leave of the court.

Overseas freezing orders

G–190a　　　**32.10.**—(1) This rule applies where a court is nominated under section 21(1) of the Crime (International Co-operation) Act 2003 to give effect to an overseas freezing order.

(2)　Where the Secretary of State serves a copy of such an order on the court officer—

(a) the general rule is that the court will consider the order no later than the next business day;

(b) exceptionally, the court may consider the order later than that, but not more than 5 business days after service.

(3) The court must not consider the order unless—

(a) it is satisfied that the chief officer of police for the area in which the evidence is situated has had notice of the order; and

(b) that chief officer of police has had an opportunity to make representations, at a hearing if that officer wants.

(4) The court may consider the order—

(a) without a hearing; or

(b) at a hearing, in public or in private.

PART 33 EXPERT EVIDENCE

Contents of this Part

Reference to expert

G–191　　　**33.1.** A reference to an 'expert' in this Part is a reference to a person who is required to give or prepare expert evidence for the purpose of criminal proceedings, including evidence required to determine fitness to plead or for the purpose of sentencing.

Expert's duty to the court

G–192　　　**33.2.**—(1) An expert must help the court to achieve the overriding objective by giving objective, unbiased opinion on matters within his expertise.

(2)　This duty overrides any obligation to the person from whom he receives instructions or by whom he is paid.

(3) This duty includes an obligation to inform all parties and the court if the expert's opinion changes from that contained in a report served as evidence or given in a statement.

Content of expert's report

33.3.—(1) An expert's report must— **G–193**

(a) give details of the expert's qualifications, relevant experience and accreditation;

(b) give details of any literature or other information which the expert has relied on in making the report;

(c) contain a statement setting out the substance of all facts given to the expert which are material to the opinions expressed in the report, or upon which those opinions are based;

(d) make clear which of the facts stated in the report are within the expert's own knowledge;

(e) say who carried out any examination, measurement, test or experiment which the expert has used for the report and—

  (i) give the qualifications, relevant experience and accreditation of that person,

  (ii) say whether or not the examination, measurement, test or experiment was carried out under the expert's supervision, and

  (iii) summarise the findings on which the expert relies;

(f) where there is a range of opinion on the matters dealt with in the report—

  (i) summarise the range of opinion, and

  (ii) give reasons for his own opinion;

(g) if the expert is not able to give his opinion without qualification, state the qualification;

(h) contain a summary of the conclusions reached;

(i) contain a statement that the expert understands his duty to the court, and has complied and will continue to comply with that duty; and

(j) contain the same declaration of truth as a witness statement.

(2) Only sub-paragraphs (i) and (j) of rule 33.3(1) apply to a summary by an expert of his conclusions served in advance of that expert's report.

Service of expert evidence

33.4.—(1) A party who wants to introduce expert evidence must— **G–194**

(a) serve it on—

  (i) the court officer, and

  (ii) each other party;

(b) serve it—

  (i) as soon as practicable, and in any event

  (ii) with any application in support of which that party relies on that evidence; and

(c) if another party so requires, give that party a copy of, or a reasonable opportunity to inspect—

  (i) a record of any examination, measurement, test or experiment on which the expert's findings and opinion are based, or that were carried out in the course of reaching those findings and opinion, and

  (ii) anything on which any such examination, measurement, test or experiment was carried out.

(2) A party may not introduce expert evidence if that party has not complied with this rule, unless—

(a) every other party agrees; or

(b) the court gives permission.

Expert to be informed of service of report

33.5. A party who serves on another party or on the court a report by an expert must, at once, inform that expert of that fact. **G–195**

Pre-hearing discussion of expert evidence

33.6.—(1) This rule applies where more than one party wants to introduce expert evidence. **G–196**

(2) The court may direct the experts to—

(a) discuss the expert issues in the proceedings; and

(b) prepare a statement for the court of the matters on which they agree and disagree, giving their reasons.

(3) Except for that statement, the content of that discussion must not be referred to without the court's permission.

(4) A party may not introduce expert evidence without the court's permission if the expert has not complied with a direction under this rule.

Court's power to direct that evidence is to be given by a single joint expert

G–197   **33.7.**—(1) Where more than one defendant wants to introduce expert evidence on an issue at trial, the court may direct that the evidence on that issue is to be given by one expert only.

(2) Where the co-defendants cannot agree who should be the expert, the court may—

(a) select the expert from a list prepared or identified by them; or

(b) direct that the expert be selected in another way.

Instructions to a single joint expert

G–198   **33.8.**—(1) Where the court gives a direction under rule 33.7 for a single joint expert to be used, each of the co-defendants may give instructions to the expert.

(2) When a co-defendant gives instructions to the expert he must, at the same time, send a copy of the instructions to the other co-defendant(s).

(3) The court may give directions about—

(a) the payment of the expert's fees and expenses; and

(b) any examination, measurement, test or experiment which the expert wishes to carry out.

(4) The court may, before an expert is instructed, limit the amount that can be paid by way of fees and expenses to the expert.

(5) Unless the court otherwise directs, the instructing co-defendants are jointly and severally liable for the payment of the expert's fees and expenses.

Court's power to vary requirements under this Part

G–198a   **33.9.**—(1) The court may—

(a) extend (even after it has expired) a time limit under this Part;

(b) allow the introduction of expert evidence which omits a detail required by this Part.

(2) A party who wants an extension of time must—

(a) apply when serving the expert evidence for which it is required; and

(b) explain the delay.

PART 34 HEARSAY EVIDENCE

Contents of this Part

When this Part applies

G–199   **34.1.** This Part applies—

(a) in a magistrates' court and in the Crown Court;

(b) where a party wants to introduce hearsay evidence, within the meaning of section 114 of the *Criminal Justice Act* 2003.

Notice to introduce hearsay evidence

G–200   **34.2.**—(1) This rule applies where a party wants to introduce hearsay evidence for admission under any of the following sections of the *Criminal Justice Act* 2003—

(a) section 114(1)(d) (evidence admissible in the interests of justice);

(b) section 116 (evidence where a witness is unavailable);

(c) section 121 (multiple hearsay).

(2) That party must—

(a) serve notice on—

(i) the court officer, and

(ii) each other party;

(b) in the notice—

(i) identify the evidence that is hearsay,

(ii) set out any facts on which that party relies to make the evidence admissible,

(iii) explain how that party will prove those facts if another party disputes them, and

(iv) explain why the evidence is admissible; and

(c) attach to the notice any statement or other document containing the evidence that has not already been served.

(3) A prosecutor who wants to introduce such evidence must serve the notice not more than 14 days after the defendant pleads not guilty.

(4) A defendant who wants to introduce such evidence must serve the notice as soon as reasonably practicable.

(5) A party entitled to receive a notice under this rule may waive that entitlement by so informing—

(a) the party who would have served it; and

(b) the court.

Opposing the introduction of hearsay evidence

34.3.—(1) This rule applies where a party objects to the introduction of hearsay evidence. **G–201**

(2) That party must—

(a) apply to the court to determine the objection;

(b) serve the application on—

(i) the court officer, and

(ii) each other party;

(c) serve the application as soon as reasonably practicable, and in any event not more than 14 days after—

(i) service of notice to introduce the evidence under rule 34.2,

(ii) service of the evidence to which that party objects, if no notice is required by that rule, or

(iii) the defendant pleads not guilty whichever of those events happens last; and

(d) in the application, explain—

(i) which, if any, facts set out in a notice under rule 34.2 that party disputes,

(ii) why the evidence is not admissible,

(iii) any other objection to the application.

(3) The court—

(a) may determine an application—

(i) at a hearing, in public or in private, or

(ii) without a hearing;

(b) must not determine the application unless the party who served the notice—

(i) is present, or

(ii) has had a reasonable opportunity to respond;

(c) may adjourn the application; and

(d) may discharge or vary a determination where it can do so under—

(i) section 8B of the *Magistrates' Courts Act* 1980 (ruling at pre-trial hearing in a magistrates' court), or (ii) section 9 of the *Criminal Justice Act* 1987, or section 31 or 40 of the *Criminal Procedure and Investigations Act* 1996 (ruling at preparatory or other pre-trial hearing in the Crown Court).

Unopposed hearsay evidence

34.4.—(1) This rule applies where— **G–202**

171

    (a) a party has served notice to introduce hearsay evidence under rule 34.2; and

    (b) no other party has applied to the court to determine an objection to the introduction of the evidence.

(2) The court will treat the evidence as if it were admissible by agreement.

Court's power to vary requirements under this Part

G–203　　**34.5.**—(1) The court may—

    (a) shorten or extend (even after it has expired) a time limit under this Part;

    (b) allow an application or notice to be in a different form to one set out in the Practice Direction, or to be made or given orally;

    (c) dispense with the requirement for notice to introduce hearsay evidence.

(2) A party who wants an extension of time must—

    (a) apply when serving the application or notice for which it is needed; and

    (b) explain the delay.

[The next paragraph is § G-207.]

PART 35 EVIDENCE OF BAD CHARACTER

Contents of this Part

When this Part applies

G–207　　**35.1.** This Part applies—

    (a) in a magistrates' court and in the Crown Court;

    (b) where a party wants to introduce evidence of bad character, within the meaning of section 98 of the *Criminal Justice Act* 2003.

Content of application or notice

G–208　　**35.2.**—(1) A party who wants to introduce evidence of bad character must—

    (a) make an application under rule 35.3, where it is evidence of a non-defendant's bad character;

    (b) give notice under rule 35.4, where it is evidence of a defendant's bad character; and

(2) An application or notice must—

    (a) set out the facts of the misconduct on which that party relies,

    (b) explain how that party will prove those facts (whether by certificate of conviction, other official record, or other evidence), if another party disputes them, and

    (c) explain why the evidence is admissible.

Application to introduce evidence of a non-defendant's bad character

G–209　　**35.3.**—(1) This rule applies where a party wants to introduce evidence of the bad character of a person other than the defendant.

(2) That party must serve an application to do so on—

    (a) the court officer; and

    (b) each other party.

(3) The applicant must serve the application—

    (a) as soon as reasonably practicable; and in any event

(b) not more than 14 days after the prosecutor discloses material on which the application is based (if the prosecutor is not the applicant).

(4) A party who objects to the introduction of the evidence must—

(a) serve notice on—

    (i) the court officer, and

    (ii) each other party not more than 14 days after service of the application; and

(b) in the notice explain, as applicable—

    (i) which, if any, facts of the misconduct set out in the application that party disputes,

    (ii) what, if any, facts of the misconduct that party admits instead,

    (iii) why the evidence is not admissible, and

    (iv) any other objection to the application.

(5) The court—

(a) may determine an application—

    (i) at a hearing, in public or in private, or

    (ii) without a hearing;

(b) must not determine the application unless each party other than the applicant—

    (i) is present, or

    (ii) has had at least 14 days in which to serve a notice of objection;

(c) may adjourn the application; and

(d) may discharge or vary a determination where it can do so under—

    (i) section 8B of the *Magistrates' Courts Act* 1980 (ruling at pre-trial hearing in a magistrates' court), or

    (ii) section 9 of the*Criminal Justice Act* 1987, or section 31 or 40 of the *Criminal Procedure and Investigations Act* 1996 (ruling at preparatory or other pre-trial hearing in the Crown Court).

Notice to introduce evidence of a defendant's bad character

35.4.—(1) This rule applies where a party wants to introduce evidence of a defendant's bad **G–210** character.

(2) That party must serve notice on—

(a) the court officer; and

(b) each other party.

(3) A prosecutor who wants to introduce such evidence must serve the notice not more than 14 days after the defendant pleads not guilty.

(4) A co-defendant who wants to introduce such evidence must serve the notice—

(a) as soon as reasonably practicable; and in any event

(b) not more than 14 days after the prosecutor discloses material on which the notice is based.

(5) A party who objects to the introduction of the evidence must—

(a) apply to the court to determine the objection;

(b) serve the application on—

    (i) the court officer, and

    (ii) each other party not more than 14 days after service of the notice; and

(c) in the application explain, as applicable—

    (i) which, if any, facts of the misconduct set out in the notice that party disputes,

    (ii) what, if any, facts of the misconduct that party admits instead,

    (iii) why the evidence is not admissible,

    (iv) why it would be unfair to admit the evidence, and

    (v) any other objection to the notice.

(6) The court—

(a) may determine an application—

    (i) at a hearing, in public or in private, or

    (ii) without a hearing;

(b) must not determine the application unless the party who served the notice—

      (i) is present, or

      (ii) has had a reasonable opportunity to respond;

  (c) may adjourn the application; and

  (d) may discharge or vary a determination where it can do so under—

      (i) section 8B of the Magistrates' Courts Act 1980 (ruling at pre-trial hearing in a magistrates' court), or

      (ii) section 9 of the Criminal Justice Act 1987, or section 31 or 40 of the Criminal Procedure and Investigations Act 1996 (ruling at preparatory or other pre-trial hearing in the Crown Court).

(7) A party entitled to receive a notice may waive that entitlement by so informing—

  (a) the party who would have served it; and

  (b) the court.

Reasons for decisions

G–211　　**35.5.** The court must announce at a hearing in public (but in the absence of the jury, if there is one) the reasons for a decision—

  (a) to admit evidence as evidence of bad character, or to refuse to do so; or

  (b) to direct an acquittal or a retrial under section 107 of the *Criminal Justice Act 2003*.

Court's power to vary requirements under this Part

G–212　　**35.6.**—(1) The court may—

  (a) shorten or extend (even after it has expired) a time limit under this Part;

  (b) allow an application or notice to be in a different form to one set out in the Practice Direction, or to be made or given orally;

  (c) dispense with a requirement for notice to introduce evidence of a defendant's bad character.

(2) A party who wants an extension of time must—

  (a) apply when serving the application or notice for which it is needed; and

  (b) explain the delay.

[The next paragraph is § G-216.]

PART 36 EVIDENCE OF A COMPLAINANT'S PREVIOUS SEXUAL BEHAVIOUR

Contents of this Part

When this Part applies

G–216　　**36.1.** This Part applies in magistrates' courts and in the Crown Court where a defendant wants to—

  (a) introduce evidence; or

  (b) cross-examine a witness about a complainant's sexual behaviour despite the prohibition in section 41 of the *Youth Justice and Criminal Evidence Act* 1999.

Application for permission to introduce evidence or cross-examine

G–217　　**36.2.** The defendant must apply for permission to do so—

(a) in writing; and

(b) not more than 28 days after the prosecutor has complied or purported to comply with section 3 of the *Criminal Procedure and Investigations Act* 1996 (disclosure by prosecutor).

Content of application

36.3. The application must—　　　　　　　　　　　　　　　　　　　　**G–218**

(a) identify the issue to which the defendant says the complainant's sexual behaviour is relevant;

(b) give particulars of—

    (i) any evidence that the defendant wants to introduce, and

    (ii) any questions that the defendant wants to ask;

(c) identify the exception to the prohibition in section 41 of the *Youth Justice and Criminal Evidence Act* 1999 on which the defendant relies; and

(d) give the name and date of birth of any witness whose evidence about the complainant's sexual behaviour the defendant wants to introduce.

Service of application

36.4. The defendant must serve the application on the court officer and all other parties.　　**G–219**

Reply to application

36.5. A party who wants to make representations about an application under rule 36.2 **G–220** must—

(a) do so in writing not more than 14 days after receiving it; and

(b) serve those representations on the court officer and all other parties.

Application for special measures

36.6. If the court allows an application under rule 36.2 then—　　　　　　　　**G–221**

(a) a party may apply not more than 14 days later for a special measures direction or for the variation of an existing special measures direction; and

(b) the court may shorten the time for opposing that application.

Court's power to vary requirements under this Part

36.7. The court may shorten or extend (even after it has expired) a time limit under this **G–222** Part.

PART 37 TRIAL AND SENTENCE IN A MAGISTRATES' COURT

Contents of this Part

Duty of justices' legal adviser rule	r.37.14 (*post*, G-229g)
Duty of court officer	r.37.15 (*post*, G-229h)

When this Part applies

G–223
    37.1.—(1) This Part applies in a magistrates' court where—
      (a) the court tries a case; or
      (b) the defendant pleads guilty.
    (2) Where the defendant is under 18, in this Part—
      (a) a reference to convicting the defendant includes a reference to finding the defendant guilty of an offence; and
      (b) a reference to sentence includes a reference to an order made on a finding of guilt.

General rules

G–224
    37.2.—(1) Where this Part applies—
      (a) the general rule is that the hearing must be in public; but
      (b) the court may exercise any power it has to—
        (i) impose reporting restrictions,
        (ii) withhold information from the public, or
        (iii) order a hearing in private; and
      (c) unless the court otherwise directs, only the following may attend a hearing in a youth court—
        (i) the parties and their legal representatives,
        (ii) a defendant's parents, guardian or other supporting adult,
        (iii) a witness,
        (iv) anyone else directly concerned in the case, and
        (v) a representative of a news-gathering or reporting organisation.
    (2) Unless already done, the justices' legal adviser or the court must—
      (a) read the allegation of the offence to the defendant;
      (b) explain, in terms the defendant can understand (with help, if necessary)—
        (i) the allegation, and
        (ii) what the procedure at the hearing will be;
      (c) ask whether the defendant has been advised about the potential effect on sentence of a guilty plea;
      (d) ask whether the defendant pleads guilty or not guilty; and
      (e) take the defendant's plea.
    (3) The court may adjourn the hearing—
      (a) at any stage, to the same or to another magistrates' court; or
      (b) to a youth court, where the court is not itself a youth court and the defendant is under 18.

Procedure on plea of not guilty

G–225
    37.3.—(1) This rule applies—
      (a) if the defendant has—
        (i) entered a plea of not guilty, or
        (ii) not entered a plea; or
      (b) if, in either case, it appears to the court that there may be grounds for making a hospital order without convicting the defendant.
    (2) If a not guilty plea was taken on a previous occasion, the justices' legal adviser or the court must ask the defendant to confirm that plea.
    (3) In the following sequence—
      (a) the prosecutor may summarise the prosecution case, identifying the relevant law and facts;
      (b) the prosecutor must introduce the evidence on which the prosecution case relies;
      (c) at the conclusion of the prosecution case, on the defendant's application or on its own initiative, the court—

   (i) may acquit on the ground that the prosecution evidence is insufficient for any reasonable court properly to convict, but

   (ii) must not do so unless the prosecutor has had an opportunity to make representations;

(d) the justices' legal adviser or the court must explain, in terms the defendant can understand (with help, if necessary)—

   (i) the right to give evidence, and

   (ii) the potential effect of not doing so at all, or of refusing to answer a question while doing so;

(e) the defendant may introduce evidence;

(f) a party may introduce further evidence if it is then admissible (for example, because it is in rebuttal of evidence already introduced) ;

(g) the prosecutor may make final representations in support of the prosecution case, where—

   (i) the defendant is represented by a legal representative, or

   (ii) whether represented or not, the defendant has introduced evidence other than his or her own; and

(h) the defendant may make final representations in support of the defence case.

(4) Where a party wants to introduce evidence or make representations after that party's opportunity to do so under paragraph (3), the court—

(a) may refuse to receive any such evidence or representations; and

(b) must not receive any such evidence or representations after it has announced its verdict.

(5) If the court—

(a) convicts the defendant; or

(b) makes a hospital order instead of doing so, it must give sufficient reasons to explain its decision.

(6) If the court acquits the defendant, it may—

(a) give an explanation of its decision; and

(b) exercise any power it has to make—

   (i) a civil behaviour order,

   (ii) a costs order.

Evidence of a witness in person

37.4.—(1) This rule applies where a party wants to introduce evidence by calling a witness to **G–226** give that evidence in person.

(2) Unless the court otherwise directs—

(a) a witness waiting to give evidence must not wait inside the courtroom, unless that witness is—

   (i) a party, or

   (ii) an expert witness;

(b) a witness who gives evidence in the courtroom must do so from the place provided for that purpose; and

(c) a witness' address must not be announced unless it is relevant to an issue in the case.

(3) Unless other legislation otherwise provides, before giving evidence a witness must take an oath or affirm.

(4) In the following sequence—

(a) the party who calls a witness must ask questions in examination-in-chief;

(b) every other party may ask questions in cross-examination;

(c) the party who called the witness may ask questions in re-examination;

(d) at any time while giving evidence, a witness may refer to a record of that witness' recollection of events, if other legislation so permits;

(e) the party who calls a witness, in examination-in-chief may ask that witness to adopt all or part of such a record as part of that witness' evidence, but only if—

   (i) the parties agree, and

   (ii) the court so permits;

(f) if the witness adopts any part of such a record—

   (i) that part must be read aloud, or

   (ii) with the court's permission, its contents may be summarised aloud.

  (5) The justices' legal adviser or the court may—

   (a) ask a witness questions; and in particular

   (b) where the defendant is not represented, ask any question necessary in the defendant's interests.

Evidence by written statement

G–227 **37.5.**—(1) This rule applies where a party introduces in evidence the written statement of a witness.

  (2) The party introducing the statement must read or summarise aloud those parts that are relevant to the issues in the case.

Evidence by admission

G–228 **37.6.**—(1) This rule applies where—

   (a) a party introduces in evidence a fact admitted by another party; or

   (b) parties jointly admit a fact.

  (2) Unless the court otherwise directs, a written record must be made of the admission.

Procedure on plea of guilty

G–229 **37.7.**—(1) This rule applies if—

   (a) the defendant pleads guilty; and

   (b) the court is satisfied that the plea represents a clear acknowledgement of guilt.

  (2) The court may convict the defendant without receiving evidence.

Written guilty plea: special rules

G–229a **37.8.**—(1) This rule applies where—

   (a) the offence alleged—

    (i) can be tried only in a magistrates' court, and

    (ii) is not one specified under section 12(1)(a) of the Magistrates' Courts Act 1980;

   (b) the defendant is at least 16 years old;

   (c) the prosecutor has served on the defendant—

    (i) the summons or requisition,

    (ii) the material on which the prosecutor relies to set out the facts of the offence and to provide information relevant to sentence,

    (iii) a notice that the procedure set out in this rule applies, and

    (iv) a notice for the defendant's use if the defendant wants to plead guilty without attending court; and

   (d) the prosecutor has served on the court officer—

    (i) copies of those documents, and

    (ii) a certificate of service of those documents on the defendant.

  (2) A defendant who wants to plead guilty without attending court must, before the hearing date specified in the summons or requisition—

   (a) serve a notice of guilty plea on the court officer; and

   (b) include with that notice any representations that the defendant wants the court to consider on that date.

  (3) A defendant who wants to withdraw such a notice must notify the court officer in writing before the hearing date.

  (4) The court may accept such a guilty plea on the hearing date, and if it does so must take account only of—

   (a) the material served by the prosecutor on the defendant under this rule; and

   (b) any representations by the defendant.

  (5) With the defendant's agreement, the court may deal with the case in the same way as under paragraph (4) where the defendant—

   (a) is present; and

   (b) has served a notice of guilty plea under paragraph (2); or

   (c) pleads guilty there and then.

Application to withdraw a guilty plea

37.9.—(1) This rule applies where the defendant wants to withdraw a guilty plea.   **G–229b**

(2) The defendant must apply to do so—

    (a) as soon as practicable after becoming aware of the reasons for doing so; and

    (b) before sentence.

(3) Unless the court otherwise directs, the application must be in writing and the defendant must serve it on—

    (a) the court officer; and

    (b) the prosecutor.

(4) The application must—

    (a) explain why it would be unjust not to allow the defendant to withdraw the guilty plea;

    (b) identify—

        (i) any witness that the defendant wants to call, and

        (ii) any other proposed evidence; and

    (c) say whether the defendant waives legal professional privilege, giving any relevant name and date.

Procedure if the court convicts

37.10.—(1) This rule applies if the court convicts the defendant.   **G–229c**

(2) The court—

    (a) may exercise its power to require—

        (i) a statement of the defendant's financial circumstances,

        (ii) a pre-sentence report; and

    (b) may (and in some circumstances must) remit the defendant to a youth court for sentence where—

        (i) the defendant is under 18, and

        (ii) the convicting court is not itself a youth court.

(3) The prosecutor must—

    (a) summarise the prosecution case, if the sentencing court has not heard evidence;

    (b) identify any offence to be taken into consideration in sentencing;

    (c) provide information relevant to sentence; and

    (d) where it is likely to assist the court, identify any other matter relevant to sentence, including—

        (i) aggravating and mitigating factors,

        (ii) the legislation applicable, and

        (iii) any guidelines issued by the Sentencing Guidelines Council, or guideline cases.

(4) The defendant must provide information relevant to sentence, including details of financial circumstances.

(5) Where the defendant pleads guilty but wants to be sentenced on a different basis to that disclosed by the prosecution case—

    (a) the defendant must set out that basis in writing, identifying what is in dispute;

    (b) the court may invite the parties to make representations about whether the dispute is material to sentence; and

    (c) if the court decides that it is a material dispute, the court will—

        (i) invite such further representations or evidence as it may require, and

        (ii) decide the dispute.

(6) Where the court has power to order the endorsement of the defendant's driving licence, or power to order the disqualification of the defendant from holding or obtaining one—

    (a) if other legislation so permits, a defendant who wants the court not to exercise that power must introduce the evidence or information on which the defendant relies;

    (b) the prosecutor may introduce evidence; and

    (c) the parties may make representations about that evidence or information.

(7) Before the court passes sentence—

    (a) the court must—

    (i) give the defendant an opportunity to make representations and introduce evidence relevant to sentence, and

    (ii) where the defendant is under 18, give the defendant's parents, guardian or other supporting adult, if present, such an opportunity as well; and

  (b) the justices' legal adviser or the court must elicit any further information relevant to sentence that the court may require.

(8) If the court requires more information, it may exercise its power to adjourn the hearing for not more than—

  (a) 3 weeks at a time, if the defendant will be in custody; or

  (b) 4 weeks at a time.

(9) When the court has taken into account all the evidence, information and any report available, the general rule is that the court will—

  (a) pass sentence there and then;

  (b) explain the sentence, the reasons for it, and its effect, in terms the defendant can understand (with help, if necessary); and

  (c) consider exercising any power it has to make a costs or other order.

(10) Despite the general rule—

  (a) the court must adjourn the hearing if—

    (i) the case started with a summons or requisition, and the defendant is absent, and

    (ii) the court considers passing a custodial sentence, or

    (iii) the court considers imposing a disqualification (unless it has already adjourned the hearing to give the defendant an opportunity to attend);

  (b) the court may exercise any power it has to—

    (i) commit the defendant to the Crown Court for sentence (and in some cases it must do so), or

    (ii) defer sentence for up to 6 months.

Procedure where a party is absent

G–229d   **37.11.**—(1) This rule—

  (a) applies where a party is absent; but

  (b) does not apply where the defendant has served a notice of guilty plea under rule 37.8 (written guilty plea: special rules).

(2) Where the prosecutor is absent, the court may—

  (a) if it has received evidence, deal with the case as if the prosecutor were present; and

  (b) in any other case—

    (i) enquire into the reasons for the prosecutor's absence, and

    (ii) if satisfied there is no good reason, exercise its power to dismiss the allegation.

(3) Where the defendant is absent—

  (a) the general rule is that the court will proceed as if the defendant—

    (i) were present, and

    (ii) had pleaded not guilty (unless a plea already has been taken) and the court must give reasons if it does not do so; but

  (b) the general rule does not apply if the defendant is under 18;

  (c) the general rule is subject to the court being satisfied that—

    (i) any summons or requisition was served on the defendant a reasonable time before the hearing, or

    (ii) in a case in which the hearing has been adjourned, the defendant had reasonable notice of where and when it would resume;

  (d) the general rule is subject also to rule 37.10(10)(a) (restrictions on passing sentence in the defendant's absence); and

  (e) the hearing must be treated as if it had not taken place at all if—

    (i) the case started with a summons or requisition,

    (ii) the defendant makes a statutory declaration of not having found out about the case until after the hearing began, and

    (iii) the defendant serves that declaration on the court officer not more than 21 days after the date of finding out about the case, unless the court extends that time limit.

(4) Where the defendant is absent, the court—

(a) must exercise its power to issue a warrant for the defendant's arrest, if it passes a custodial sentence; and

(b) may exercise its power to do so in any other case, if it does not apply the general rule in paragraph (3)(a) of this rule about proceeding in the defendant's absence.

Provision of documents for the court

37.12.—(1) This rule applies where a party—   **G–229e**

(a) introduces in evidence any document; or

(b) relies on any other document in the presentation of that party's case

(2) Unless the court otherwise directs, that party must supply sufficient copies of such a document for—

(a) each other party;

(b) the court; and

(c) the justices' legal adviser.

Place of trial

37.13.—(1) Unless the court otherwise directs, the hearing must take place in a courtroom **G–229f** provided by the Lord Chancellor.

(2) Where the hearing takes place in Wales—

(a) any party or witness may use the Welsh language; and

(b) if practicable, at least one member of the court must be Welsh-speaking.

Duty of justices' legal adviser

37.14.—(1) A justices' legal adviser must attend, unless the court—   **G–229g**

(a) includes a District Judge (Magistrates' Courts); and

(b) otherwise directs.

(2) A justices' legal adviser must—

(a) give the court legal advice; and

(b) if necessary, attend the members of the court outside the courtroom to give such advice; but

(c) inform the parties of any such advice given outside the courtroom.

(3) A justices' legal adviser must—

(a) assist an unrepresented defendant;

(b) assist the court by—

   (i) making a note of the substance of any oral evidence or representations, to help the court recall that information,

   (ii) if the court rules inadmissible part of a written statement introduced in evidence, marking that statement in such a way as to make that clear,

   (iii) ensuring that an adequate record is kept of the court's decisions and the reasons for them, and

   (iv) making any announcement, other than of the verdict or sentence.

(4) Where the defendant has served a notice of guilty plea to which rule 37.8 (written guilty plea: special rules) applies, a justices' legal adviser must read aloud to the court—

(a) the material on which the prosecutor relies to set out the facts of the offence and to provide information relevant to sentence (or summarise any written statement included in that material, if the court so directs); and

(b) any written representations by the defendant.

Duty of court officer

37.15. The court officer must—   **G–229h**

(a) serve on each party notice of where and when an adjourned hearing will resume, unless—

   (i) the party was present when that was arranged, or

   (ii) the defendant has served a notice of guilty plea to which rule 37.8 applies, and the adjournment is for not more than 4 weeks;

(b) if the reason for the adjournment was to postpone sentence, include that reason in any such notice to the defendant;

(c) unless the court otherwise directs, make available to the parties any written report to which rule 37.10 applies;

(d) where the court has ordered a defendant to provide information under section 25 of the *Road Traffic Offenders Act* 1988, serve on the defendant notice of that order unless the defendant was present when it was made;

(e) serve on the prosecutor—

   (i) any notice of guilty plea to which rule 37.8 applies, and

   (ii) any declaration served under rule 37.11(3)(e) that the defendant did not know about the case;

(f) record in the magistrates' court register the court's reasons for not proceeding in the defendant's absence where rule 37.11(3)(a) applies; and

(g) give the court such other assistance as it requires.

[The next paragraph is § G-238.]

PART 40 TAINTED ACQUITTALS

Contents of this Part

Time of certification

G–238   **40.1.** Where a person is convicted of an offence as referred to in section 54(1)(b) of the *Criminal Procedure and Investigations Act* 1996 and it appears to the court before which the conviction has taken place that the provisions of section 54(2) are satisfied, the court shall make the certification referred to in section 54(2) at any time following conviction but no later than—

(a) immediately after the court sentences or otherwise deals with that person in respect of the offence; or

(b) where the court, being a magistrates' court, commits that person to the Crown Court, or remits him to another magistrates' court, to be dealt with in respect of the offence, immediately after he is so committed or remitted, as the case may be; or

(c) (c) where that person is a child or young person and the court, being the Crown Court, remits him to a youth court to be dealt with in respect of the offence, immediately after he is so remitted.

Form of certification in the Crown Court

G–239   **40.2.** A certification referred to in section 54(2) of the *Criminal Procedure and Investigations Act* 1996 by the Crown Court shall be drawn up in the form set out in the Practice Direction.

Service of a copy of the certification

G–240   **40.3.** Where a magistrates' court or the Crown Court makes a certification as referred to in section 54(2) of the *Criminal Procedure and Investigations Act* 1996, the court officer shall, as soon as practicable after the drawing up of the form, serve a copy on the acquitted person referred to in the certification, on the prosecutor in the proceedings which led to the acquittal, and, where the acquittal has taken place before a court other than, or at a different place to, the court where the certification has been made, on—

    (a) the clerk of the magistrates' court before which the acquittal has taken place; or

    (b) the Crown Court officer at the place where the acquittal has taken place.

Entry in register or records in relation to the conviction which occasioned certification

40.4. A clerk of a magistrates' court or an officer of a Crown Court which has made a certifi- **G–241** cation under section 54(2) of the *Criminal Procedure and Investigations Act* 1996 shall enter in the register or records, in relation to the conviction which occasioned the certification, a note of the fact that certification has been made, the date of certification, the name of the acquitted person referred to in the certification, a description of the offence of which the acquitted person has been acquitted, the date of the acquittal, and the name of the court before which the acquittal has taken place.

Entry in the register or records in relation to the acquittal

40.5. . The court officer of the court before which an acquittal has taken place shall, as soon **G–242** as practicable after receipt of a copy of a form recording a certification under section 54(2) of the *Criminal Procedure and Investigations Act* 1996 relating to the acquittal, enter in the register or records a note that the certification has been made, the date of the certification, the name of the court which has made the certification, the name of the person whose conviction occasioned the making of the certification, and a description of the offence of which that person has been convicted. Where the certification has been made by the same court as the court before which the acquittal has occurred, sitting at the same place, the entry shall be made as soon as practicable after the making of the certification. In the case of an acquittal before a magistrates' court, the entry in the register shall be signed by the clerk of the court.

Display of copy certification form

40.6.—(1) Where a court makes a certification as referred to in section 54(2) of the *Criminal* **G–243** *Procedure and Investigations Act* 1996, the court officer shall, as soon as practicable after the drawing up of the form, display a copy of that form at a prominent place within court premises to which place the public has access.

(2) Where an acquittal has taken place before a court other than, or at a different place to, the court which has made the certification under section 54(2) of the 1996 Act in relation to the acquittal, the court officer at the court where the acquittal has taken place shall, as soon as practicable after receipt of a copy of the form recording the certification, display a copy of it at a prominent place within court premises to which place the public has access.

(3) The copy of the form referred to in paragraph (1), or the copy referred to in paragraph (2), shall continue to be displayed as referred to, respectively, in those paragraphs at least until the expiry of 28 days from, in the case of paragraph (1), the day on which the certification was made, or, in the case of paragraph (2), the day on which the copy form was received at the court.

Entry in the register or records in relation to decision of High Court

40.7.—(1) The court officer at the court where an acquittal has taken place shall, on receipt **G–244** from the Administrative Court Office of notice of an order made under section 54(3) of the *Criminal Procedure and Investigations Act* 1996 quashing the acquittal, or of a decision not to make such an order, enter in the register or records, in relation to the acquittal, a note of the fact that the acquittal has been quashed by the said order, or that a decision has been made not to make such an order, as the case may be.

(2) The court officer of the court which has made a certification under section 54(2) of the 1996 Act shall, on receipt from the Administrative Court Office of notice of an order made under section 54(3) of that Act quashing the acquittal referred to in the certification, or of a decision not to make such an order, enter in the register or records, in relation to the conviction which occasioned the certification, a note that the acquittal has been quashed by the said order, or that a decision has been made not to make an order, as the case may be.

(3) The entries in the register of a magistrates' court referred to, respectively, in paragraphs (1) and (2) above shall be signed by the magistrates' court officer.

Display of copy of notice received from High Court

G–245   **40.8.**—(1) Where the court officer of a court which has made a certification under section 54(2) of the *Criminal Procedure and Investigations Act* 1996 or before which an acquittal has occurred to which such a certification refers, receives from the Administrative Court Office notice of an order quashing the acquittal concerned, or notice of a decision not to make s uch an order, he shall, as soon as practicable after receiving the notice, display a copy of it at a prominent place within court premises to which place the public has access.

(2) The copy notice referred to in paragraph (1) shall continue to be displayed as referred to in that paragraph at least until the expiry of 28 days from the day on which the notice was received at the court.

[The next paragraph is § G-263.]

PART 42 REMITTAL FROM ONE MAGISTRATES' COURT TO ANOTHER FOR SENTENCE

Contents of this Part

Remittal for sentence

G–263   **42.1.**—(1) Where a magistrates' court remits an offender to some other magistrates' court under section 10 of the *Powers of Criminal Courts (Sentencing) Act* 2000 after convicting him of an offence, the court officer for the convicting court shall send to the court officer for the other court—

  (a) a copy signed by the court officer for the convicting court of the minute or memorandum of the conviction and remittal entered in the register;

  (b) a copy of any note of the evidence given at the trial of the offender, any written statement tendered in evidence and any deposition;

  (c) such documents and articles produced in evidence before the convicting court as have been retained by that court;

  (d) any report relating to the offender considered by the convicting court;

  (e) if the offender is remitted on bail, a copy of the record made by the convicting court in pursuance of section 5 of the Bail Act 1976 relating to such bail and also any recognizance entered into by any person as his surety;

  (f) if the convicting court makes an order under section 148 of the 2000 Act (restitution orders), a copy signed by the court officer for the convicting court of the minute or memorandum of the order entered in the register;

  (g) a copy of any representation order previously made in the same case; and (h) a copy of any application for a representation order.

(2) Where a magistrates' court remits an offender to some other magistrates' court as aforesaid and the other court remits him back to the convicting court under section 10(5) of the 2000 Act, the court officer for the other court shall send to the court officer for the convicting court—

  (a) a copy signed by the court officer for the other court of the minute or memorandum of the remittal back entered in the register;

  (b) if the offender is remitted back on bail, a copy of the record made by the other court in pursuance of section 5 of the Bail Act 1976 relating to such bail and also any recognizance entered into by any person as his surety; and

  (c) all documents and articles sent in pursuance of paragraph (1) of this rule. (3) In this rule 'the offender', 'the convicting court' and 'the other court' have the same meanings as in section 10 of the 2000 Act.

PART 43 COMMITTAL TO THE CROWN COURT FOR SENTENCE

Contents of this Part

Committals for sentence, etc

43.1.—(1) Where a magistrates' court commits an offender to the Crown Court under the **G–264** *Vagrancy Act* 1824, sections 3, 6, 116(3)(b) or 120(2)(a) of the*Powers of Criminal Courts (Sentencing) Act* 2000 or section 6 of the *Bail Act* 1976 after convicting him of an offence, the magistrates' court officer shall send to the Crown Court officer—

- (a) a copy signed by the magistrates' court officer of the minute or memorandum of the conviction entered in the register;
- (b) copy of any note of the evidence given at the trial of the offender, any written statement tendered in evidence and any deposition;
- (c) such documents and articles produced in evidence before the court as have been retained by the court;
- (d) any report relating to the offender considered by the court;
- (e) if the offender is committed on bail, a copy of the record made in pursuance of section 5 of the 1976 Act relating to such bail and also any recognizance entered into by any person as his surety;
- (f) if the court imposes under section 26 of the *Road Traffic Offenders Act* 1988 an interim disqualification for holding or obtaining a licence under Part III of the *Road Traffic Act* 1988, a statement of the date of birth and sex of the offender;
- (g) if the court makes an order under section 148 of the 2000 Act (restitution orders), a copy signed by the clerk of the convicting court of the minute or memorandum of the order entered in the register; and
- (h) any documents relating to an appeal by the prosecution against the granting of bail.

(2) Where a magistrates' court commits an offender to the Crown Court under the *Vagrancy Act* 1824 or sections 3, 6 or 120(2) of the 2000 Act and the magistrates' court on that occasion imposes, under section 26 of the *Road Traffic Offenders Act* 1988, an interim disqualification for holding or obtaining a licence under Part III of the *Road Traffic Act* 1988, the magistrates' court officer shall give notice of the interim disqualification to the Crown Court officer.

(3) Where a magistrates' court commits a person on bail to the Crown Court under any of the enactments mentioned in paragraph (2) of this rule or under section 6 of the *Bail Act* 1976 the magistrates' court officer shall give notice thereof in writing to the governor of the prison to which persons of the sex of the person committed are committed by that court if committed in custody for trial and also, if the person committed is under the age of 21, to the governor of the remand centre to which he would have been committed if the court had refused him bail.

Committal for order restricting discharge, etc

43.2. Where a magistrates' court commits an offender to the Crown Court either—   **G–265**

- (a) under section 43 of the *Mental Health Act* 1983 with a view to the making of a hospital order with an order restricting his discharge; or
- (b) under section 3 of the *Powers of Criminal Courts (Sentencing) Act* 2000, as modified by section 43(4) of the 1983 Act, with a view to the passing of a more severe sentence than the magistrates' court has power to inflict if such an order is not made, the magistrates' court officer shall send to the Crown Court officer—
  - (i) the copies, documents and articles specified in rule 43.1,
  - (ii) any written evidence about the offender given by a medical practitioner under section 37 of the 1983 Act or a copy of a note of any oral evidence so given,

    (iii) the name and address of the hospital the managers of which have agreed to admit the offender if a hospital order is made, and

    (iv) if the offender has been admitted to a hospital under section 37 of the 1983 Act, the name and address of that hospital.

PART 45 BREACH, REVOCATION AND AMENDMENT OF COMMUNITY AND OTHER ORDERS IN A MAGISTRATES' COURT

Contents of this Part

G–266   **44.1.** This Part applies in a magistrates' court where—

  (a) the officer responsible for a defendant's compliance with an order to which applies—

    (i) Schedule 3, 5, 7 or 8 to the *Powers of Criminal Courts (Sentencing) Act* 2000,

    (ii) Schedule 8 to the *Criminal Justice Act* 2003, or

    (iii) Schedule 2 to the *Criminal Justice and Immigration Act* 2008 wants the court to deal with that defendant for failure to comply;

  (b) one of the following wants the court to exercise any power it has to revoke or amend such an order—

    (i) the responsible officer,

    (ii) the defendant, or

    (iii) a person affected by the order; or

  (c) the court considers exercising on its own initiative any power it has to revoke or amend such an order

Application by responsible officer

G–267   **44.2.**—(1) This rule applies where—

  (a) the responsible officer wants the court to—

    (i) deal with a defendant for failure to comply with an order to which this Part applies, or

    (ii) revoke or amend such an order; or

  (b) the court considers exercising on its own initiative any power it has to—

    (i) revoke or amend such an order, and

    (ii) summon the defendant to attend for that purpose.

    (2) Rules 7.2 to 7.4, which deal, among other things, with starting a prosecution in a magistrates' court by information and summons, apply—

  (a) as if—

    (i) a reference in those rules to an allegation of an offence included a reference to an allegation of failure to comply with an order to which this Part applies, and

    (ii) a reference to the prosecutor included a reference to the responsible officer; and

  (b) with the necessary consequential modifications.

Application by defendant or person affected

G–267a   **44.3.**—(1) This rule applies where—

  (a) the defendant wants the court to exercise any power it has to revoke or amend an order to which this Part applies; or

(b) a person affected by such an order wants the court to exercise any such power.

(2)   That defendant, or person affected, must—

    (a) apply in writing, explaining why the order should be revoked or amended; and

    (b) serve the application on—

        (i)   the court officer,

        (ii) the responsible officer, and

        (iii) as appropriate, the defendant or the person affected.

Procedure on application by responsible officer

44.4.—(1) Except for rule 37.8, the rules in Part 37, which deal with the procedure at a trial **G–267b**
in a magistrates' court, apply—

    (a) as if—

        (i)   a reference in those rules to an allegation of an offence included a refer-
ence to an allegation of failure to comply with an order to which this Part
applies,

        (ii) a reference to the court's verdict included a reference to the court's deci-
sion to revoke or amend such an order, or to exercise any other power it
has to deal with the defendant, and

        (iii) a reference to the court's sentence included a reference to the exercise of
any such power; and

    (b) with the necessary consequential modifications.

(2)   The court officer must serve on each party any order revoking or amending an order to which this Part applies.

PART 46 DEFERRED SENTENCE

Contents of this Part

Further conviction in magistrates' court after sentence deferred

45.1. Where under section 1 of the *Powers of Criminal Courts (Sentencing) Act* 2000 a **G–268**
court has deferred passing sentence on an offender and before the expiration of the period of
deferment he is convicted of any offence by a magistrates' court, the court officer for the convicting court shall, if the court which deferred passing sentence on the earlier occasion was another
magistrates' court or the Crown Court, give notice of the conviction to the court officer for that
court.

[The next paragraph is § G-270.]

PART 47 SUSPENDED SENTENCES OF IMPRISONMENT

Contents of this Part

Entries in magistrates' court register in respect of suspended sentences

47.1.—(1) Where under section 119 of the *Powers of Criminal Courts (Sentencing) Act* **G–270**
2000 a magistrates' court deals with a person in respect of a suspended sentence otherwise than
by making an order under section 119(1)(a), the court shall cause to be entered in the register its
reasons for its opinion that it would be unjust to make such an order.

(2) Where an offender is dealt with under section 119 of the 2000 Act in respect of a suspended sentence passed by a magistrates' court, the court officer shall note this in the register, or where the suspended sentence was not passed by that court, shall notify the court officer for the court by which it was passed who shall note it in the register.

Suspended sentence supervision orders

G–271   **47.2.**—(1) Where a magistrates' court makes an order under section 119(1)(a) or (b) of the Powers of Criminal Courts (Sentencing) Act 2000 in respect of a person who is subject to a suspended sentence supervision order, the court officer shall note this in the register, or where that order was not made by that court, shall—

(a) if the order was made by another magistrates' court, notify the court officer for that court who shall note the court register accordingly; or

(b) if the order was made by the Crown Court, notify the Crown Court officer.

(2) Where a magistrates' court discharges a suspended sentence supervision order under section 124(1) of the 2000 Act, the court officer shall note this in the register, or where that order was not made by that court, shall—

(a) if the order was made by another magistrates' court, notify the court officer for that court who shall note the court register accordingly; or

(b) if the order was made by the Crown Court, notify the Crown Court officer.

PART 48 COMMUNITY PENALTIES

Contents of this Part

Curfew order or requirement with electronic monitoring requirement

G–272   **48.1.**—(1) This rule applies where the Crown Court makes—

(a) a curfew order with an electronic monitoring requirement under section 35 of the Crime (Sentences) Act 1997 or under sections 37 and 36B of the *Powers of Criminal Courts (Sentencing) Act* 2000; or

(b) a community rehabilitation order with curfew and electronic monitoring requirements under section 41 of and paragraph 7 of Schedule 2 to the 2000 Act.

(2) The court officer shall serve notice of the order on the person in respect of whom it is made by way of pages 1 and 2 of the form set out in the Practice Direction.

(3) The court officer shall serve notice of the order on the person responsible for electronically monitoring compliance with it by way of the form set out in the Practice Direction.

(4) Where any community order additional to the curfew order has been made in respect of the offender, the court officer shall serve a copy of the notice required by paragraph (3) on the local probation board or Youth Offending Team responsible for the offender.

PART 49 HOSPITAL AND GUARDIANSHIP ORDERS

Contents of this Part

Remand by magistrates' court for medical inquiries

G–273   **49.1.** On exercising the powers conferred by section 11 of the *Powers of Criminal Courts (Sentencing) Act* 2000 a magistrates' court shall—

(a) where the accused is remanded in custody, send to the institution or place to which he is committed; or

(b) where the accused is remanded on bail, send to the institution or place at which, or the person by whom, he is to be examined, a statement of the reasons why the court is of opinion that an inquiry ought to be made into his physical or mental condition and of any information before the court about his physical or mental condition.

Hospital or guardianship order imposed by a magistrates' court

49.2.—(1) The magistrates' court by which a hospital order is made under section 37 of the **G–274** *Mental Health Act* 1983 shall send to the hospital named in the order such information in the possession of the court as it considers likely to be of assistance in dealing with the patient to whom the order relates, and in particular such information about the mental condition, character and antecedents of the patient and the nature of the offence.

(2) The magistrates' court by which a guardianship order is made under section 37 of the 1983 Act shall send to the local health authority named therein as guardian or, as the case may be, the local health authority for the area in which the person so named resides, such information in the possession of the court as it considers likely to be of assistance in dealing with the patient to whom the order relates and in particular such information about the mental condition, character and antecedents of the patient and the nature of the offence.

(3) The magistrates' court by which an offender is ordered to be admitted to hospital under section 44 of the 1983 Act shall send to the hospital such information in the possession of the court as it considers likely to assist in the treatment of the offender until his case is dealt with by the Crown Court.

PART 50 CIVIL BEHAVIOUR ORDERS AFTER VERDICT OR FINDING

Contents of this Part

When this Part applies

50.1.—(1) This Part applies in magistrates' courts and in the Crown Court where the court **G–275** could decide to make, vary or revoke a civil order—

    (a) under a power that the court can exercise after reaching a verdict or making a finding, and

    (b) that requires someone to do, or not do, something.

(2) A reference to a 'behaviour order' in this Part is a reference to any such order.

(3) A reference to 'hearsay evidence' in this Part is a reference to evidence consisting of hearsay within the meaning of section 1(2) of the*Civil Evidence Act* 1995.

Behaviour orders: general rules

50.2.—(1) The court must not make a behaviour order unless the person to whom it is **G–276** directed has had an opportunity—

    (a) to consider what order is proposed and why; and

    (b) to make representations at a hearing (whether or not that person in fact attends).

(2) That restriction does not apply to making an interim behaviour order.

(3) But an interim behaviour order has no effect unless the person to whom it is directed—

(a) is present when it is made; or

(b) is handed a document recording the order not more than 7 days after it is made.

Application for behaviour order: special rules

G–277   **50.3.**—(1) This rule applies where a prosecutor wants the court to make—

(a) an anti-social behaviour order; or

(b) a serious crime prevention order, if the defendant is convicted.

(2) The prosecutor must serve a notice of intention to apply for such an order on—

(a) the court officer;

(b) the defendant against whom the prosecutor wants the court to make the order; and

(c) any person on whom the order would be likely to have a significant adverse effect, as soon as practicable (without waiting for the verdict).

(3) The notice must be in the form set out in the Practice Direction and must—

(a) summarise the relevant facts;

(b) identify the evidence on which the prosecutor relies in support;

(c) attach any written statement that the prosecutor has not already served; and

(d) specify the order that the prosecutor wants the court to make.

(4) The defendant must then—

(a) serve written notice of any evidence on which the defendant relies on—

(i) the court officer, and

(ii) the prosecutor, as soon as practicable (without waiting for the verdict); and

(b) in the notice, identify that evidence and attach any written statement that has not already been served.

(5) This rule does not apply to an application for an interim anti-social behaviour order.

Evidence to assist the court: special rules

G–278   **50.4.**—(1) This rule applies where the court indicates that it may make on its own initiative—

(a) a football banning order;

(b) a restraining order;

(c) an anti-social behaviour order; or

(d) a drinking banning order.

(2) A party who wants the court to take account of any particular evidence before making that decision mustμ

(a) serve notice in writing on—

(i) the court officer, and

(ii) every other party, as soon as practicable (without waiting for the verdict); and

(b) in that notice identify that evidence and attach any written statement that has not already been served.

Application to vary or revoke behaviour order

G–278a   **50.5.**—(1) The court may vary or revoke a behaviour order if—

(a) the legislation under which it is made allows the court to do so; and

(b) one of the following applies—

(i) the prosecutor,

(ii) the person to whom the order is directed,

(iii) any other person mentioned in the order,

(iv) the relevant authority or responsible officer,

(v) the relevant Chief Officer of Police, or

(vi) the Director of Public Prosecutions.

(2) A person applying under this rule must—

(a) apply in writing as soon as practicable after becoming aware of the grounds for doing so, explaining why the order should be varied or revoked; and

(b) serve the application, and any notice under paragraph (3), on the court officer and, as appropriate, anyone listed in paragraph (1)(b).

(3) A party who wants the court to take account of any particular evidence before making its decision must, as soon as practicable—

    (a) serve notice in writing on—
        (i) the court officer, and
        (ii) as appropriate, anyone listed in paragraph (1)(b); and
    (b) in that notice identify the evidence and attach any written statement that has not already been served.

(4) The court may decide an application under this rule with or without a hearing.

(5) But the court must not—
    (a) dismiss an application under this rule unless the applicant has had an opportunity to make representations at a hearing (whether or not the applicant in fact attends); or
    (b) allow an application under this rule unless everyone served with the application has had at least 14 days in which to make representations, including representations about whether there should be a hearing.

(6) Where a person applies under this rule to a magistrates' court—
    (a) the application must be by complaint; and
    (b) the court officer must give notice by summons of any hearing.

Notice of hearsay evidence

50.6.—(1) A party who wants to introduce hearsay evidence must—   **G–278b**
    (a) serve a notice in writing on—
        (i) the court officer, and
        (ii) every other party directly affected; and
    (b) in that notice—
        (i) explain that it is a notice of hearsay evidence,
        (ii) identify that evidence,
        (iii) identify the person who made the statement which is hearsay, or explain why if that person is not identified, and
        (iv) explain why that person will not be called to give oral evidence.

(2) A party may serve one notice under this rule in respect of more than one notice and more than one witness.

Cross-examination of maker of hearsay statement

50.7.—(1) This rule applies where a party wants the court's permission to cross-examine a **G–278c** person who made a statement which another party wants to introduce as hearsay.

(2) The party who wants to cross-examine that person must—
    (a) apply in writing, with reasons, not more than 7 days after service of the notice of hearsay evidence; and
    (b) serve the application on—
        (i) the court officer,
        (ii) the party who served the hearsay evidence notice, and
        (iii) every party on whom the hearsay evidence notice was served.

(3) The court may decide an application under this rule with or without a hearing.

(4) But the court must not—
    (a) dismiss an application under this rule unless the applicant has had an opportunity to make representations at a hearing (whether or not the applicant in fact attends); or
    (b) allow an application under this rule unless everyone served with the application has had at least 7 days in which to make representations, including representations about whether there should be a hearing.

Credibility and consistency of maker of hearsay statement

50.8.—(1) This rule applies where a party wants to challenge the credibility or consistency of **G–278d** a person who made a statement which another party wants to introduce as hearsay.

(2) The party who wants to challenge the credibility or consistency of that person must—
    (a) serve a written notice of intention to do so on—
        (i) the court officer, and
        (ii) the party who served the notice of hearsay evidence not more than 7 days after service of that hearsay evidence notice; and

(b) in the notice, identify any statement or other material on which that party relies.

(3) The party who served the hearsay notice—

(a) may call that person to give oral evidence instead; and

(b) if so, must serve a notice of intention to do so on—

(i) the court officer, and

(ii) every party on whom he served the hearsay notice not more than 7 days after service of the notice under paragraph (2).

Court's power to vary requirements under this Part

G–278e   **50.9.** The court may—

(a) shorten a time limit or extend it (even after it has expired);

(b) allow a notice or application to be given in a different form, or presented orally.

[The next paragraph is § G-280.]

PART 52 ENFORCEMENT OF FINES

Contents of this Part

Notice to defendant of fine or forfeited recognizance

G–280   **52.1.** Where under section 140(1) of the *Powers of Criminal Courts (Sentencing) Act* 2000 or section 67(2) of the *Criminal Justice Act* 1988 a magistrates' court is required to enforce payment of a fine imposed or recognizance forfeited by the Crown Court or where a magistrates' court allows time for payment of a sum adjudged to be paid by a summary conviction, or directs that the sum be paid by instalments, or where the offender is absent when a sum is adjudged to be paid by a summary conviction, the magistrates' court officer shall serve on the offender notice in writing stating the amount of the sum and, if it is to be paid by instalments, the amount of the instalments, the date on which the sum, or each of the instalments, is to be paid and the places and times at which payment may be made; and a warrant of distress or commitment shall not be issued until the preceding provisions of this rule have been complied with.

Payment of fine to be made to magistrates' court officer

G–281   **52.2.**—(1) A person adjudged by the conviction of a magistrates' court to pay any sum shall, unless the court otherwise directs, pay that sum, or any instalment of that sum, to the court officer.

(2) Where payment of any sum or instalment of any sum adjudged to be paid by the conviction or order of a magistrates' court is made to any person other than the court officer, that person, unless he is the person to whom the court has directed payment to be made or, in the case of a child, is the person with whom the child has his home, shall, as soon as may be, account for and, if the court officer so requires, pay over the sum or instalment to the court officer.

(3) Where payment of any sum adjudged to be paid by the conviction or order of a magistrates' court, or any instalment of such a sum, is directed to be made to the court officer for another court, the court officer for the court that adjudged the sum to be paid shall pay over any sums received by him on account of the said sum or instalment to the court officer for that other court.

Duty of magistrates' court officer to give receipt

52.3. The court officer for a magistrates' court shall give or send a receipt to any person who **G–282** makes a payment to him in pursuance of a conviction or order of a magistrates' court and who asks for a receipt.

Application to magistrates' court for further time

52.4. An application under section 75(2) of the *Magistrates' Courts Act* 1980 (further time **G–283** to pay) may, unless the court requires the applicant to attend, be made in writing.

Review of terms of postponement of warrant of commitment by magistrates' court

52.5. An application under section 77(5) of the *Magistrates' Courts Act* 1980 may be made **G–284** in writing or in person.

Notice to defendant before enforcing magistrates' court order

52.6. A warrant of commitment shall not be issued for disobedience to an order of a magis- **G–285** trates' court unless the defendant has been previously served with a copy of the minute of the order, or the order was made in his presence and the warrant is issued on that occasion:

Provided that this paragraph shall not apply to an order to pay money.

Execution of magistrates' court distress warrant

52.7.—(1) A warrant of distress issued for the purpose of levying a sum adjudged to be paid **G–286** by a summary conviction or order—

   (a) shall name or otherwise describe the person against whom the distress is to be levied;

   (b) shall be directed to the constables of the police area in which the warrant is issued or to the civilian enforcement officers for the area in which they are employed, or to a person named in the warrant and shall, subject to, and in accordance with, the provisions of this rule, require them to levy the said sum by distress and sale of the goods belonging to the said person; and

   (c) may where it is directed to the constables of a police area, instead of being executed by any of those constables, be executed by any person under the direction of a constable.

(2) The warrant shall authorise the person charged with the execution of it to take as well any money as any goods of the person against whom the distress is levied; and any money so taken shall be treated as if it were the proceeds of the sale of goods taken under the warrant.

(3) The warrant shall require the person charged with the execution to pay the sum to be levied to the court officer for the court that issued the warrant.

(4) A warrant to which this rule applies may be executed by the persons to whom it was directed or by any of the following persons, whether or not the warrant was directed to them—

   (a) A constable for any police area in England and Wales, acting in his own police area;

   (b) where the warrant is one to which section 125A of the *Magistrates' Courts Act* 1980 applies, a civilian enforcement officer within the meaning of section 125A of the 1980 Act; and

(c) where the warrant is one to which section 125A of the 1980 Act applies, any of the individuals described in section 125B(1) of the 1980 Act; and in this rule any reference to the person charged with the execution of a warrant includes any of the above persons who is for the time being authorised to execute the warrant, whether or not they have the warrant in their possession at the time.

(5) A person executing a warrant of distress shall—

(a) either—

  (i) if he has the warrant with him, show it to the person against whom the distress is levied, or

  (ii) otherwise, state where the warrant is and what arrangements may be made to allow the person against whom distress is levied to inspect it;

(b) explain, in ordinary language, the sum for which distress is levied and the reason for the distress;

(c) where the person executing the warrant is one of the persons referred to in paragraph (4)(b) or (c) above, show the person against whom distress is levied a written statement under section 125A(4) of 125B(4) as appropriate; and

(d) in any case, show documentary proof of his identity.

(6) There shall not be taken under the warrant the clothing or bedding of any person or his family or the tools, books, vehicles or other equipment which he personally needs to use in his employment, business or vocation, provided that in this paragraph the word 'person' shall not include a corporation.

(7) The distress levied under any such warrant as aforesaid shall be sold within such period beginning not earlier than the 6th day after the making of the distress as may be specified in the warrant, or if no period is specified in the warrant, within a period beginning on the 6th day and ending on the 14th day after the making of the distress: Provided that with the consent in writing of the person against whom the distress is levied the distress may be sold before the beginning of the said period.

(8) The clerk of the court which issued the warrant may, on the application of the person charged with the execution of it, extend the period within which the distress must be sold by any number of days not exceeding 60; but following the grant of such an application there shall be no further variation or extension of that period.

(9) The said distress shall be sold by public auction or in such other manner as the person against whom the distress is levied may in writing allow.

(10) Notwithstanding anything in the preceding provisions of this rule, the said distress shall not be sold if the sum for which the warrant was issued and the charges of taking and keeping the distress have been paid.

(11) Subject to any direction to the contrary in the warrant, where the distress is levied on household goods, the goods shall not, without the consent in writing of the person against whom the distress is levied, be removed from the house until the day of sale; and so much of the goods shall be impounded as is in the opinion of the person executing the warrant sufficient to satisfy the distress, by affixing to the articles impounded a conspicuous mark.

(12) The person charged with the execution of any such warrant as aforesaid shall cause the distress to be sold, and may deduct out of the amount realised by the sale all costs and charges incurred in effecting the sale; and he shall return to the owner the balance, if any, after retaining the amount of the sum for which the warrant was issued and the proper costs and charges of the execution of the warrant.

(13) The person charged with the execution of any such warrant as aforesaid shall as soon as practicable send to the court officer for the court that issued it a written account of the costs and charges incurred in executing it; and the court officer shall allow the person against whom the distress was levied to inspect the account within one month after the levy of the distress at any reasonable time to be appointed by the court.

(14) If any person pays or tenders to the person charged with the execution of any such warrant as aforesaid the sum mentioned in the warrant, or produces a receipt for that sum given by the court officer for the court that issued the warrant, and also pays the amount of the costs and charges of the distress up to the time of the payment or tender or the production of the receipt, the person as aforesaid shall not execute the warrant, or shall cease to execute it, as the case may be.

Payment after imprisonment imposed by magistrates' court

G–287　　**52.8.**—(1) The persons authorised for the purposes of section 79(2) of the *Magistrates' Courts Act* 1980 to receive a part payment are—

(a) unless there has been issued a warrant of distress or commitment, the court officer for the court enforcing payment of the sum, or any person appointed under section 88 of that Act to supervise the offender;

(b) where the issue of a warrant of commitment has been suspended on conditions which provide for payment to be made to the court officer for another magistrates' court, that court officer;

(c) any constable holding a warrant of distress or commitment or, where the warrant is directed to some other person, that person; and

(d) the governor or keeper of the prison or place in which the defaulter is detained, or other person having lawful custody of the defaulter: Provided that—

　　(i) the said governor or keeper shall not be required to accept any sum tendered in part payment under the said section 79(2) of the 1980 Act except on a week-day between 9 o'clock in the morning and 5 o'clock in the afternoon, and

　　(ii) no person shall be required to receive in part payment under the said subsection (2) an amount which, or so much of an amount as, will not procure a reduction of the period for which the defaulter is committed or ordered to be detained.

(2) Where a person having custody of a defaulter receives payment of any sum he shall note receipt of the sum on the warrant of commitment.

(3) Where the magistrates' court officer for a court other than the court enforcing payment of the sums receives payment of any sum he shall inform the magistrates' court officer for the other court.

(4) Where a person appointed under section 88 of the 1980 Act to supervise an offender receives payment of any sum, he shall send it forthwith to the magistrates' court officer for the court which appointed him.

Order for supervision made by magistrates' court

52.9.—(1) Unless an order under section 88(1) of the *Magistrates' Courts Act* 1980 is made **G–288** in the offender's presence, the court officer for the court making the order shall deliver to the offender, or serve on him by post, notice in writing of the order.

(2) It shall be the duty of any person for the time being appointed under the said section to advise and befriend the offender with a view to inducing him to pay the sum adjudged to be paid and thereby avoid committal to custody and to give any information required by a magistrates' court about the offender's conduct and means.

Transfer of magistrates' court fine order

52.10.—(1) The court officer for a magistrates' court which has made a transfer of fine order **G–289** under section 89 or 90 or section 90 as applied by section 91 of the Magistrates' Courts Act 1980 shall send to the clerk of the court having jurisdiction under the order a copy of the order.

(2) Where a magistrates' court has made a transfer of fine order in respect of a sum adjudged to be paid by a court in Scotland or in Northern Ireland the court officer shall send a copy of the order to the clerk of the Scottish court or to the clerk of the Northern Irish court, as the case may be.

(3) Where a court officer receives a copy of a transfer of fine order (whether made in England and Wales, or in Scotland or in Northern Ireland) specifying his court as the court by which payment of the sum in question is to be enforceable, he shall thereupon, if possible, deliver or send by post to the offender notice in writing.

(4) Where under a transfer of fine order a sum adjudged to be paid by a Scottish court or by a Northern Irish court is enforceable by a magistrates' court—

(a) if the sum is paid, the court officer shall send it to the clerk of the Scottish court or to the clerk of the Northern Irish court, as the case may be; or

(b) if the sum is not paid, the court officer shall inform the clerk of the Scottish court or the clerk of the Northern Irish court, as the case may be, of the manner in which the adjudication has been satisfied or that the sum, or any balance thereof, appears to be irrecoverable.

Directions by magistrates' court that money found on defaulter shall not be applied in satisfaction of debt

52.11. Where the defaulter is committed to, or ordered to be detained in, a prison or other **G–290**

place of detention, any direction given under section 80(2) of the *Magistrates' Courts Act* 1980 shall be endorsed on the warrant of commitment.

Particulars of fine enforcement to be entered in magistrates' court register

G–291   **52.12.**—(1) Where the court on the occasion of convicting an offender of an offence issues a warrant of commitment for a default in paying a sum adjudged to be paid by the conviction or, having power to issue such a warrant, fixes a term of imprisonment under section 77(2) of the *Magistrates' Courts Act* 1980, the reasons for the court's action shall be entered in the register, or any separate record kept for the purpose of recording particulars of fine enforcement.

(2) There shall be entered in the register, or any such record, particulars of any—

   (a) means inquiry under section 82 of the 1980 Act;

   (b) hearing under subsection (5) of the said section 82;

   (c) allowance of further time for the payment of a sum adjudged to be paid by a conviction;

   (d) direction that such a sum shall be paid by instalments including any direction varying the number of instalments payable, the amount of any instalments payable and the date on which any instalment becomes payable;

   (e) distress for the enforcement of such a sum;

   (f) attachment of earnings order for the enforcement of such a sum;

   (g) decision of the Secretary of State to make deductions from income support under section 24 of the Criminal Justice Act 1991;

   (h) order under the 1980 Act placing a person under supervision pending payment of such a sum;

   (i) order under section 85(1) of the 1980 Act remitting the whole or any part of a fine;

   (j) order under section 120(4) of the 1980 Act remitting the whole or any part of any sum enforceable under that section (forfeiture of recognizance);

   (k) authority granted under section 87(3) of the 1980 Act authorising the taking of proceedings in the High Court or county court for the recovery of any sum adjudged to be paid by a conviction;

   (l) transfer of fine order made by the court;

   (m) order transferring a fine to the court;

   (n) order under section 140(1) of the *Powers of Criminal Courts (Sentencing) Act* 2000 specifying the court for the purpose of enforcing a fine imposed or a recognizance forfeited by the Crown Court; and

   (o) any fine imposed or recognizance forfeited by a coroner which has to be treated as imposed or forfeited by the court;

   (p) reference by a justice of the peace of an application under section 77(5) of the 1980 Act for a review of the terms on which a warrant of commitment is postponed; or

   (q) order under section 77(3) of the 1980 Act varying the time for which or the conditions subject to which a warrant of commitment is postponed.

Payment after Attendance Centre order

G–292   **52.13.**—(1) Where any person is ordered, under section 60 of the Powers of Criminal Courts (Sentencing) Act 2000, to attend at an attendance centre in default of payment of a sum of money, payment may thereafter be made—

   (a) of the whole of the said sum, to the court officer for the magistrates' court which made the order, or

   (b) of the whole or, subject to paragraph (2), any part of the said sum, to the officer in charge of the attendance centre specified in the order ('the officer in charge').

(2) The officer in charge may not accept a part payment that would not secure the reduction by one or more complete hours of the period of attendance specified in the order.

(3) On receiving a payment under paragraph (1) the court officer shall forthwith notify the officer in charge.

(4) The officer in charge shall pay any money received by him under paragraph (1) above to the court officer and shall note the receipt of the money in the register maintained at the attendance centre.

[The next paragraph is § G–294.]

PART 53 COMPENSATION ORDERS

Contents of this Part

Review of compensation order made by a magistrates' court

53.1.—(1) An application under section 133 of the Powers of Criminal Courts (Sentencing) **G–294** Act 2000 for the review of a compensation order shall be by complaint.

(2) The court officer for the magistrates' court to which the complaint is made shall send a letter to the person for whose benefit the compensation order was made, inviting him to make observations and to attend any hearing of the complaint and advising him of his right to be heard.

PART 54 CONDITIONAL DISCHARGE

Contents of this Part

Further offence committed after offender conditionally discharged by a magistrates' court

54.1.—(1) Where a magistrates' court deals with a person under section 13 of the *Powers of* **G–295** *Criminal Courts (Sentencing) Act* 2000 in relation to an order for conditional discharge which was not made by that court the court officer shall give notice of the result of the proceedings to the court officer for the court by which the order was made.

(2) The court officer for a magistrates' court receiving a notice under this rule shall note the decision of the other court in the register.

PART 55 ROAD TRAFFIC PENALTIES

Contents to this Part

G–295a

Endorsement of driving licence by a magistrates' court

55.1.—(1) Where a magistrates' court convicts a person of an offence and, under section 44 **G–296** of the *Road Traffic Offenders Act* 1988 orders that particulars of the conviction, and, if the court orders him to be disqualified, particulars of the disqualification, shall be endorsed on any licence held by him, the particulars to be endorsed shall include—

(a) the name of the local justice area for which the court is acting;

(b) the date of the conviction and the date on which sentence was passed (if different);

(c) particulars of the offence including the date on which it was committed; and

(d) particulars of the sentence of the court (including the period of disqualification, if any).

(2) Where a magistrates' court orders that the licence of an offender be endorsed as mentioned in paragraph (1) or imposes an interim disqualification as mentioned in rule 43.1(1)(f) and the court officer knows or is informed of the date of birth and sex of the offender, the court officer shall send the information to the licensing authority which granted the licence.

Application to magistrates' court for removal of a disqualification

G–297   **55.2.**—(1) An application under section 42 of the Road Traffic Offenders Act 1988 or paragraph 7 of Schedule 4 to the *Road Traffic (Consequential Provisions) Act* 1988 for an order removing a disqualification or disqualifications for holding or obtaining a licence shall be by complaint.

(2) The justice to whom the complaint is made shall issue a summons directed to the chief officer of police requiring him to appear before a magistrates' court to show cause why an order should not be made on the complaint.

(3) Where a magistrates' court makes an order under either of the provisions mentioned in paragraph (1) the court shall cause notice of the making of the order and a copy of the particulars of the order endorsed on the licence, if any, previously held by the applicant for the order to be sent to the licensing authority to which notice of the applicant's disqualification was sent.

Application to court for review of course provider's refusal to issue a certificate of satisfactory completion of driving course

G–298   **55.3.**—(1) An application to the supervising court or the relevant local court under section 34B(6) or (8) of the *Road Traffic Offenders Act* 1988 shall be served on the court officer within 28 days after the date specified in an order under section 34A(5) of the 1988 Act.

(2) An application under section 34B(6) of the 1988 Act shall be accompanied by the notice under section 34B(5) of the 1988 Act.

(3) Where such an application is served on the court officer—

(a) he shall fix a date and time for the hearing of the application; and

(b) he shall—

(i) serve a copy of the application on the course provider, and

(ii) serve notice of the hearing on the applicant and course provider.

(4) If the course provider fails to appear or be represented at the hearing of the application without reasonable excuse, the court may proceed to decide the application in his absence.

(5) In this rule, 'course provider', 'relevant local court' and 'supervising court' have the meanings assigned to them in England and Wales by section 34C of the 1988 Act.

Statutory declaration under section 72 or 73 of the Road Traffic Offenders Act 1988

G–299   **55.4.** Where a magistrates' court officer receives a statutory declaration under section 72 or 73 of the *Road Traffic Offenders Act* 1988 (fixed penalty notice or notice fixed to vehicle invalid) he shall send a copy of it to the appropriate chief officer of police.

Appeal against recognition of foreign driving disqualification

G–299a   **55.5.**—(1) This rule applies where—

(a) a minister gives a disqualification notice under section 57 of the Crime (International Co-operation) Act 2003; and

(b) the person to whom it is given wants to appeal under section 59 of the Act to a magistrates' court.

(2) That person ('the appellant') must serve an appeal notice on—

(a) the court officer, at a magistrates' court in the local justice area in which the appellant lives; and

(b) the minister, at the address given in the disqualification notice.

(3) The appellant must serve the appeal notice within the period for which section 59 of the 2003 Act provides.

(4) The appeal notice must—
  (a) attach a copy of the disqualification notice;
  (b) explain which of the conditions in section 56 of the 2003 Act is not met, and why section 57 of the Act therefore does not apply; and
  (c) include any application to suspend the disqualification, under section 60 of the Act.
(5) The minister may serve a respondent's notice, and must do so if—
  (a) the minister wants to make representations to the court; or
  (b) the court so directs.
(6) The minister must—
  (a) unless the court otherwise directs, serve any such respondent's notice not more than 14 days after—
    (i) the appellant serves the appeal notice, or
    (ii) a direction to do so;
  (b) in any such respondent's notice—
    (i) identify the grounds of opposition on which the minister relies,
    (ii) summarise any relevant facts not already included in the disqualification and appeal notices, and
    (iii) identify any other document that the minister thinks the court will need to decide the appeal (and serve any such document with the notice).
(7) Where the court determines an appeal—
  (a) the general rule is that it will do so at a hearing (which will be in public, unless the court otherwise directs); but
  (b) it may do so without a hearing.
(8) The court officer must serve on the minister—
  (a) notice of the outcome of the appeal; and
  (b) notice of any suspension of the disqualification; and
  (c) the appellant's driving licence, if surrendered to the court officer.

PART 62 CONTEMPT OF COURT

Contents of this Part

When this Part applies
  62.1.—(1) This Part applies—   **G–299b**
    (a) in the Crown Court, where a person is accused of disobeying—
      (i) an order of the Crown Court, or

       (ii) any other order, where legislation allows that person to be punished as if that were an order of the Crown Court;

    (b) in magistrates' courts and in the Crown Court, where a person is accused of contempt of court under section 18 of the*Criminal Procedure and Investigations Act* 1996.

(2) In this Part, 'respondent' means any such accused person.

Exercise of court's power to punish for contempt of court

G–299c   **62.2.** The court must not exercise its power to punish the respondent for contempt of court in the respondent's absence, unless the respondent has had at least 14 days in which to—

    (a) make any representations; and

    (b) introduce any evidence.

Application to punish for contempt of court

G–299d   **62.3.**—(1) A person who wants the court to exercise its power to punish the respondent for contempt of court must—

    (a) apply in writing and serve the application on the court officer; and

    (b) serve on the respondent—

       (i) the application, and

       (ii) notice of where and when the court will hear the application (not less than 14 days after service).

(2) The application must—

    (a) identify the respondent;

    (b) explain that it is an application for the respondent to be punished for contempt of court;

    (c) contain such particulars of the conduct constituting contempt of court as to make clear what the applicant alleges against the respondent; and

    (d) include a notice warning the respondent that the court—

       (i) can impose imprisonment, or a fine, or both, for contempt of court, and

       (ii) may deal with the application in the respondent's absence, if the respondent does not attend the hearing of the application.

Notice of suspension of punishment

G–299e   **62.4.**—(1) This rule applies where—

    (a) the court exercises its power to suspend a punishment it imposes for contempt of court—

       (i) for a period, or

       (ii) conditionally; and

    (b) the respondent is absent when the court does so.

(2) The applicant must serve on the respondent notice of the terms of the court's order.

Application to discharge an order for imprisonment

G–299f   **62.5.**—(1) This rule applies where—

    (a) the court has ordered the respondent's imprisonment for contempt of court; and

    (b) the respondent wants the court to discharge that order.

(2) The respondent must—

    (a) apply in writing;

    (b) serve the application on—

       (i) the court officer, and

       (ii) the applicant who applied for the respondent's punishment;

    (c) explain why it is appropriate for the order to be discharged; and

    (d) ask for a hearing, if the respondent wants one.

Introduction of written witness statement or other hearsay

G–299g   **62.6.**—(1) A party who wants to introduce in evidence the written statement of a witness, or other hearsay, must—

    (a) serve a copy of the statement, or notice of other hearsay, on—

       (i) the court officer, and

(ii) the other party; and

(b) serve the copy or notice—

(i) when serving the application under rule 62.3, in the case of the applicant, or

(ii) not more than 7 days after service of that application, in the case of the respondent.

(2) Such service is notice of that party's intention to introduce in evidence that written witness statement, or other hearsay, unless that party otherwise indicates when serving it.

(3) A party entitled to receive such notice may waive that entitlement by so informing the court officer and the party who would have given it.

Content of written witness statement

62.7.—(1) This rule applies to a written witness statement served under rule 62.6.   **G–299h**

(2) Such a written witness statement must contain a declaration by the person making it that it is true to the best of that person's knowledge and belief.

False statements

62.8.—(1) In the Crown Court, the court can punish for contempt of court a person who   **G–299i** makes, or causes to be made, a false statement in such a written witness statement without an honest belief in its truth.

(2) The Crown Court may exercise its power to punish that person for contempt of court—

(a) on an application by a party, with the court's permission; or

(b) on its own initiative.

(3) A person who wants the court to exercise that power must comply with the rules in this Part.

Content of notice of other hearsay

62.9.—(1) This rule applies to a notice of hearsay, other than a written witness statement,   **G–299j** served under rule 62.6.

(2) Such a notice must—

(a) set out the evidence, or attach the document that contains it; and

(b) identify the person who made the statement that is hearsay.

Cross-examination of maker of written witness statement or other hearsay

62.10.—(1) This rule applies where a party wants the court's permission to cross-examine   **G–299k** the maker of a written witness statement, or other hearsay statement, served under rule 62.6.

(2) The party who wants to cross-examine that person must—

(a) apply in writing, with reasons; and

(b) serve the application on—

(i) the court officer, and

(ii) the party who served the hearsay.

(3) A respondent who wants to cross-examine such a person must apply to do so not more than 7 days after service of the hearsay by the applicant.

(4) An applicant who wants to cross-examine such a person must apply to do so not more than 3 days after service of the hearsay by the respondent.

(5) The court—

(a) may decide an application under this rule without a hearing; but

(b) must not dismiss such an application unless the person making it has had an opportunity to make representations at a hearing.

Credibility and consistency of maker of written witness statement or other hearsay

62.11.—(1) This rule applies where a party wants to challenge the credibility or consistency   **G–299l** of the maker of a written witness statement, or other hearsay statement, served under rule 62.6.

(2) The party who wants to challenge the credibility or consistency of that person must—

(a) serve a written notice of intention to do so on—

(i) the court officer, and

(ii) the party who served the hearsay; and

(b) in it, identify any statement or other material on which that party relies.

(3) A respondent who wants to challenge such a person's credibility or consistency must serve such a notice not more than 7 days after service of the hearsay by the applicant. —

(4) An applicant who wants to challenge such a person's credibility or consistency must serve such a notice not more than 3 days after service of the hearsay by the respondent.

(5) The party who served the hearsay—

    (a) may call that person to give oral evidence instead; and

    (b) if so, must serve a notice of intention to do so on—

        (i)   the court officer, and

        (ii) the other party as soon as practicable after service of the notice under paragraph (2).

Court's power to vary requirements under this Part

G–299m   **62.12.**—(1) The court may shorten or extend (even after it has expired) a time limit under this Part.

(2) A person who wants an extension of time must—

    (a) apply when serving the statement, notice or application for which it is needed; and

    (b) explain the delay.

PART 63 APPEAL TO THE CROWN COURT

Content of this Part

When this Part applies

G–300   **63.1.**—(1) This Part applies where—

    (a) a defendant wants to appeal under—

        (i)   section 108 of the *Magistrates' Courts Act* 1980,

        (ii)   section 45 of the *Mental Health Act* 1983,

        (iii) paragraph 10 of Schedule 3 to the *Powers of Criminal Courts (Sentencing) Act* 2000, or paragraphs 9(8) or 13(5) of Schedule 8 to the *Criminal Justice Act* 2003,

        (iv)   section 10 of the *Violent Crime Reduction Act* 2006,

        (v)   section 42 of the *Counter Terrorism Act* 2008;

    (b) the Criminal Cases Review Commission refers a defendant's case to the Crown Court under section 11 of the *Criminal Appeal Act* 1995;

    (c) a prosecutor wants to appeal under—

        (i)   section 14A(5A) of the *Football Spectators Act* 1989, or

        (ii) section 147(3) of the *Customs and Excise Management Act* 1979; or

    (d) a person wants to appeal under—

        (i)   section 1 of the Magistrates' Courts (Appeals from Binding Over Orders) Act 1956,

        (ii) section 12(5) of the *Contempt of Court Act* 1981,

(iii) regulation 3C or 3H of the *Costs in Criminal Cases (General) Regulations* 1986, or

(iv) section 22 of the *Football Spectators Act* 1989.

(2) A reference to an 'appellant' in this Part is a reference to such a party or person.

Service of appeal notice

63.2.—(1) An appellant must serve an appeal notice on—   **G–301**

   (a) the magistrates' court officer; and

   (b) every other party.

(2) The appellant must serve the appeal notice—

   (a) as soon after the decision appealed against as the appellant wants; but

   (b) not more than 21 days after—

      (i) sentence or the date sentence is deferred, whichever is earlier, if the appeal is against conviction or against a finding of guilt,

      (ii) sentence, if the appeal is against sentence, or

      (iii) the order or failure to make an order about which the appellant wants to appeal, in any other case.

(3) The appellant must—

   (a) serve with the appeal notice any application for an extension of the time limit under this rule; and

   (b) in that application, explain why the appeal notice is late.

Form of appeal notice

63.3. The appeal notice must be in writing and must—   **G–302**

   (a) specify—

      (i) the conviction or finding of guilt,

      (ii) the sentence, or

      (iii) the order, or the failure to make an order about which the appellant wants to appeal;

   (b) summarise the issues;

   (c) in an appeal against conviction—

      (i) identify the prosecution witnesses whom the appellant will want to question if they are called to give oral evidence, and

      (ii) say how long the trial lasted in the magistrates' court and how long the appeal is likely to last in the Crown Court;

   (d) in an appeal against a finding that the appellant insulted someone or interrupted proceedings in the magistrates' court, attach—

      (i) the magistrates' court's written findings of fact, and

      (ii) the appellant's response to those findings;

   (e) say whether the appellant has asked the magistrates' court to reconsider the case; and

   (f) include a list of those on whom the appellant has served the appeal notice.

Duty of magistrates' court officer

63.4. The magistrates' court officer must—   **G–303**

   (a) as soon as practicable serve on the Crown Court officer—

      (i) the appeal notice and any accompanying application served by the appellant,

      (ii) details of the parties including their addresses,

      (iii) a copy of each magistrates' court register entry relating to the decision under appeal and to any application for bail pending appeal, and

      (iv) any report received for the purposes of sentencing;

   (b) keep any document or object exhibited in the proceedings in the magistrates' court, or arrange for it to be kept by some other appropriate person, until—

      (i) 6 weeks after the conclusion of those proceedings, or

      (ii) the conclusion of any proceedings in the Crown Court that begin within that 6 weeks; and

   (c) provide the Crown Court with any document, object or information for which the Crown Court officer asks, within such period as the Crown Court officer may require.

Duty of person keeping exhibit

G–304

63.5. A person who, under arrangements made by the magistrates' court officer, keeps a document or object exhibited in the proceedings in the magistrates' court must—

    (a) keep that exhibit until—

        (i) 6 weeks after the conclusion of those proceedings, or

        (ii) the conclusion of any proceedings in the Crown Court that begin within that 6 weeks, unless the magistrates' court or the Crown Court otherwise directs; and

    (b) provide the Crown Court with any such document or object for which the Crown Court officer asks, within such period as the Crown Court officer may require.

Reference by the Criminal Cases Review Commission

G–305

63.6.—(1) The Crown Court officer must, as soon as practicable, serve a reference by the Criminal Cases Review Commission on —

    (a) the appellant;

    (b) every other party; and

    (c) the magistrates' court officer.

(2) The appellant may serve an appeal notice on—

    (a) the Crown Court officer; and

    (b) every other party, not more than 21 days later.

(3) The Crown Court must treat the reference as the appeal notice if the appellant does not serve an appeal notice.

Hearings and decisions

G–306

63.7.—(1) The Crown Court as a general rule must hear in public an appeal or reference to which this Part applies, but—

    (a) may order any hearing to be in private; and

    (b) where a hearing is about a public interest ruling, must hold that hearing in private.

(2) The Crown Court officer must give as much notice as reasonably practicable of every hearing to—

    (a) the parties;

    (b) any party's custodian; and

    (c) any other person whom the Crown Court requires to be notified.

(3) The Crown Court officer must serve every decision on—

    (a) the parties;

    (b) any other person whom the Crown Court requires to be served; and

    (c) the magistrates' court officer and any party's custodian, where the decision determines an appeal.

(4) But where a hearing or decision is about a public interest ruling, the Crown Court officer must not—

    (a) give notice of that hearing to; or

    (b) serve that decision on, anyone other than the prosecutor who applied for that ruling, unless the court otherwise directs.

Abandoning an appeal

G–307

63.8.—(1) The appellant—

    (a) may abandon an appeal without the Crown Court's permission, by serving a notice of abandonment on—

        (i) the magistrates' court officer,

        (ii) the Crown Court officer, and

        (iii) every other party before the hearing of the appeal begins; but

    (b) after the hearing of the appeal begins, may only abandon the appeal with the Crown Court's permission.

(2) A notice of abandonment must be signed by or on behalf of the appellant.

(3) Where an appellant who is on bail pending appeal abandons an appeal—
  (a) the appellant must surrender to custody as directed by the magistrates' court officer; and
  (b) any conditions of bail apply until then.

Court's power to vary requirements under this Part
63.9. The Crown Court may—   **G–308**
  (a) shorten or extend (even after it has expired) a time limit under this Part;
  (b) allow an appellant to vary an appeal notice that that appellant has served;
  (c) direct that an appeal notice be served on any person;
  (d) allow an appeal notice or a notice of abandonment to be in a different form to one set out in the Practice Direction, or to be presented orally.

Constitution of the Crown Court
63.10. On the hearing of an appeal—   **G–308a**
  (a) the general rule is that the Crown Court must comprise—
      (i) a judge of the High Court, a Circuit judge or a Recorder, and
      (ii) no less than two and no more than four justices of the peace, none of whom took part in the decision under appeal; and
  (b) if the appeal is from a youth court—
      (i) each justice of the peace must be qualified to sit as a member of a youth court, and
      (ii) the Crown Court must include a man and a woman; but
  (c) the Crown Court may include only one justice of the peace and need not include both a man and a woman if—
      (i) the presiding judge decides that otherwise the start of the appeal hearing will be delayed unreasonably, or
      (ii) one or more of the justices of the peace who started hearing the appeal is absent.

PART 64 APPEAL TO THE HIGH COURT BY WAY OF CASE STATED

Contents of this Part

Application to a magistrates' court to state a case
64.1.—(1) An application under section 111(1) of the *Magistrates' Courts Act* 1980 shall be **G–309** made in writing and signed by or on behalf of the applicant and shall identify the question or questions of law or jurisdiction on which the opinion of the High Court is sought.

(2) Where one of the questions on which the opinion of the High Court is sought is whether there was evidence on which the magistrates' court could come to its decision, the particular finding of fact made by the magistrates' court which it is claimed cannot be supported by the evidence before the magistrates' court shall be specified in such application.

(3) Any such application shall be sent to a court officer for the magistrates' court whose decision is questioned.

Consideration of a draft case by a magistrates' court
64.2.—(1) Within 21 days after receipt of an application made in accordance with rule 64.1, a **G–310**

court officer for the magistrates' court whose decision is questioned shall, unless the justices refuse to state a case under section 111(5) of the *Magistrates' Courts Act* 1980, send a draft case in which are stated the matters required under rule 64.6 (content of case stated) to the applicant or his legal representative and shall send a copy thereof to the respondent or his legal representative.

(2) Within 21 days after receipt of the draft case under paragraph (1), each party may make representations thereon. Any such representations shall be in writing and signed by or on behalf of the party making them and shall be sent to the magistrates' court officer.

(3) Where the justices refuse to state a case under section 111(5) of the 1980 Act and they are required by a mandatory order of the High Court under section 111(6) to do so, this rule shall apply as if in paragraph (1)—

> (a) for the words 'receipt of an application made in accordance with rule 64.1' there were substituted the words 'the date on which a mandatory order under section 111(6) of the 1980 Act is made'; and
>
> (b) the words 'unless the justices refuse to state a case under section 111(5) of the 1980 Act' were omitted.

Preparation and submission of final case to a magistrates' court

G–311   **64.3.**—(1) Within 21 days after the latest day on which representations may be made under rule 64.2, the justices whose decision is questioned shall make such adjustments, if any, to the draft case prepared for the purposes of that rule as they think fit, after considering any such representations, and shall state and sign the case.

(2) A case may be stated on behalf of the justices whose decision is questioned by any 2 or more of them and may, if the justices so direct, be signed on their behalf by the justices' clerk.

(3) Forthwith after the case has been stated and signed a court officer for the court shall send it to the applicant or his legal representative, together with any statement required by rule 64.4.

Extension of time limits by a magistrates' court

G–312   **64.4.**—(1) If a magistrates' court officer is unable to send to the applicant a draft case under rule 64.2(1) within the time required by that paragraph, he shall do so as soon as practicable thereafter and the provisions of that rule shall apply accordingly; but in that event a court officer shall attach to the draft case, and to the final case when it is sent to the applicant or his legal representative under rule 64.3(3), a statement of the delay and the reasons for it.

(2) If a magistrates' court officer receives an application in writing from or on behalf of the applicant or the respondent for an extension of the time within which representations on the draft case may be made under rule 64.2(2), together with reasons in writing for it, the justices' clerk may, by notice in writing sent to the applicant, or respondent as the case may be, by the magistrates' court officer, extend the time and the provisions of that paragraph and of rule 64.3 shall apply accordingly; but in that event the court officer shall attach to the final case, when it is sent to the applicant or his legal representative under rule 64.3(3), a statement of the extension and the reasons for it.

(3) If the justices are unable to state a case within the time required by rule 64.3(1), they shall do so as soon as practicable thereafter and the provisions of that rule shall apply accordingly; but in that event a court officer shall attach to the final case, when it is sent to the applicant or his legal representative under rule 64.3(3), a statement of the delay and the reasons for it.

Content of case stated by a magistrates' court

G–313   **64.5.**—(1) A case stated by the magistrates' court shall state the facts found by the court and the question or questions of law or jurisdiction on which the opinion of the High Court is sought.

(2) Where one of the questions on which the opinion of the High Court is sought is whether there was evidence on which the magistrates' court could come to its decision, the particular finding of fact which it is claimed cannot be supported by the evidence before the magistrates' court shall be specified in the case.

(3) Unless one of the questions on which the opinion of the High Court is sought is whether there was evidence on which the magistrates' court could come to its decision, the case shall not contain a statement of evidence.

Application to the Crown Court to state a case

64.6.—(1) An application under section 28 of the *Senior Courts Act* 1981 to the Crown **G–314** Court to state a case for the opinion of the High Court shall be made in writing to a court officer within 21 days after the date of the decision in respect of which the application is made.

(2) The application shall state the ground on which the decision of the Crown Court is questioned.

(3) After making the application, the applicant shall forthwith send a copy of it to the parties to the proceedings in the Crown Court.

(4) On receipt of the application, the Crown Court officer shall forthwith send it to the judge who presided at the proceedings in which the decision was made.

(5) On receipt of the application, the judge shall inform the Crown Court officer as to whether or not he has decided to state a case and that officer shall give notice in writing to the applicant of the judge's decision.

(6) If the judge considers that the application is frivolous, he may refuse to state a case and shall in that case, if the applicant so requires, cause a certificate stating the reasons for the refusal to be given to him.

(7) If the judge decides to state a case, the procedure to be followed shall, unless the judge in a particular case otherwise directs, be the procedure set out in paragraphs (8) to (12) of this rule.

(8) The applicant shall, within 21 days of receiving the notice referred to in paragraph (5), draft a case and send a copy of it to the Crown Court officer and to the parties to the proceedings in the Crown Court.

(9) Each party to the proceedings in the Crown Court shall, within 21 days of receiving a copy of the draft case under paragraph (8), either—

(a) give notice in writing to the applicant and the Crown Court officer that he does not intend to take part in the proceedings before the High Court;

(b) indicate in writing on the copy of the draft case that he agrees with it and send the copy to a court officer; or

(c) draft an alternative case and send it, together with the copy of the applicant's case, to the Crown Court officer.

(10) The judge shall consider the applicant's draft case and any alternative draft case sent to the Crown Court officer under paragraph (9)(c).

(11) If the Crown Court so orders, the applicant shall, before the case is stated and delivered to him, enter before the Crown Court officer into a recognizance, with or without sureties and in such sum as the Crown Court considers proper, having regard to the means of the applicant, conditioned to prosecute the appeal without delay.

(12) The judge shall state and sign a case within 14 days after either—

(a) the receipt of all the documents required to be sent to a court officer under paragraph (9); or

(b) the expiration of the period of 21 days referred to in that paragraph, whichever is the sooner.

(13) A case stated by the Crown Court shall state the facts found by the Crown Court, the submissions of the parties (including any authorities relied on by the parties during the course of those submissions), the decision of the Crown Court in respect of which the application is made and the question on which the opinion of the High Court is sought.

(14) Any time limit referred to in this rule may be extended either before or after it expires by the Crown Court.

(15) If the judge decides not to state a case but the stating of a case is subsequently required by a mandatory order of the High Court, paragraphs (7) to (14) shall apply to the stating of the case save that—

(a) in paragraph (7) the words 'If the judge decides to state a case' shall be omitted; and

(b) in paragraph (8) for the words 'receiving the notice referred to in paragraph (5)' there shall be substituted the words 'the day on which the mandatory order was made'.

[The next paragraph is § G-315a.]

PART 75 REQUEST TO THE EUROPEAN COURT FOR A PRELIMINARY RULING

Contents of this Part

When this Part applies

G–315a   **75.1.** This Part applies where the court can request the Court of Justice of the European Union ('the European Court') to give a preliminary ruling, under Article 267 of the Treaty on the Functioning of the European Union.

Preparation of request

G–315b   **75.2.**—(1) The court may—
    (a) make an order for the submission of a request—
        (i) on application by a party, or
        (ii) on its own initiative;
    (b) give directions for the preparation of the terms of such a request.
    (2) The court must—
    (a) include in such a request—
        (i) the identity of the court making the request,
        (ii) the parties' identities,
        (iii) a statement of whether a party is in custody,
        (iv) a succinct statement of the question on which the court seeks the ruling of the European Court,
        (v) a succinct statement of any opinion on the answer that the court may have expressed in any judgment that it has delivered,
        (vi) a summary of the nature and history of the proceedings, including the salient facts and an indication of whether those facts are proved, admitted or assumed,
        (vii) the relevant rules of national law,
        (viii) a summary of the relevant contentions of the parties,
        (ix) an indication of the provisions of European Union law that the European Court is asked to interpret, and
        (x) an explanation of why a ruling of the European Court is requested;
    (b) express the request in terms that can be translated readily into other languages; and
    (c) set out the request in a schedule to the order.

Submission of request

G–315c   **75.3.**—(1) The court officer must serve the order for the submission of the request on the Senior Master of the Queen's Bench Division of the High Court.
    (2) The Senior Master will—
    (a) submit the request to the European Court; but
    (b) unless the court otherwise directs, postpone the submission of the request until—
        (i) the time for any appeal against the order has expired, and
        (ii) any appeal against the order has been determined.

Postponement of case pending request

G–315d   **75.4.** Where the court orders the submission of a request—
    (a) the general rule is that it will adjourn or postpone any further hearing; but
    (b) it may otherwise direct.

PART 76 COSTS

Contents of this Part

SECTION 1: GENERAL

When this Part applies

76.1.—(1) This Part applies where the court can make an order about costs under—   **G–316**

    (a) Part II of the *Prosecution of Offences Act* 1985 and Part II, IIA or IIB of the *Costs in Criminal Cases (General) Regulations* 1986;

    (b) section 109 of the *Magistrates' Courts Act* 1980;

    (c) section 52 of the *Senior Courts Act* 1981 and rule 76.6;

    (d) section 8 of the *Bankers Books Evidence Act* 1879;

    (e) section 2C(8) of the *Criminal Procedure (Attendance of Witnesses) Act* 1965;

    (f) section 36(5) of the Criminal Justice Act 1972;

    (g) section 159(5) and Schedule 3, paragraph 11, of the *Criminal Justice Act* 1988;

    (h) section 14H(5) of the *Football Spectators Act* 1989; or

    (i) Part 3 of the *Serious Crime Act* 2007 (Appeals under Section 24) Order 2008.

  (2) In this Part, 'costs' means—

    (a) the fees payable to a legal representative;

    (b) the disbursements paid by a legal representative; and

    (c) any other expenses incurred in connection with the case.

Costs orders: general rules

76.2.—(1) The court must not make an order about costs unless each party and any other **G–317** person directly affected—

    (a) is present; or

    (b) has had an opportunity—

　　　　　(i)　to attend, or
　　　　　(ii)　to make representations.
　　(2)　The court may make an order about costs—
　　　　(a)　at a hearing in public or in private; or
　　　　(b)　without a hearing.
　　(3)　In deciding what order, if any, to make about costs, the court must have regard to all the circumstances, including—
　　　　(a)　the conduct of all the parties; and
　　　　(b)　any costs order already made.
　　(4)　If the court makes an order about costs, it must—
　　　　(a)　specify who must, or must not, pay what, to whom; and
　　　　(b)　identify the legislation under which the order is made, where there is a choice of powers.
　　(5)　The court must give reasons if it—
　　　　(a)　refuses an application for a costs order; or
　　　　(b)　rejects representations opposing a costs order.
　　(6)　If the court makes an order for the payment of costs—
　　　　(a)　the general rule is that it will be for an amount that is sufficient reasonably to compensate the recipient for costs—
　　　　　(i)　actually, reasonably and properly incurred, and
　　　　　(ii)　reasonable in amount; but
　　　　(b)　the court may order the payment of—
　　　　　(i)　a proportion of that amount,
　　　　　(ii)　a stated amount less than that amount,
　　　　　(iii)　costs from or until a certain date only,
　　　　　(iv)　costs relating only to particular steps taken, or
　　　　　(v)　costs relating only to a distinct part of the case.
　　(7)　On an assessment of the amount of costs, relevant factors include—
　　　　(a)　the conduct of all the parties;
　　　　(b)　the particular complexity of the matter or the difficulty or novelty of the questions raised;
　　　　(c)　the skill, effort, specialised knowledge and responsibility involved;
　　　　(d)　the time spent on the case;
　　　　(e)　the place where and the circumstances in which work or any part of it was done; and
　　　　(f)　any direction or observations by the court that made the costs order.
　　(8)　If the court orders a party to pay costs to be assessed under rule 76.11, it may order that party to pay an amount on account.
　　(9)　An order for the payment of costs takes effect when the amount is assessed, unless the court exercises any power it has to order otherwise.

Court's power to vary requirements under Sections 2, 3 and 4

G–318　　**76.2.**—(1)　The court may—
　　　　(a)　extend a time limit for serving an application or representations under section 2, 3 or 4 of this Part, even after it has expired; and
　　　　(b)　consider an application or representations—
　　　　　(i)　made in a different form to one set out in the Practice Direction, or
　　　　　(ii)　made orally instead of in writing.
　　(2)　A person who wants an extension of time must—
　　　　(a)　apply when serving the application or representations for which it is needed; and
　　　　(b)　explain the delay.

SECTION 2: COSTS OUT OF CENTRAL FUNDS

Costs out of central funds

G–319　　**76.3.**—(1)　This rule applies where the court can order the payment of costs out of central funds.

(2) In this rule, costs—
   (a) include—
      (i) on an appeal, costs incurred in the court that made the decision under appeal, and
      (ii) at a retrial, costs incurred at the initial trial and on any appeal; but
   (b) do not include costs funded by the Legal Services Commission.
(3) The court may make an order—
   (a) on application by the person who incurred the costs; or
   (b) on its own initiative.
(4) Where a person wants the court to make an order that person must—
   (a) apply as soon as practicable; and
   (b) outline the type of costs and the amount claimed, if that person wants the court to direct an assessment; or
   (c) specify the amount claimed, if that person wants the court to assess the amount itself.
(5) The general rule is that the court will make an order, but—
   (a) the court may decline to make a defendant's costs order if, for example—
      (i) the defendant is convicted of at least one offence, or
      (ii) the defendant's conduct led the prosecutor reasonably to think the prosecution case stronger than it was; and
   (b) the court may decline to make a prosecutor's costs order if, for example, the prosecution was started or continued unreasonably.
(6) If the court makes an order—
   (a) it may direct an assessment under, as applicable—
      (i) regulations 4 to 12 of the *Costs in Criminal Cases (General) Regulations* 1986, or
      (ii) articles 21 to 28 of the *Serious Crime Act 2007 (Appeals under Section 24) Order* 2008;
   (b) it may assess the amount itself, if the recipient agrees; or
   (c) it must assess the amount itself, in a case in which it decides not to allow an amount that is reasonably sufficient to compensate the recipient for expenses properly incurred in the proceedings.

SECTION 3: PAYMENT OF COSTS BY ONE PARTY TO ANOTHER

Costs on conviction and sentence

76.5.—(1) This rule applies where the court can order a defendant to pay the prosecutor's **G–320** costs if the defendant is—
   (a) convicted or found guilty;
   (b) dealt with in the Crown Court after committal for sentence there; or
   (c) dealt with for breach of a sentence.
(2) The court may make an order—
   (a) on application by the prosecutor; or
   (b) on its own initiative.
(3) Where the prosecutor wants the court to make an order—
   (a) the prosecutor must—
      (i) apply as soon as practicable, and
      (ii) specify the amount claimed; and
   (b) the general rule is that the court will make an order if it is satisfied that the defendant can pay; but
   (c) the court may decline to do so.
(4) A defendant who wants to oppose an order must make representations as soon as practicable.
(5) If the court makes an order, it must assess the amount itself.

Costs on appeal

76.6.—(1) This rule— **G–321**

    (a) applies where a magistrates' court, the Crown Court or the Court of Appeal can order a party to pay another person's costs on an appeal, or an application for permission to appeal;

    (b) authorises the Crown Court, in addition to its other powers, to order a party to pay another party's costs on an appeal to that court, except on an appeal under—

        (i) section 108 of the *Magistrates' Courts Act* 1980, or

        (ii) section 45 of the *Mental Health Act* 1983.

(2) In this rule, costs include—

    (a) costs incurred in the court that made the decision under appeal; and

    (b) costs funded by the Legal Services Commission.

(3) The court may make an order—

    (a) on application by the person who incurred the costs; or

    (b) on its own initiative.

(4) A person who wants the court to make an order must—

    (a) apply as soon as practicable;

    (b) notify each other party;

    (c) specify—

        (i) the amount claimed, and

        (ii) against whom; and

    (d) where an appellant abandons an appeal to the Crown Court by serving a notice of abandonment—

        (i) apply in writing not more than 14 days later, and

        (ii) serve the application on the appellant and on the Crown Court officer.

(5) A party who wants to oppose an order must—

    (a) make representations as soon as practicable; and

    (b) where the application was under paragraph (4)(d), serve written representations on the applicant, and on the Crown Court officer, not more than 7 days after it was served.

(6) Where the application was under paragraph (4)(d), the Crown Court officer may—

    (a) submit it to the Crown Court; or

    (b) serve it on the magistrates' court officer, for submission to the magistrates' court.

(7) If the court makes an order, it may direct an assessment under rule 76.11, or assess the amount itself where—

    (a) the appellant abandons an appeal to the Crown Court;

    (b) the Crown Court decides an appeal, except an appeal under—

        (i) section 108 of the *Magistrates' Courts Act* 1980, or

        (ii) section 45 of the *Mental Health Act* 1983; or

    (c) the Court of Appeal decides an appeal to which Part 69 applies (appeal to the Court of Appeal regarding reporting or public access restriction).

(8) If the court makes an order in any other case, it must assess the amount itself.

Costs on an application

G–322   **76.7.**—(1) This rule applies where the court can order a party to pay another person's costs in a case in which—

    (a) the court decides an application for the production in evidence of a copy of a bank record;

    (b) a magistrates' court or the Crown Court decides an application to terminate a football banning order; or (c) the Crown Court allows an application to withdraw a witness summons.

(2) The court may make an order—

    (a) on application by the person who incurred the costs; or

    (b) on its own initiative.

(3) A person who wants the court to make an order must—

    (a) apply as soon as practicable;

    (b) notify each other party; and

    (c) specify—

        (i) the amount claimed, and

        (ii) against whom.

(4) A party who wants to oppose an order must make representations as soon as practicable.

(5) If the court makes an order, it may direct an assessment under rule 76.11, or assess the amount itself.

Costs resulting from unnecessary or improper act, etc.

76.8.—(1) This rule applies where the court can order a party to pay another party's costs **G–323** incurred as a result of an unnecessary or improper act or omission by or on behalf of the first party.

(2) In this rule, costs include costs funded by the Legal Services Commission.

(3) The court may make an order—

    (a) on application by the party who incurred such costs; or

    (b) on its own initiative.

(4) A party who wants the court to make an order must—

    (a) apply in writing as soon as practicable after becoming aware of the grounds for doing so;

    (b) serve the application on—

        (i)   the court officer (or, in the Court of Appeal, the Registrar), and

        (ii) each other party;

    (c) in that application specify—

        (i)   the party by whom costs should be paid,

        (ii)   the relevant act or omission,

        (iii) the reasons why that act or omission meets the criteria for making an order,

        (iv)   the amount claimed, and

        (v)   those on whom the application has been served.

(5) Where the court considers making an order on its own initiative, it must—

    (a) identify the party against whom it proposes making the order; and

    (b) specify—

        (i)   the relevant act or omission,

        (ii)   the reasons why that act or omission meets the criteria for making an order, and

        (iii) with the assistance of the party who incurred the costs, the amount involved.

(6) A party who wants to oppose an order must—

    (a) make representations as soon as practicable; and

    (b) in reply to an application, serve written representations on the applicant and on the court officer (or Registrar) not more than 7 days after it was served.

(7) If the court makes an order, it must assess the amount itself.

SECTION 4: OTHER COSTS ORDERS

Costs against a legal representative

76.9.—(1) This rule applies where—   **G–324**

    (a) a party has incurred costs—

        (i)   as a result of an improper, unreasonable or negligent act or omission by a legal or other representative or representative's employee, or

        (ii) which it has become unreasonable for that party to have to pay because of such an act or omission occurring after those costs were incurred; and

    (b) the court can—

        (i)   order the representative responsible to pay such costs, or

        (ii) prohibit the payment of costs to that representative.

(2) In this rule, costs include costs funded by the Legal Services Commission.

(3) The court may make an order—

    (a) on application by the party who incurred such costs; or

    (b) on its own initiative.

(4) A party who wants the court to make an order must—

    (a) apply in writing as soon as practicable after becoming aware of the grounds for doing so;

    (b) serve the application on—

        (i) the court officer (or, in the Court of Appeal, the Registrar),

        (ii) the representative responsible,

        (iii) each other party, and

        (iv) any other person directly affected;

    (c) in that application specify—

        (i) the representative responsible,

        (ii) the relevant act or omission,

        (iii) the reasons why that act or omission meets the criteria for making an order,

        (iv) the amount claimed, and

        (v) those on whom the application has been served.

(5) Where the court considers making an order on its own initiative, it must—

    (a) identify the representative against whom it proposes making that order; and

    (b) specify—

        (i) the relevant act or omission,

        (ii) the reasons why that act or omission meets the criteria for making an order, and

        (iii) with the assistance of the party who incurred the costs, the amount involved.

(6) A representative who wants to oppose an order must—

    (a) make representations as soon as practicable; and

    (b) in reply to an application, serve written representations on the applicant and on the court officer (or Registrar) not more than 7 days after it was served.

(7) If the court makes an order—

    (a) the general rule is that it will do so without waiting until the end of the case, but it may postpone making the order; and

    (b) it must assess the amount itself.

(8) Instead of making an order, the court may make adverse observations about the representative's conduct for use in an assessment where—

    (a) a party's costs are—

        (i) funded by the Legal Services Commission, or

        (ii) to be paid out of central funds; or

    (b) there is to be an assessment under rule 76.11.

Costs against a third party

G–325   **76.10.**—(1) This rule applies where—

    (a) there has been serious misconduct by a person who is not a party; and

    (b) the court can order that person to pay a party's costs.

(2) In this rule, costs include costs funded by the Legal Services Commission.

(3) The court may make an order—

    (a) on application by the party who incurred the costs; or

    (b) on its own initiative.

(4) A party who wants the court to make an order must—

    (a) apply in writing as soon as practicable after becoming aware of the grounds for doing so;

    (b) serve the application on—

        (i) the court officer (or, in the Court of Appeal, the Registrar),

        (ii) the person responsible,

        (iii) each other party, and

        (iv) any other person directly affected;

    (c) in that application specify—

        (i) the person responsible,

        (ii) the relevant misconduct,

        (iii) the reasons why the criteria for making an order are met,

    (iv) the amount claimed, and

    (v) those on whom the application has been served.

(5) Where the court considers making an order on its own initiative, it must—

    (a) identify the person against whom it proposes making that order; and

    (b) specify—

        (i) the relevant misconduct,

        (ii) the reasons why the criteria for making an order are met, and

        (iii) with the assistance of the party who incurred the costs, the amount involved.

(6) A person who wants to oppose an order must—

    (a) make representations as soon as practicable; and

    (b) in reply to an application, serve written representations on the applicant and on the court officer (or Registrar) not more than 7 days after it was served.

(7) If the court makes an order—

    (a) the general rule is that it will do so at the end of the case, but it may do so earlier; and

    (b) it must assess the amount itself.

SECTION 5: ASSESSMENT OF COSTS

Assessment and re-assessment

76.11.—(1) This rule applies where the court directs an assessment under— **G–326**

    (a) rule 61.20 (*Proceeds of Crime Act* 2002 – rules applicable to restraint and receivership proceedings, assessment of costs);

    (b) rule 76.6 (costs on appeal); or

    (c) rule 76.7 (costs on an application).

(2) The assessment must be carried out by the relevant assessing authority, namely—

    (a) the court officer, where the direction was given by a magistrates' court or by the Crown Court; or

    (b) the Registrar of Criminal Appeals, where the direction was given by the Court of Appeal.

(3) The party in whose favour the court made the costs order ('the applicant') must—

    (a) apply for an assessment—

        (i) in writing, in any form required by the assessing authority, and

        (ii) not more than 3 months after the costs order; and

    (b) serve the application on—

        (i) the assessing authority, and

        (ii) the party against whom the court made the costs order ('the respondent').

(4) The applicant must—

    (a) summarise the work done;

    (b) specify—

        (i) each item of work done, giving the date, time taken and amount claimed,

        (ii) any disbursements or expenses, including the fees of any advocate, and

        (iii) any circumstances of which the applicant wants the assessing authority to take particular account; and

    (c) supply—

        (i) receipts or other evidence of the amount claimed, and

        (ii) any other information or document for which the assessing authority asks, within such period as that authority may require.

(5) A respondent who wants to make representations about the amount claimed must—

    (a) do so in writing; and

    (b) serve the representations on the assessing authority, and on the applicant, not more than 21 days after service of the application.

(6) The assessing authority must—

    (a) if it seems likely to help with the assessment, obtain any other information or document;

(b)　resolve in favour of the respondent any doubt about what should be allowed; and

(c)　serve the assessment on the parties.

(7)　Where either party wants the amount allowed re-assessed—

    (a)　that party must—

        (i)　apply to the assessing authority, in writing and in any form required by that authority,

        (ii)　serve the application on the assessing authority, and on the other party, not more than 21 days after service of the assessment,

        (iii)　explain the objections to the assessment,

        (iv)　supply any additional supporting information or document, and

        (v)　ask for a hearing, if that party wants one; and

    (b)　a party who wants to make representations about an application for re-assessment must—

        (i)　do so in writing,

        (ii)　serve the representations on the assessing authority, and on the other party, not more than 21 days after service of the application, and

        (iii)　ask for a hearing, if that party wants one;

    (c)　the assessing authority—

        (i)　must arrange a hearing, in public or in private, if either party asks for one,

        (ii)　subject to that, may re-assess the amount allowed with or without a hearing,

        (iii)　must re-assess the amount allowed on the initial assessment, taking into account the reasons for disagreement with that amount and any other representations,

        (iv)　may maintain, increase or decrease the amount allowed on the assessment,

        (v)　must serve the re-assessment on the parties, and

        (vi)　must serve written reasons on the parties, if not more than 21 days later either party asks for such reasons.

(8)　A time limit under this rule may be extended even after it has expired—

    (a)　by the assessing authority, or

    (b)　by the Senior Costs Judge, if the assessing authority declines to do so.

Appeal to a costs judge

G–327　　76.12.—(1) This rule applies where—

    (a)　the assessing authority has re-assessed the amount allowed under rule 76.11; and

    (b)　either party wants to appeal against that amount.

(2)　That party must—

    (a)　serve an appeal notice on—

        (i)　the Senior Costs Judge,

        (ii)　the other party, and

        (iii)　the assessing authority not more than 21 days after service of the written reasons for the re-assessment;

    (b)　explain the objections to the re-assessment;

    (c)　serve on the Senior Costs Judge with the appeal notice—

        (i)　the applications for assessment and re-assessment,

        (ii)　any other information or document considered by the assessing authority,

        (iii)　the assessing authority's written reasons for the re-assessment, and

        (iv)　any other information or document for which a costs judge asks, within such period as the judge may require; and

    (d)　ask for a hearing, if that party wants one.

(3)　A party who wants to make representations about an appeal must—

    (a)　serve representations in writing on—

        (i)　the Senior Costs Judge, and

        (ii)　the applicant not more than 21 days after service of the appeal notice; and

    (b)　ask for a hearing, if that party wants one.

(4)　Unless a costs judge otherwise directs, the parties may rely only on—

    (a)　the objections to the amount allowed on the initial assessment; and

(b) any other representations and material considered by the assessing authority.

(5) A costs judge—

(a) must arrange a hearing, in public or in private, if either party asks for one;

(b) subject to that, may determine an appeal with or without a hearing;

(c) may—

    (i) consult the assessing authority,

    (ii) consult the court which made the costs order, and

    (iii) obtain any other information or document;

(d) must reconsider the amount allowed by the assessing authority, taking into account the objections to the re-assessment and any other representations;

(e) may maintain, increase or decrease the amount allowed on the re-assessment;

(f) may provide for the costs incurred by either party to the appeal; and

(g) must serve reasons for the decision on—

    (i) the parties, and

    (ii) the assessing authority.

(6) A costs judge may extend a time limit under this rule, even after it has expired.

Appeal to a High Court judge

76.13.—(1) This rule applies where— **G–328**

(a) a costs judge has determined an appeal under rule 76.12; and

(b) either party wants to appeal against the amount allowed.

(2) A party who wants to appeal—

(a) may do so only if a costs judge certifies that a point of principle of general importance was involved in the decision on the review; and

(b) must apply in writing for such a certificate and serve the application on—

    (i) the costs judge,

    (ii) the other party not more than 21 days after service of the decision on the review.

(3) That party must—

(a) appeal to a judge of the High Court attached to the Queen's Bench Division as if it were an appeal from the decision of a master under Part 52 of the Civil Procedure Rules 1998; and

(b) serve the appeal not more than 21 days after service of the costs judge's certificate under paragraph (2).

(4) A High Court judge—

(a) may extend a time limit under this rule even after it has expired;

(b) has the same powers and duties as a costs judge under rule 76.12; and

(c) may hear the appeal with one or more assessors.

Application for an extension of time under Section 5

76.14. . A party who wants an extension of time under rule 76.11, 76.12 or 76.13 must— **G–329**

(a) apply in writing;

(b) explain the delay; and

(c) attach the application, representations or appeal for which the extension of time is needed.

INDEX

LEGAL TAXONOMY
FROM SWEET & MAXWELL

This index has been prepared using Sweet and Maxwell's Legal Taxonomy. Main index entries conform to keyworks provided by the Legal Taxonomy except where references to specific documents or non-standard terms (denoted by quotation marks) have been included. These keywords provide a means of identifying similar concepts in other Sweet & Maxwell publications and online services to which keywords from the Legal Taxonomy have been applied. Readers may find some minor differences between terms used in the text and those which appear in the index. Suggestions to *taxonomy@sweetandmaxwell.co.uk*

(All references are to paragraph number)